Praise for *First Nations? Second Thoughts*

"Provocative is not a cliché when describing this book." *Choice*

"Fascinating, factual, frank." *Edmonton Journal*

"Flanagan literally takes the bull by the horns in his latest offering ... an excellent read." *Alberta Native News*

"No reader will come away from Tom Flanagan's Provocative *First Nations? Second Thoughts* without some opinion about aboriginal peoples." *The Beaver*

"Tom Flanagan has written an important critique of the 'aboriginal orthodoxy' in Canada. *First Nations? Second Thoughts* will elicit strong reactions from readers." *Perspectives on Political Science*

"Flanagan's arguments are, without question, the most thoughtful and comprehensive of the critiques of aboriginal policy that have been offered so far. His views are controversial and, whether or not you agree with him, there is a clear need for his arguments to be publicly available and debated." Alan Cairns, Faculty of Law, University of British Columbia

Second Edition

First Nations?
Second Thoughts

TOM FLANAGAN

McGill-Queen's University Press
Montreal & Kingston · London · Ithaca

© McGill-Queen's University Press 2008
ISBN 978-0-7735-3443-8 (cloth)
ISBN 978-0-7735-3444-5 (paper)

Legal deposit third quarter 2008
Bibliothèque nationale du Québec

Printed in Canada on acid-free paper that is 100%
ancient forest free (100% post-consumer recycled),
processed chlorine free

First edition 2000. Reprinted 2001, 2005

McGill-Queen's University Press acknowledges the
support of the Canada Council for the Arts for our
publishing program. We also acknowledge the financial
support of the Government of Canada through the
Book Publishing Industry Development Program
(BPIDP) for our publishing activities.

Canadian Cataloguing in Publication Data

Flanagan, Thomas, 1944–
    First nations? Second thoughts / Tom Flanagan. –
    2nd ed.
    Includes bibliographical references and index.
    ISBN 978-0-7735-3443-8 (cloth)
    ISBN 978-0-7735-3444-5 (paper)
    1. Indians of North America – Canada – Politics and
    government. 2. Indians of North America – Canada –
    Government relations – 1951– . 3. Indians of North
    America – Legal status, laws, etc. – Canada. I. Title.
    E92.F614 2008   323.1197'071   C2008-903411-2

Typeset in Sabon 10.5/13
by Infoscan Collette, Quebec

Contents

Preface to the Second Edition

The first edition of *First Nations? Second Thoughts* attracted more attention than the usual academic book. Greeted with acclaim in some quarters, it won two prizes in 2001: the Donner Prize for the best book on Canadian public policy, and the Donald Smiley Prize, awarded by the Canadian Political Science Association, for the best book on Canadian politics and government. Fortuitously, my book appeared in the same year as Alan Cairns's fine work *Citizens Plus: Aboriginal Peoples and the Canadian State.*[1] Although our viewpoints were by no means the same,[2] we both expressed misgivings about the tendency of aboriginal political leaders to emphasize sovereignty over integration into Canadian society. Since some of our ideas were picked up and amplified by journalists and media columnists, they may even have had an effect upon the climate of opinion in Canada.

On the other side, many aboriginal authors and spokesmen vigorously attacked *First Nations? Second Thoughts,* calling it racist, poorly researched, and out of date. The attacks continued as I went on to spend a few years in politics as campaign manager for Stephen Harper and the Conservative Party of Canada.[3] During the federal election campaigns of 2004 and 2005–06, aboriginal organizations, as well as the Liberal Party of Canada, issued press releases condemning my sinister presence in the councils of the Conservative Party and calling on Mr. Harper "to provide a clear answer as to whether or not he agrees with the antiquated, ill-informed, regressive and offensive writings of Mr. Flanagan in articles and books such as *First Nations? Second Thoughts.*"[4]

Given that the book played a role in public debate, I thought it better not to revise it when Philip Cercone, executive director of McGill-Queen's University Press, asked me to consider a second edition. The first edition was a critique of the worldview expressed in the report of the Royal Commission on Aboriginal Peoples and has to be understood in the context of the debate that swirled around that report when it was released in 1996. There is no point in trying to rewrite *First Nations? Second Thoughts* now that that debate is over. I propose, instead, to leave the first edition unchanged so that readers can see why it was controversial in the context of its day but to add a ten-year update in the form of a new concluding chapter. The first edition was published in 2000, but I did much of the research and writing in 1998, so 2008 is approximately the ten-year anniversary of the work.

Since I first published *First Nations? Second Thoughts*, other authors have made notable contributions to the critique of aboriginal orthodoxy. Jean Allard, himself a Metis and a former member of Ed Schreyer's NDP cabinet in Manitoba, put forward the radical proposal that treaty benefits be commuted into cash payments to individual status Indians to give them more control over their own governments.[5] Also in Manitoba, Cree writer Don Sandberg is leading a study of aboriginal local government, sponsored by the Frontier Centre for Public Policy.[6] Policy analyst John Richards has studied the truly awful conditions of health, welfare, and education experienced by many aboriginal people, especially on Indian reserves, and concluded, along with Alan Cairns, that aboriginal problems cannot be solved "by an exaggerated stress on 'otherness.'"[7] Tsimshian lawyer and businessman Calvin Helin, in his book *Dances with Dependency: Indigenous Success Through Self-Reliance,* challenges native people to become economically self-supporting.[8] Frances Widdowson and Albert Howard, in their forthcoming book *Disrobing the Global Aboriginal Industry: The Deception Behind Indigenous Cultural Preservation,* raise hitherto taboo questions about the validity of so-called "traditional knowledge" and the difficulty of adapting Neolithic cultures to modern conditions.[9]

These critiques come from many different perspectives. I have no idea what politics Sandberg, Cairns, and Helin might have, but I do know that Allard and Richards are social democrats, at least by origin, Widdowson and Howard are orthodox Marxists, and I am a political conservative. That in spite of our many differences we all see inherent problems in the aboriginal orthodoxy suggests that these problems are real and not just the biased imaginings of one or two bigoted observers. By publishing an updated edition of *First Nations? Second Thoughts*, I hope to renew my contribution to this ongoing debate, which is so essential for the future well-being of aboriginal people and all Canadians.

Acknowledgments

FIRST EDITION

I am grateful to the Donner Canadian Foundation for financially supporting my research as well as the publication of this book. I would also like to thank Philip J. Cercone, executive director and editor of McGill-Queen's University Press, for taking interest in a manuscript that is bound to provoke some hostile reactions. Finally, I am grateful to Judith Turnbull for her careful copy-editing and to Christopher Matthews for preparing the index.

SECOND EDITION

Philip Cercone, executive director of McGill-Queen's University Press, suggested a new edition of this book, and Joan McGilvray, coordinating editor, saw it through press. Dan Beavon generously sent me copies of research studies conducted by the Strategic Research and Analysis Directorate, Indian and Northern Affairs Canada. Ph.D candidate Mike Zekulin indexed the new material added to this edition. I am grateful to all of you but remain solely responsible for the sometimes controversial opinions expressed in the book.

FIRST NATIONS?
SECOND THOUGHTS

CHAPTER 1

The Aboriginal Orthodoxy

The Royal Commission on Aboriginal Peoples (RCAP) released its final report – five volumes and thirty-five hundred pages – in the fall of 1996.[1] The report had taken over five years to prepare and cost more than $50 million. Because of the inordinate expense and time involved, the RCAP may be the last royal commission we will see for some time. Nonetheless, it was extraordinarily important, and the appearance of its final report touched off a round of conferences to discuss its recommendations. The experience of participating in one of these talk-fests led me to write this book.

At a conference entitled "Forging a New Relationship," sponsored by the McGill Institute for the Study of Canada,[2] I turned out to be one of the no more than half dozen of the roughly 120 speakers to suggest that the RCAP's recommendations pointed in the wrong direction.[3] A couple of delegates told me that they "admired my courage," even though they disagreed with my views; but for the most part I was politely ignored. Canadians, especially aboriginal Canadians, are almost always polite. The whole experience made me realize that I was confronting not just the report of a royal commission, but a new orthodoxy, widely and firmly accepted in all circles exercising any influence over aboriginal policy.

I then decided that I wanted to write my own book, not as a commentary on the RCAP report, but as an analysis of the principles that support it. I had been doing research on aboriginal issues for a quarter of a century, writing highly detailed historical studies on subjects such as Louis Riel and the North-West Rebellion, Metis land claims in Manitoba, and the never-ending Lubicon conflict in northern Alberta.[4] Now I wanted to step back from microscopically focused historical research and think systematically about the central ideas of the new consensus.

What I call the aboriginal orthodoxy is an emergent consensus on fundamental issues. It is widely shared among aboriginal leaders, government officials, and academic experts. It weaves together threads from historical revisionism, critical legal studies, and the aboriginal political activism of the last thirty years. Although its ideas are expressed in many books,[5] it has no Marx and Engels, that is, no canonical writers to authoritatively define the ideology. In the course of questioning the aboriginal orthodoxy, *First Nations? Second Thoughts* pieces together its tenets from many sources, including government reports, books and articles, speeches, and judicial decisions. The resulting synthesis may not fully and accurately represent the thinking of any particular individual, but it captures the dominant trends of thought among those who now make and influence aboriginal policy.

The book contains a series of essays on topics such as sovereignty, nationhood, self-government, property rights, and treaties. Although not a complete dissection of the aboriginal orthodoxy, it deals with the main tenets, probing for logical inconsistencies and raising objections based on historical evidence. I do not claim to say the last word on these difficult and controversial issues, only to offer some viewpoints that are seldom heard today. In particular, I do not present a plan for curing all the ills besetting aboriginal peoples. I do not believe in the validity of such plans. Nonetheless, I think it is valid to raise questions about the direction in which we are obviously headed.

Indeed, it is vital to do so, even though the RCAP *Report* may have less practical effect in the short run than the commission members and their supporters hoped. The RCAP's recommendations were too sweeping and too expensive for the cautious, economy-minded government of Jean Chrétien. In early 1998, the Liberal government announced an Aboriginal Action Plan that cost far less than the RCAP proposals and avoided formalizing aboriginal government as a "third order of government" in the federal system. The centrepiece of the new plan was an apology from the government for Indian residential schools. A "healing fund" was established, costing $350 million over four years. There was also supposed to be an increase of about

$250 million in the next year's budget for a variety of measures in support of self-government and economic development.[6] Skeptics may be forgiven for suspecting that some or all of the alleged new money would have been spent anyway because of aboriginal population growth and the internal dynamics of existing programs.

Native reaction to the Aboriginal Action Plan was mixed. Phil Fontaine, national chief of the Assembly of First Nations (AFN), was appreciative, even though it was much less than the RCAP had called for. He believed that the plan represented the best that could be achieved at the present time. Leaders of the Inuit, Metis, and non-status Indians were critical, however, because the plan offered far more to AFN status Indians than to their groups.

But even though only a few of the RCAP proposals have been implemented, the *Report* itself stands as a monument to the new orthodoxy, and the people who share those beliefs are actively pushing the federal government to move in that direction. Unless there is serious public debate, sooner or later we are likely to end up where the RCAP wanted us to go. Canada will be redefined as a multinational state embracing an archipelago of aboriginal nations that own a third of Canada's land mass, are immune from federal and provincial taxation, are supported by transfer payments from citizens who do pay taxes, are able to opt out of federal and provincial legislation, and engage in "nation to nation" diplomacy with whatever is left of Canada. That is certainly not the vision of Canada I had when I immigrated in 1968 and decided to become a Canadian citizen in 1973; I doubt it's what most Canadians want for themselves and their children. But it's what we may get if we don't open the debate on the aboriginal orthodoxy.

Perhaps the damage to Canada would be tolerable if it meant that aboriginal peoples would escape from the social pathologies in which they are mired to become prosperous, self-supporting citizens. But I believe the actual outcome of implementing the aboriginal orthodoxy would be quite different. Although aboriginal leaders might achieve rewarding political careers, most aboriginal people would remain poor and dependent, marginalized on reserves and other territorial enclaves. This would be a lose-lose situation in which Canada and aboriginal peoples would both become worse off than they should be.

Eight of the propositions in the aboriginal orthodoxy are particularly dubious. They are stated below in italics, followed by my own contrarian positions. The rest of the book consists of eight chapters, each devoted to one of these propositions, plus a short conclusion.

1. *Aboriginals differ from other Canadians because they were here first. As "First Nations," they have unique rights, including the inherent right of self-government.*

Aboriginal peoples were in almost constant motion as they contested with each other for control of land. In much of Canada, their present place of habitation postdates the arrival of European settlers. Europeans are, in effect, a new immigrant wave, taking control of land just as earlier aboriginal settlers did. To differentiate the rights of earlier and later immigrants is a form of racism.

2. *Aboriginal cultures were on the same level as those of the European colonists. The distinction between civilized and uncivilized is a racist instrument of oppression.*

European civilization was several thousand years more advanced than the aboriginal cultures of North America, both in technology and in social organization. Owing to this tremendous gap in civilization, the European colonization of North America was inevitable and, if we accept the philosophical analysis of John Locke and Emer de Vattel, justifiable.

3. *Aboriginal peoples possessed sovereignty. They still do, even if they choose to call it the "inherent right of self-government."*

Sovereignty is an attribute of statehood, and aboriginal peoples in Canada had not arrived at the state level of political organization prior to contact with Europeans. The "inherent right of self-government" would be acceptable in contemporary Canada if it had the same meaning as the American formula of "domestic dependent nations" possessing "tribal sovereignty"; but in fact it means much, much more.

4. *Aboriginal peoples were and are nations in both the cultural and political senses of this term. Their nationhood is concomitant with their sovereignty.*

The European concept of nation does not properly describe aboriginal tribal communities. Unless we want to turn Canada into a modern version of the Ottoman Empire, there can be only one political community at the highest level – one nation – in Canada. Subordinate communities, such as provinces, cities, and ethnic or religious groups, cannot be nations.

5. *Aboriginal peoples can succesfully exercise their inherent right of self-government on Indian reserves.*

Aboriginal government is fraught with difficulties stemming from small size, an overly ambitious agenda, and dependence on transfer payments. In practice, aboriginal government produces wasteful, destructive, familistic factionalism.

6. *Aboriginal property rights should be recognized as full owner-ship rights in Canadian law and entrenched, not extinguished, through land-claims agreements.*

Contemporary judicial attempts to redefine aboriginal rights are producing little but uncertainty. Recent Supreme Court of Canada decisions define aboriginal title in a way that will make its use impossible in a modern economy.

7. *The land-surrender treaties in Ontario and the prairie provinces mean something other than their words indicate. Their wording needs to be "modernized" – reinterpreted or renegotiated – to recognize an ongoing relationship between nations.*

The treaties mean what they say. Their reinterpretation, while it might not be as far-reaching as the redefinition of aboriginal title in British Columbia and Atlantic Canada, has the potential to be both expensive and mischievous for the economies of all provinces in which treaties have been signed.

8. *Aboriginal people, living and working on their own land base, will become prosperous and self-sufficient by combining transfer payments, resource revenues, and local employment.*

Prosperity and self-sufficiency in the modern economy require a willingness to integrate into the economy, which means, among other things, a willingness to move to where jobs and investment opportunities exist. Heavy subsidies for reserve economies are pro-ducing two extremes in the reserve population – a well-to-do entrepreneurial and professional elite and increasing numbers of welfare-dependent Indians.

There is now a huge and rapidly growing literature on aboriginal issues. To have taken full account of what has been written, each of the book's chapters, indeed many of the sections within these chapters, would have had to become books in their own right. I am keenly aware that I have omitted some major contemporary issues, such as Nunavut and the Nisga'a Treaty, and have dealt hardly at all with the Inuit and only glancingly with the Metis and non-status Indians. I focus instead on issues associated with status Indians because it is in relation to these issues that the aboriginal orthodoxy is most clearly expressed. In short, this book is not an encyclopedia of aboriginal issues. It is my attempt to reflect on a few key topics and see them in relation to each other.

On a trip to New Zealand and Australia in early 1999, I was reminded that the aboriginal orthodoxy is an international phenomenon. Although each country offers its own legal and political setting, the public debate is remarkably similar in all of them. I have drawn a few comparisons between the debate in Canada and that in New Zealand and Australia where I thought they would illuminate the Canadian situation, but I have not tried to make the book fully international. Not only would the reach of such a project be beyond my grasp, it would produce a book that would be inaccessible to most Canadians. I hope that *First Nations? Second Thoughts* will be read by more than a few academic specialists, because the issues it addresses are vital matters of contemporary public policy.

Finally, because I presume to analyse the political views of others, I should briefly sketch out my own. In terms of contemporary labels, I am happy to be called either conservative or libertarian, if that means "classical liberal." My views on politics and society owe a great debt to Friedrich Hayek, now widely recognized as one of the most influential thinkers of the late twentieth century. On issues relevant to this book, I hold certain core beliefs:

• Society is a spontaneous order that emerges from the choices of individual human beings. The indispensable role of government is to make and enforce rules of conduct that allow society to function. Individuals naturally congregate in families and other associations, but these must be voluntary if society is to be free and prosperous. When government sorts people into categories with different legal rights, especially when those categories are based on immutable characteristics such as race and sex, it interferes with social processes based on free association.

- Although it is imperfect, representative government under the constitutional rule of law is the only form of government yet discovered that promotes individual freedom while protecting the spontaneous order of society.

- The only economic system that has brought a high standard of living to a complex society is the free market. Like representative government, it has many imperfections, but it is the most effective method ever discovered for inducing self-interested individuals to serve the needs of others.

- Threads of progress are visible in the fabric of civilization. Developments in science and technology have led to a cumulative increase in mastery over nature. Advances in social organization have created larger and more complex societies, thus making the division of labour more elaborate and effective. These developments have led to increases in human numbers and longevity, the flowering of the arts and sciences, and a refinement of human relationships, manifest in the abolition of slavery, democratic control over government, and legal equality between women and men. Although the word "progress" is out of fashion, there is no other term to describe such achievements. Although human history does not march towards a utopia, it has brought about demonstrable betterment of the human condition.

Although I call these points "beliefs," they are not untestable value commitments but empirical propositions to be weighed against historical evidence. I think the evidence supports them, but I realize that people at least as intelligent and well-informed as I am do not agree with my views. This doesn't cause me to change my assessment of the evidence, but it reminds me that I (like everyone else) may be wrong in my conclusions. Respect for individual belief and decison is important precisely because every person's intellect and knowledge is so limited. In a world where everyone might conceivably be mistaken about almost everything, the only corrective is constant testing through the confrontation of ideas and evidence.

It is in that spirit that I publish *First Nations? Second Thoughts*. Even if my second thoughts turn out to be misguided, they may still be useful in the way that John Stuart Mill described the utility of mistaken viewpoints: "He who knows only his own side of the case knows little of that. His reasons may be good, and no one may have been able to refute them. But if he is equally unable to refute the reasons on the opposite side, if he does not so much as know what they are, he has no ground for preferring either opinion."[7] And further: "if opponents of all-important truths do not exist, it is indispensable to imagine them and supply them with the strongest arguments which the most skillful devil's advocate can conjure up."[8]

Although I think that the proponents of the new aboriginal orthodoxy are mistaken, I admire their energy and moral conviction. As a political scientist, I particularly admire their success in influencing both public opinion and the decisions of the federal government. They are among the most talented players in the contemporary game of politics. In this book I pay them the highest compliment of taking their ideas seriously. I invite them to reply in kind.

CHAPTER 2

We Were Here First

"The fact is, we are a special people. We were here first."
– Phil Fontaine, national chief, Assembly of First Nations,
speaking on the CBC Radio news, 23 September 1998.

ABORIGINALITY

One of the most powerful themes in the aboriginal orthodoxy is that special rights flow from having been here first. It is implied in the phrase "First Nations" – now an almost obligatory label for Indians – as well as in the more technical term "aboriginal," derived from the Latin words *ab,* meaning "from," and *origo,* meaning "origin." To be the people who were here from the beginning – put here by the Creator, as Indians often say – is the basic idea of aboriginality. The same notion is prominent in Australia, where most Aboriginals claim to have occupied their particular homelands forever, since the time of the Dreaming, the mythical time of origins when supernatural beings shaped the features of the earth and created its population of plants, animals, and human beings.

Aboriginal people routinely use phrases such as "thirty thousand years of history" to emphasize the supposedly great period of time in which they have occupied Canada.[1] Even professional historians such as J.R. Miller speak in the same vein of the Indians' ancestors having "entered North America from Siberia by way of the Bering Strait in search of game perhaps as long as 40,000 years ago ... Evidence of what were undoubtedly the original human occupiers of the continent that was unearthed in the Yukon indicates that they were there as long as 27,000 years ago."[2] Arthur Ray follows a similar rhetorical strategy when he entitles his history of Indians in Canada *I Have Lived Here Since the World Began.*[3] The archaeological evidence, however, does not support such great time depth. The famous Old Crow hide flesher to which Miller refers, once thought to be twenty-seven thousand years old, has been radiocarbon dated to less than three thousand years before the present (BP).[4]

The archaeological record of human habitation in the New World is reasonably secure for only the last twelve thousand years. Four well-known authorities on early human migration, who have no emotional or political stake in the dispute, either prefer to stay with the traditional date of 12,000 BP for the first human entry into the Americas (Clive Gamble, Jared Diamond) or regard the issue as uncertain (Luigi Cavalli-Sforza, Christopher Stringer).[5] The dating of the Monte Verde site in southern Chile at almost 13,000 BP is now widely accepted, but its implications are still unclear. If human beings were in southern Chile thirteen thousand years ago, they must have crossed over from northeast Asia at least a thousand years earlier, and perhaps much earlier than that; but there is no verified route of migration.

There are many claims for sites with earlier dates, but all are controversial in one way or another.[6] None of the alleged Early Man sites contain fossilized human bones that can be dated directly through techniques such as carbon-14 analysis. Because dating depends on the geological context in which stone tools, animal bones, and cinders are found, there is much room for dispute and error. Some archaeologists defend the early dates with great passion, but passionate conviction is not the same as scientific certainty.

Regardless of how this controversy is eventually resolved, three things seem reasonably certain:

• The physical appearance of Indians from the Arctic to Tierra del Fuego is remarkably similar. Moreover, equatorial South America is the only tropical region in the world where the indigenous people are not dark-skinned, suggesting that the South American tropics were settled as part of a relatively recent and rapid wave of immigration across the New World.
• Second, if Early Man did live in the New World before 12,000 BP, the numbers were scanty. How else to explain the absence of any fossilized human remains or the very small numbers of alleged artifacts from that early period? Also, it is surely relevant that the extinction of numerous species of megafauna, such as

mammoths, mastodons, and giant ground sloths, took place shortly after 12,000 BP ("In no more than 3,000 years, between 12,000 and 9,000 years ago, nearly 40 species of large mammals became extinct)."[7] The most plausible explanation is that Early Man entered the Americas at this point in some numbers and had a field day hunting large animals that, having evolved apart from human beings for hundreds of thousands of years, did not have a healthy wariness of human hunters.[8] If human beings were present earlier, their numbers must have been small, for they would otherwise have exterminated these species earlier. A possible explanation favoured by University of Alberta archaeologist Ruth Gruhn is that the very early human settlements were along the seaboard, such as Monte Verde in Chile, and that Early Man penetrated only much later into the interior plains of North and South America where the megafauna lived.[9]

• Third, and most relevant to the theme of this chapter, even if Early Man was present in the New World long before the conventional date of 12,000 BP, he would have lived in South America, Central America, or what is now the United States; he could not have lived in Canada because it was totally covered with glacial ice, except for a few islands and promontories along the coast of British Columbia and the dry, cold plains of the northern Yukon.

Around twenty-five thousand years ago, in the Late Wisconsin ice age, the glaciers in Canada began to expand. The peak of glacial coverage occurred about fifteen thousand years ago. At that point, the Laurentide glacier expanding from Hudson Bay met the Cordilleran glacier coming down from the Rockies.[10] It used to be thought that there was an ice-free corridor along the eastern foothills of the Rockies, but the latest research, based on a new method of dating the glacial erratics (large isolated boulders) in the Alberta foothills, shows that the two glaciers met and merged.[11] Canada was one vast ice sheet for thousands of years. Some bits of the British Columbia coast as well as the northern Yukon were probably unglaciated, but these were mere fragments of what we now call Canada. (It is also possible that parts of the continental shelf off British Columbia, and perhaps off Newfoundland, were raised above sea level because of the great mass of water contained in the glaciers.)

As the ice receded, Canada slowly became habitable. By 12,000 BP, it might have been possible to live in the eastern foothills of the Rockies and in Atlantic Canada.[12] Some early stone implements found on Canadian soil are projectile points from the Yukon (before 11,000 BP); Charlie Lake Cave north of Fort St John, BC (10,500 BP); Sibbald Creek near Calgary (9570 BP); and the Debert site in central Nova Scotia (10,600 BP).[13] There are also traces of human habitation on the British Columbia coast from 9000 to 10,000 BP.[14] By 9000 BP, southern Ontario and Quebec were habitable,[15] and people moved further north into the Canadian Shield as the glaciers receded.

The science of linguistics also may have something to tell us, although linguists, as in Harry Truman's famous aphorism about economists, refuse to point the same way even if you line them up end to end. Along the Pacific coast, from Alaska to California, are dozens of mutually unintelligible, perhaps unrelated, native languages. It is a general principle of historical linguistics that such diversity is strong evidence of ancient and continuous habitation.[16] The linguistic situation in the rest of Canada is much simpler in comparison. There are only five linguistic families: the Inuit languages of the Arctic; the Athapaskan languages of the Yukon and the Mackenzie Valley, with their southern projections; the Algonquian languages spoken almost everywhere else; the Sioux dialects that came north from the United States into the southern Canadian prairies in the seventeenth and eighteenth centuries;[17] and the Iroquoian languages (related to the Cherokee languages of the southeastern United States), which were more prominent in the United States but were also found in the St Lawrence lowlands and southern Great Lakes region.

The Algonquian family is by far the most far-flung. It includes Blackfoot on the prairies, the Cree dialects across the Canadian Shield, Ojibwa in southern Ontario, and the Eastern Algonquian languages of Quebec and the Maritimes (the affiliation of the poorly attested Beothuk language of Newfoundland is unclear). Cree and Ojibwa are so closely related to each other that their various dialects are mutually intelligible to some degree. In his *History of the Ojebway Indians*, the Mississauga Methodist missionary Peter Jones classified Cree as a dialect of Ojibwa, which he called "the most extensive of the North American languages, being understood and spoken by all the tribes found on both sides of the Lakes Huron, Michigan, and Superior, and so on to the head-waters of the Mississippi and Red River. It is true that some of the tribes find it difficult to understand each other when they first meet, but after a short intercourse they are enabled to converse with one another."[18]

Many words are almost identical in Cree and Ojibwa, as shown by a few examples that Jones gave:[19]

English Meaning	Cree	Ojibwa
Man	Eye-new	E-ne-ne
Woman	Isk-wao	E-qua
Earth	Us-keo	Uh-ke
Bear	Mus-kwu	Muh-quuh

This degree of mutual intelligibility is similar to that among Danish, Norwegian, and Swedish, or between Dutch and Low German, and would imply a separation of only about a thousand or fifteen hundred years. Relationships with Blackfoot and Eastern Algonquian are not as close but are still demonstrable. Much more tenuous relationships, discernible only to linguists and still debated within that fraternity, may exist between Algonquian and various languages of British Columbia, such as Kootenay and Salish.[20]

A likely implication for migration and habitation is that, whatever the remote history may have been, the direct ancestors of the Indians living in Canada (other than coastal British Columbia) at the time of contact with European explorers could not have arrived at those locations earlier than a few thousand years before; otherwise their languages would have become more divergent.[21] (Of course, the Algonquian and Iroquoian peoples may have absorbed or driven away earlier inhabitants). This is a conclusion about the continuous existence of peoples as identified by their language, not about human habitation as such.

Another approach comes from the work of the linguist Joseph Greenberg, who in 1987 proposed that all Indian languages, except the Athapaskan group, should be classified as belonging to a macro-family he called Amerind.[22] There are, according to Greenberg, eleven subfamiles of Amerind, quite different from one another but all sharing certain basic features, such as a first-person pronominal marker in -n and a second-person marker in -m, resemblances impossible to attribute to chance or borrowing.

If Greenberg is right about Amerind, the Athapaskan speakers must stem from a separate and more recent immigration to the New World. The languages of that family are clearly related to each other and are concentrated in Alaska, Yukon, the western Northwest Territories, and northern British Columbia, Alberta, and Saskatchewan, with a few outriders in Washington, Oregon, and the southwestern United States. The greatest linguistic variety within the Athapaskan family is found in the north, particularly in Alaska, suggesting longer residence there followed by more recent expansion into the other areas where Athapaskan languages are now found.[23] The more ambitious linguistic theorists claim that a relationship can be demonstrated between the Athapaskan languages and the Yeniseian family of Siberia,[24] and even the great Sino-Tibetan family of East Asia.[25]

Confirmatory evidence comes from biological research into the dentition and mitochondrial DNA of American Indians, both showing that there is a strong division between the Athapaskan-speaking peoples and all other indigenous inhabitants of the Americas.[26] The differences in dentition are particularly striking. American Indians, except for those who speak Athapaskan languages, tend to have the so-called Sinodont pattern of shovel-shaped incisors, triple-rooted lower first molars, and single-rooted upper first premolars. This pattern was common in northern China twenty thousand years ago but is rare there today. Athapaskan speakers, in contrast, have dental features similar to those of the modern inhabitants of northeast Asia.[27] This strongly suggests that the Athapaskan speakers constitute a second wave of immigration more recent than the original arrivals in the New World.[28]

The Inuit are the most recent of all. Again, their language is obviously different from either Amerind or Athapaskan. Some linguists, including Greenberg, classify it as part of a macro-family known as Eurasiatic or Nostratic, very distantly related to Indo-European and other families sharing a first-person pronominal marker in -m and a second-person marker in -t.[29] Be that as it may, Inuit does not seem to belong to any other language family of North America.

The earliest evidence of habitation in the Canadian Arctic is from about 4000 BP. These so-called Paleo-Eskimos, who penetrated as far east as northern Greenland, were perhaps related to the modern Inuit. They were followed by the pre-Dorset and Dorset cultures, distinguished by differences in stone and bone technology. The Inuit as we know them today are descended from the so-called Thule culture, which expanded out of Alaska from about 1100 BP onward, either absorbing or displacing the people of the Dorset culture.[30]

The Amerind family posited by Greenberg and his followers is highly controversial, indeed rejected by most specialists in native American languages, who regard Amerind as the worst sort of "lumping."[31] Johanna Nichols, another prominent linguist, argues that, even if Amerind forms a genuine unit at some level, its internal differentiation is so great that its time depth would have to be closer to forty-thousand years than to the twelve thousand years that Greenberg posited when he took over the conventional dating for the first human arrival in the New World. Nichols concludes that "the New World has been inhabited for tens of millennia."[32]

Although there is no consensus among archaeologists and linguists about these very early dates, the differences between Inuit, Athapaskan, and others seem more widely accepted. That alone means that the now popular image of aboriginal rights based on "30,000 years of history" is highly misleading. There must have been three or even more major waves of immigration from Siberia to America: the Amerind, perhaps earlier or even much earlier, but certainly by 12,000 BP; the Athabaskan, perhaps 5000–10,000 BP; and the Inuit, from about 4000 BP onward (if the Paleo-Eskimos and Dorset people were Inuit). As the glaciers covering Canada retreated, groups took up settlement at various times and places.

Moreover, it seems very unlikely that bands, tribes, or peoples occupied land as the glaciers receded and then stayed there continuously until the arrival of the French and English. Theories of conquest or displacement based purely on archaeological evidence are conjectural because the presence of a new style of pottery, tool, or grave neither proves nor disproves the arrival of a new people. Cultural practices can be transferred by imitation and diffusion as well as by conquest and displacement. However, from the sixteenth century onward, as soon as European explorers could report their observations, we have strong evidence that aboriginal peoples contested with each other for the control of territory and that conquest, absorption, displacement, and even extermination were routine phenomena. Below are a few examples.

Jacques Cartier met Iroquoian-speaking people on his voyages up and down the St Lawrence in 1534–36, but when Samuel

Champlain came back to establish a permanent settlement in 1608, the Iroquois were gone, replaced by Algonquian-speaking Montaignais.[33] Later in the century the Iroquois returned with a vengeance. Having obtained metal implements and guns from Dutch fur traders, they expanded west as far as Illinois and north into the St Lawrence valley.[34] They killed off or carried away most of the Huron, Neutral, and Petun tribes that lived north of Lake Erie and Lake Ontario, depopulating southern Ontario for a century and leaving it open for new waves of settlement. As Peter Desbarats, dean of journalism at the University of Western Ontario, has remarked, "The ancestors of today's Southern Ontario population of natives and non-natives all arrived in this part of Canada about the same time."[35]

Similar dramas were enacted further west. Peguis, the Ojibwa or Saulteaux chief who signed the Selkirk Treaty at Red River in 1817, had been born near Sault Sainte-Marie in Ontario; his people only started to settle along the lower Red River in the 1790s. Earlier in the eighteenth century, after securing guns from both French and English fur traders, they pushed west from their home north of Lake Huron and into what are now the states of Minnesota and North Dakota, driving the Cheyenne and Hidatsa before them. "The Chippeways silently collected in the forests, and made war on the nearest village, destroying it with fire," wrote the explorer David Thompson about one of these attacks on the Hidatsa.[36]

When the Cree, armed with guns acquired from the Hudson's Bay Company, moved onto the prairies in the seventeenth or early eighteenth century, they soon encountered the Blackfoot. The Blackfoot were being pushed north and east by tribes such as the Shoshone, Gros Ventres, and Kootenay, who had procured horses through trade with the Spanish further south. At first the Cree befriended the Blackfoot and gave them guns, which the Blackfoot used to drive their enemies back to Montana or across the mountains to present-day British Columbia.[37] In the mid-nineteenth century, however, the Cree started to attack the Blackfoot because they stood between them and the failing population of buffalo; but the Blackfoot, now getting better guns from American traders to the south, soundly defeated a large party of Cree warriors at a famous battle in 1870 on the Oldman River.[38] In any case, the buffalo were quickly disappearing, and within a few years both peoples had to settle on reserves and be kept alive by rations from the government.

These population movements were not caused by aboriginal people losing their own lands to white settlers, but by their taking advantage of new technology secured through trade. Thus, even though the events occurred after contact with European colonists, they suggest a pattern of behaviour that likely prevailed in earlier centuries; it seems clear that the Indian peoples' collective control of land was fundamentally based on power. An increase of numbers or an improvement in technology led one people to probe the territory of another, with results depending on the relative balance of power.

All of this means that the standard definition of aboriginal rights is a legal fiction; aboriginal peoples cannot justifiably claim "property rights which inure to native peoples by virtue of their occupation upon certain lands from time immemorial."[39] There may be specific cases where a native community has dwelled continuously upon the same territory for thousands of years (if such cases exist in Canada, they lie on the coast of British Columbia), but, in general, native peoples in Canada, like hunter-collectors around the world, moved a great deal. In many cases, the patterns of habitation upon which the land-surrender agreements of the nineteenth century were based were only a few decades old. "From time immemorial" means only "prior" – not necessarily "a long, long time, a very long time, or even a long time."[40]

Indeed, a great many of the current locations of aboriginal peoples in Canada are more recent than the arrival of European colonists. The presence of the French in Acadia and New France, the Dutch and English in New York and New England, the Hudson's Bay Company in the Canadian Shield country, and the Spanish in the American southwest set off waves of movement among aboriginal popoulations. The chief mechanisms were depopulation due to Old World diseases; adoption of new technologies such as metal implements, firearms, and horseback riding; competition to exploit newly profitable resources, such as beaver pelts and buffalo robes; and flight from warfare. Whatever the remote ancestry of aboriginal peoples may be, their current presence in most parts of Canada is quite recent, historically speaking.

This line of thought is confirmed by the situation in New Zealand, where the Maori claim aboriginal rights even though their ancestors arrived on the islands little more than a thousand years ago. They do not pretend to have lived there since the beginning of time; their own oral traditions tell the story of travelling in great canoes from far-away islands, landing on the north island of what is now New Zealand, spreading over both the north and south islands, and engaging in almost constant warfare for control of territory.

PRIORITY

Chief Justice Lamer wrote in his *Van der Peet* decision (1996) that

the doctrine of aboriginal rights exists, and is recognized and affirmed by s. 35(1) [of the Constitution Act, 1982], because of one simple fact: when Europeans arrived in North America, aboriginal peoples *were already here* [emphasis in original], living in communities on the land, and participating in distinctive cultures, as they had done for centuries. It is this fact, and this fact above all others, which separates aboriginal peoples from all other minority groups in Canadian society, and which mandates their special legal, and now constitutional, status.[41]

With respect to the chief justice, emphasis is not a substitute for logic. His statement offers no reason *why* ancestral priority requires creation of a special legal regime.

Admittedly, temporal priority is one of the great ordering principles of human society, memorialized in proverbs such as "first come, first served." We follow rules of priority in such daily-life situations as standing in line to pay a cashier or waiting for a speaker to finish rather than interrupting. When I go trout fishing on a stream and I find another fisherman already working a pool, I don't cast into the same pool, I walk away to find one that is unoccupied (by fishermen, not by trout!).

The importance of temporal priority is shown by how people react when it is violated. How angry do you feel when someone cuts in ahead of you in a queue or zips into a parking place for which you've been waiting? Yet we do not follow temporal priority blindly and inflexibly. Passing in traffic is allowed as long as conditions are safe. Parents in today's world are expected to love all their children equally, not to favour the first-born. When children are small, their age, which is a reflection of temporal priority, makes a difference in the way they are treated, but not once they are grown. We have to look more closely, therefore, at the role of temporal priority in aboriginal politics.

Let us start with an obvious but often overlooked distinction between individual and ancestral priority. As an immigrant from the United States, I arrived in Canada in 1968. I have now been here over thirty years, longer than most aboriginal people now alive have lived in Canada (in the 1996 census, 53 per cent of aboriginal people were younger than twenty-five).[42] But even though I am individually prior to most aboriginal people in Canada, they would all claim to be ancestrally prior to me by virtue of having one or more direct ancestors who lived in Canada (in some cases, actually in the United States) before any of my ancestors lived in North America.

In Canada, as in most contemporary liberal democracies, individual temporal priority figures only indirectly and accidentally in public policy. Examples are the age requirement to obtain a driver's licence and the residency requirement to obtain citizenship. Arriving in Canada ahead of another immigrant means that I will be eligible to become a citizen before him or her, but only as an indirect consequence of the legislated residency requirement. Once we are citizens, we will both have the same legal rights, which will also be the same as the rights of all other citizens, both natural-born and naturalized.

There are, to be sure, some exceptions to this general rule. Only someone born in the United States can be elected president, and it has been suggested in both the United States and Canada that immigrants should not be eligible for welfare for a number of years after acquiring citizenship, which would create a legal distinction between natural-born and naturalized citizens. But it is still generally true that individual temporal priority has little to do with rights.

In any case, the issue is not individual but ancestral priority as far as aboriginal people are concerned. At this level, there is no doubt that some (but not all) aboriginal peoples in Canada receive benefits from the federal government partly because of who their ancestors were – benefits that are not available to others. For example, the federal government, under the rubric of Non-insured Health Benefits, pays medical expenses for status Indians – drugs, eyeglasses, prostheses, ambulances – beyond what Medicare provides for everyone else. This program cost over half a billion dollars a year in the mid-1990s.[43] It is not an unalloyed benefit, since the provision of free prescriptions increases drug abuse among aboriginal people,[44] but it is nevertheless a financial advantage. Non-insured Health Benefits are not treaty provisions obtained by bargaining, which would raise additional issues; they are provided legislatively to all registered Indians, whether or not they have adhered to any treaty. In this and other respects, Indians have become what the Hawthorn Commission of the mid-1960s called for them to become – "citizens plus."[45]

Because of complicated legal definitions of who is a status Indian, not all persons with aboriginal ancestry receive these benefits. According to the 1996 census, about 210,000 people thought of themselves as Metis, and a large but unknown additional number have some degree of aboriginal ancestry but do not identify themselves with any aboriginal label.[46] But even if aboriginal ancestry is not sufficient to qualify for special treatment, it is necessary. In that somewhat qualified sense, Canada treats status Indians as a separate racial group. Call them Siberian-Canadians.[47] The attribution of privileges to Siberian-Canadians on the basis of ancestry is anomalous in a liberal democracy because it contradicts a fundamental aspect of the rule of law – treating people for what they do rather than for who they are. Indians did not do anything to achieve their status except to be born, and no one else can do anything to join them in that status because no action can affect one's ancestry.

This is not just a logical problem; this contradiction of a fundamental principle has all the practical consequences pointed out by Thomas Sowell in his worldwide survey of ethnic and racial preferential policies.[48] It leads to deadweight losses (people tend not to economize on things that come to them without cost). It helps some who do not need help (there are some wealthy Indians who could easily pay for their own medicines and university educations) while failing to help others who do need help (there are many non-Indians who have trouble paying for these things). It creates a sense of entitlement among those inside the magic circle while fostering resentment among those who are excluded, thus poisoning the political atmosphere.

A rejoinder to this line of argument is sure to take the following form: Aboriginals are not like other Canadians. They are not simply ethnic groups but members of ancient political communities forcibly or perhaps semi-voluntarily incorporated into Canada. All other Canadians, or at least their ancestors, chose to come here and thereby to become part of Canada. But Canada was thrust upon the ancestors of aboriginal peoples by the incursion of the

Europeans. Hence, as the "First Nations," they are entitled to rights of self-government that no other race or ethnic group can claim.[49]

This assertion, so central to the aboriginal orthodoxy, depends on several propositions. The first assumption is that aboriginal peoples were self-governing political communities before the European discovery of the Americas. At one level, this is self-evidently true. Before the Europeans arrived, only aboriginals were here, and they, like all human communities, engaged in the collective decision-making process that we call politics. However, as explained at greater length in the next chapter, aboriginal government had not achieved the level of organization and formality that characterizes civilized states.

Second, statements about self-government usually assume continuity, making it seem that aboriginal communities have been living in the same places under the same governments for thousands of years. But, as shown above, the facts are rather different. Indians and Inuit are not a single people. They probably stem from at least three migrations into Canada at different times. Only the first migrants, whoever they were and whenever they came, found a truly empty continent. Later arrivals had to push their way in just as the European colonists did.

Once in North America, the basic stocks differentiated themselves into many peoples who did not follow a rule of temporal priority among themselves. They sometimes negotiated non-aggression pacts, as the Cree and Blackfoot repeatedly did in the nineteenth century; but these did not establish peace, merely stand-offs after periods of open warfare.[50] Aboriginal peoples contested with each other vigorously for control of land, resulting in conquest, assimilation, displacement, and extermination.

It is routine today for aboriginal spokesmen to downplay warfare among native peoples. According to Georges Erasmus, "our people were not a war-like people, but they did defend their interests. Our territorial boundaries were clearly defined. Although First Nations had many disputes with neighbours in their history, they eventually arrived at peaceful arrangements with one another."[51] But these words hardly do justice to the war of extermination waged by the Iroquois against the Huron, or to the ferocious struggles between the Cree and the Blackfoot over access to the buffalo herds. The historical record clearly shows that, while aboriginal peoples exercised a kind of collective control over territories, the boundaries were neither long-lasting nor well defined and communities must have been repeatedly formed, dissolved, and reconstituted with different identities.

Third, the assertion of continuing self-government assumes that aboriginal communities did not lose control of their own affairs even after the advent of the European settlers. Aboriginal spokesmen in Canada take every opportunity to repeat that because their nations were never conquered and never voluntarily gave up their right of self-government, they must still possess it. "It is essential to understand," writes the lawyer Derek T. Ground, "that Aboriginal peoples have never forfeited their right to govern themselves. In Canada, no Aboriginal nation was ever defeated at war."[52]

But this assertion is highly questionable. All treaties, from the covenants of submission of the eighteenth century to the land-surrender agreements of the nineteenth and twentieth centuries, explicitly recognized the sovereignty of the Crown. It is true that no treaties were signed in some provinces, but the historical record shows that the power of the Crown was as irresistible in these provinces as elsewhere. Even without formal negotiation and agreement, aboriginal communities accepted land reserves and regulation under the Indian Act. They may have disliked the outcome, but they were powerless to change it. In other words, they no longer had the capacity to implement their supposed right of self-government.

To cite a late example, when the commissioners for Treaty 8 negotiated with the Cree at Lesser Slave Lake in 1899, they told the Indians that "whether treaty was made or not, they were subject to the law, bound to obey it, and liable to punishment for any infringement of it. We pointed out that the law was designed for the protection of all, and must be respected by all the inhabitants of the country, irrespective of colour or origin; and that, in requiring them to live at peace with white men who came into the country, and not to molest them in person or in property, it only required them to do what white men were required to do as to the Indians."[53] This is not the way that one speaks to another independent government; this is how one addresses subjects. It does not matter that British or Canadian military forces had never defeated the Cree of northern Alberta in war; the Indians had become subject *de facto* to the sovereignty of the Crown. They knew it and everyone else knew it at the time.

The recent practice of calling the right of aboriginal self-government "inherent" is a way of claiming that history doesn't matter, that aboriginal communities had, have, and always will have the right to govern themselves, no matter what happens. But history does matter. Government depends on power. New and more powerful tribes – the European tribes – entered Canada and established a new political order, as must have repeatedly happened before the arrival of the Europeans. It is true that there was not a conquest in most of Canada in the same way that there was in Mexico and Peru or in much of the United States. But can anyone seriously doubt that the conquest would have been carried out if necessary, just as Canada suppressed the Metis and Indians who rose in the North-West Rebellion? Does it make sense to respect power established by brutal conquest but not power that was, for the most part, established peacefully and humanely?

Why not consider the coming of the Europeans as a fourth migration, a new set of tribes pushing others in front of them? Should we hesitate to do so because the European colonists had lighter-coloured skin, hair, and eyes than the older inhabitants? At bottom, the assertion of an inherent right of aboriginal self-government is a kind of racism. It contends that the only legitimate inhabitants of the Americas have been the Indians and Inuit. According to this view, they had the right to drive each other from different territories as much as they liked, even to the point of destroying whole peoples and taking over their land, but Europeans had no similar right to push their way in.

Another distinction between Europeans and Siberians in the Americas is that the Europeans were civilized, while the earlier inhabitants were not. The sixteenth-century Spanish *conquistadores* were civilized, yet they set upon the Aztecs, Mayas, and Incas – the only civilized aboriginal inhabitants of the Americas – without mercy, overthrowing their governments, killing their leaders, and enslaving their people. The French in the seventeenth century were not nearly as harsh in Acadia or New France, although they, too, did not recognize any independent rights of the Indians to their own land and government. It was only the British, most notably through the Royal Proclamation of 1763, who gave some formal recognition to Indian rights. The recognition of Indians and Inuit as aboriginal peoples, with certain special rights adhering to that status, is thus a product of Western, particularly British, civilization in its Enlightenment phase.

Even as I write these lines, I can hear the hoots of derision. Civilization? Today, almost all writers on aboriginal topics put that word into sneer quotes, to indicate that the distinction between civilization and savagery has no meaning, or they maintain that Indians and Europeans both had civilizations – different, perhaps, but equal in stature.[54] This issue is so vexing that it requires its own chapter. Turn the page.

CHAPTER 3

What Ever Happened
to Civilization?

In contemporary discussions of aboriginal affairs, the distinction between civilized and uncivilized has virtually disappeared. For example, Alberta Stoney chief John Snow once said that "a migratory people are not necessarily a people who lack civilization, not if 'civilization' is taken in the sense of a law-abiding and caring society."[1] Ontario Ojibwa chief Fred Plain wrote at greater length: "Civilization is the accumulation of the traditions and culture of a people: their ability to express themselves in a variety of ways – in dance, music, art, law, religion, the telling of stories, the writing of books, and so on. The aboriginal people of North and South America constituted a number of different civilizations."[2] In this perspective, civilization is the same as what most writers mean by culture, that is, the life ways of a people; just as every people has a culture, so every people is civilized.

From another angle, aboriginal spokesmen attack the concept of civilization as a tool of oppression. Cree chief Stanley Arcand, for example, used the *Globe and Mail* to denounce what he called the "frontier thesis" that "there was a collision between an advanced civilization and a savage, primitive one. In the ensuing collision, the advanced civilization triumphed and prospered while the savage, primitive one withered away."[3] Likewise, the Royal Commission on Aboriginal Peoples denied that the concept of civilization was relevant to understanding the entry of Europeans into the New World. In its view, only European ethnocentrism converted differences between cultures into the alleged superiority of civilization over savagery.[4]

Although the views of Snow, Plain, Arcand, and the RCAP are not identical, they all have one thing in common – they reject any notion of superiority of European civilization over aboriginal cultures. Understanding this complicated issue and all its implications requires archaeological excavation of two talismanic words of our time – "civilization" and "culture."

CIVILIZATION

A whole family of terms, including "civil," "civic," "citizen," and "civilization," is derived from the Latin word *civis,* usually translated as "citizen." *Civis* did not originally have the legal implications that we now associate with citizenship; its Indo-European cognates include the English word "home" and a Greek word for "village." The original meaning of *civis* must have been simply someone who lives here rather than elsewhere. Because of its sense of fixed place (it is also related to the Latin word that gave us "cemetery"), it must have taken on its meaning after the adoption of agriculture as a sedentary way of life.

In classical Greek, *polis* meant "city-state," *polites* "citizen," and *politikos* "statesman" (as a noun) and "political" (as an adjective). With the translation of Greek philosophy into Latin, words of the *civis* family took on parallel meanings: *civitas* became "city-state," *civis* "citizen," and *civilis* "political" (as an adjective). But the Greek adjective was also borrowed directly into Latin as *politicus,* and that duplication was repeated as English acquired its philosophical vocabulary from Latin.

This explains why in those seventeenth-century masterpieces of social-contract theory, *Leviathan* by Thomas Hobbes and *The Second Treatise of Government* by John Locke, the words "civil" and "political" are synonyms for each other. Human beings are said to leave the "state of nature" and enter "civil society" or "political society" when they agree to form a sovereign government with the power to enforce the law. Both Hobbes and Locke thought that organized government was essential to peaceful existence. Hobbes expressed it most memorably when he wrote that in the state of nature there is "continual fear, and danger of violent death," and that the life of man there is "solitary, poor, nasty, brutish, and short."[5]

There were two major lines of development after Hobbes and Locke. One led to the contemporary concept of civil society, which has separated itself from government and politics. Civil society today is understood to be a self-ordering network of voluntary associations that spring up and function independently of government.[6] The other line led through the French and Scottish Enlightenments to the concept of civilization.

Whatever their other differences, eighteenth-century authors as divergent as Adam Smith and Jean-Jacques Rousseau exhibited a growing appreciation of historical growth. They began to portray civil society as resulting not from a single decision at a moment in time – the mythical social contract – but from a long and gradual process of development. In this evolutionary view, civil society implied not just the existence of formal government but also the flowering of the arts and sciences and the refinement of manners and mores. A new meaning required a new word – civilization. As late as 1772, Dr Johnson refused to put "civilization" in his dictionary, preferring "civility" instead, but he was fighting a losing battle. The term became general in the nineteenth century.[7]

John Stuart Mill's well-known essay "Civilization," published in 1836, set forth an ethnocentric understanding of the term that is still often encountered today.[8] He saw Europe as the only really civilized part of the world, and Great Britain as the most civilized country of Europe. Although Mill included in his characterization of civilization some of the elements that we find in later, more scientific definitions, such as agriculture, division of labour, and organized government, his parochial bias was unfortunate. One encounters the same problem today when American officials denounce Iraq as uncivilized because of the cruelty of Saddam Hussein's regime, or when Canadian editorial writers call the United States uncivilized because capital punishment is still administered there. All three countries – Iraq, the United States, and Canada – obviously count as civilized under a more neutral and scientific application of the term.

The American anthropologist Lewis Henry Morgan gave some precision to the concept of civilization. In *Ancient Society* (1877), he argued that human history moved through three phases, which he called savagery, barbarism, and civilization. Savagery, in Morgan's lexicon, corresponded roughly to the hunting-gathering way of life; barbarism to horticulture or non-intensive agriculture; and civilization to societies with intensive agriculture, formalized government (the state), and literacy.[9] (Morgan's scheme was actually more complicated than this, because he postulated three subordinate periods in both savagery and barbarism, but here we can omit the secondary details.) Morgan's evolutionary theory of civilization dominated anthropology for two generations before being overthrown by the rival theory of cultural relativism.

CULTURE

The word "culture" comes from the Latin *colere*, meaning to inhabit, honour, or tend. Inhabiting leads to the word "colony," honouring to "cult," and tending to words such as "cultivate," "agriculture," and "culture." The German writer J.G. Herder, in his *Ideas on the Philosophy of the History of Mankind* (1784–1791), was the first to make the concept of culture relevant to political and social philosophy. In rejecting the prevailing Enlightenment notion of a unilinear process of development culminating in Western civilization, he spoke of cultures in the plural, writing that "the very thought of a superior European culture is a blatant insult to the majesty of Nature."[10]

Herder's concept of culture had to wait almost a century before taking hold. A landmark was the book *Primitive Culture* (1871), the work of the British anthropologist E.B. Tylor, who defined culture as "the knowledge, belief, arts, morals, customs and any other capabilities and habits acquired by man as a member of society."[11] Although he discerned the plurality of cultures, Tylor also postulated an evolutionary process of advance and agreed with Morgan about the three stages of savagery, barbarism, and civilization.[12]

The real triumph of culture as an anthropological concept came through the influence of Franz Boas and the brilliant students he attracted to Columbia University, including Margaret Mead, Ruth Benedict, Alfred Kroeber, Robert Lowie, and Melville Herskovits.[13] Using Tylor's notion of culture, Boas developed a research program that entailed encountering non-Western cultures on their own terms. He put an emphasis on discovering the internal logic and coherence of such cultures – how they functioned to meet universal human needs – rather than on ranking them on a scale of advancement. "Anthropolgy," wrote Boas, "was by definition impossible

as long as these distinctions between ourselves and the primitive,
ourselves and the barbarian, ourselves and the pagan, held sway
over people's minds. It was necessary first to arrive at that degree
of sophistication where we no longer set our own beliefs over
against our neighbor's superstition."[14]

Books such as Boas's *The Mind of Primitive Man* (1911), Mead's
Coming of Age in Samoa (1928), and Benedict's *Patterns of Culture*
(1934) entrenched relativism in the new discipline of cultural
anthropology as well as in the larger realm of educated public opinion. Generations of students learned that all cultures were equivalent, each had its own way of meeting human needs, each functioned
in its own terms, and none was superior to any other. Initially,
however, the change was more a matter of emphasis than of total
rejection of earlier evolutionary theories of civilization. Although
they discarded the schema of savagery, barbarism, and civilization,
Boas and his students still used words such as "civilization" and
"primitive." They held it to be especially useful to study primitive
cultures because, being simple, they were more integrated, exhibit-
ing "one well-defined general pattern" that an anthropologist could
grasp through careful observation.[15] But if one culture is simple and
another complex, is not the latter also superior to the former in
some sense? Increasing complexity is a hallmark of progress in
scholarship and science, as well as of technical advances in engineering, commerce, and athletics. Why not in culture generally?
Boas and his school did not dwell on such problems.

At the end of the twentieth century, Boasian relativism still rules
cultural anthropology. In one textbook, the word "civilization"
does not even appear in the index, although there is a mention of
primitive societies: "First, it must be made clear that nothing
pejorative is implied in the anthropological use of the term 'primitive.' It refers only to societies and not to people, as such, and
means merely that the society is nonliterate and is relatively unseg-
mented by divisions of class, ethnicity, and occupation, a simplicity
of social organization that is commonly the result of a simple
technology. There is, however, nothing simple or backward about
the mentalities or languages of primitives."[16] Civilization gets one
paragraph in another textbook, in the restricted context of a discussion of intensive agriculture. Civilization, defined there laconi-
cally as "living in cities," is said to have emerged as a result of
intensive agriculture. End of story.[17]

THE PERSISTENCE OF CIVILIZATION

Civilization, however, is still a central concept in archaeology and prehistory, even though these are often considered subfields of anthropology. One archaeology textbook even uses the term "civilization" in its title, with an implication of evolutionary progress: *Ascent to Civilization: The Archaeology of Early Man.*[18] The author's definition is a little vague: "The two essential elements in any civilization were modern man with the brain to organize, and food production, the economic base that made it possible. Food production made high population density inevitable – but that could only work if the human society was organized. Not all civilizations have cities, but all have food production and complex social organization. Higher technology is helpful but not essential in every respect – the wheel was unknown in the New World."[19]

Another textbook, with a whole chapter entitled "The Development of Civilization," offers a clearer discussion:

The word *civilization* has a ready, everyday meaning. It implies "civility," a measure of decency in the behavior of the individual in a civilization. Such definitions inevitably reflect ethnocentrism or value judgments because what is "civilized" behavior in one civilization might be antisocial or baffling in another. These simplistic understandings are of no use to students of prehistoric civilizations seeking basic definitions and cultural processes.

Some special attributes that separate civilizations from other societies can be listed as follows:

- Urbanized societies, based on cities, with large, very complex social organizations. The early civilization was invariably based on a specific territory, such as the Nile Valley, as opposed to smaller areas owned by individual kin groups.
- Symbiotic economies based on the centralized accumulation of capital and social status through tribute and taxation. This type of economy allows the support of hundreds, often thousands, of nonfood producers such as smiths and priests. Long-distance trade and the division of labor, as well as craft specialization, are often characteristic of early civilizations.
- Advances toward record keeping, science and mathematics, and some form of written script.
- Impressive public buildings and monumental architecture.

The attributes are by no means common to all early civilizations, for they take different forms in each.[20]

The archaeological concept of civilization does not mean that cultural relativism is entirely wrong; indeed, it obviously contains important truths. There have been and still are many societies with different cultures. Standards of goodness and beauty exist only within a cultural context and hence are inherently, though not infinitely, variable; they are not infinitely variable because all human beings belong to the same species and therefore share certain patterns of behaviour. Cultural universals exist in the sense that all societies have conceptions of family and kinship, norms of reciprocity and justice, and ways of making collective decisions.

But, in addition to this horizontal tableau of variability within wide limits, there is also a vertical dimension of development through time. Human history and prehistory record an evolutionary process of increasing technical mastery over nature and increasing size and complexity of social organization. Cultural relativists implicitly recognize this when they distinguish between simple and complex societies.

I use the term "civilization" as archaeologists still do, to refer to societies that have passed a certain threshold of technology and complexity. The threshold of civilization is crossed when a society acquires a combination of certain attributes:

- Intensive agriculture – long-term cultivation of the same ground, assisted by some combination of irrigation, fertilization, and animal husbandry
- Urbanization – permanent settlements of several thousand residents
- Division of labour among cultivators, craftsmen, merchants, soldiers, rulers, and priests
- Intellectual advances such as record-keeping, writing, and astronomy. All early civilizations except the Incas developed writing, and the latter had both an astronomically based calendar and a system of record-keeping using knotted strings.
- Advanced technology. New World civilizations did not have the wheel, and their metallurgy was in the early stages, but they performed impressive feats of architecture and engineering.
- Formalized, hierarchial government – that is, a state.

These attributes are all matters of degree. Agriculture can be more or less intensive, technology more or less advanced, government more or less organized. Qualified observers can disagree in particular cases as to whether the term "civilization" applies. Without quibbling over details, I would apply it to the Old World civilizations of Egypt, Mesopotamia, India, and China, as well as to the New World civilizations of the Andes and Meso-America, bearing in mind that all these were centres from which civilization radiated outward to be adopted by many peoples other than the originators.

Civilization is not a unilinear process. Even though there was contact and diffusion among both the Old World and New World civilizations (though not between the two hemispheres), multiple civilizations advanced along their own lines. But the lines of development were parallel; they did not go off in unrelated directions. The New World civilizations the Spaniards conquered were remarkably like Old World civilizations of about five thousand years earlier, with their stone tools, metal ornaments, monumental architecture, divine kingship, and hieroglyphic writing.

Civilization is a process of collective advance. Individual human beings who live in an uncivilized society – the "savages" or "barbarians" – are not necessarily any less intelligent, wise, kind, courageous, or trustworthy than their counterparts in a civilized society; indeed, they may possess more of all these virtues. But the collective advance of civilization places superior resources in the hands of the individual. The bard may have a better memory, but the scholar can resort to a library of books. The warrior may be braver, but the soldier has deadlier weapons as well as the advantage of belonging to a larger, more disciplined fighting force. The chief may be wiser, but the head of state can call upon an entire bureaucracy for advice.

"Civilization" as I use the term here is a factual, not a normative, concept. It describes a certain type of social organization that has gradually emerged and spread around the entire world. It is not that savagery is bad and civilization is good; both are stages of social development that have arisen sequentially in the historical process. Civilization is not the preordained goal of history. Particular civilizations have collapsed in the past, and it is conceivable that civilization as a specific kind of social structure could collapse or be replaced by some other, as yet inconceivable, form of social organization.

But even if civilization is a factually descriptive concept, the worldwide spread of civilization has certain moral implications. If we pretend that civilization as defined here does not exist or that it does not absorb and replace earlier forms of society, we ignore basic aspects of the contemporary human condition at our peril, for any political program based on ignorance or rejection of reality is bound to fail.

To take one example, only the complex economies that are part of civilization can support the existence of the numbers of human beings, including aboriginal people, who are now alive. Though one might dislike many aspects of civilization, would it be morally defensible to call for a radical decline in population, necessitating early death and reproductive failure for billions of people now living? The answer is clearly no if morality means treating other people as ends in themselves rather than as elements in a scheme you wish to impose.

WHAT DIFFERENCE DOES IT MAKE?

Even though it remains central to archaeology, the distinction between civilized and uncivilized societies has virtually vanished from the discussion of aboriginal politics and history in Canada. There is now the assumption that native American cultures did not differ fundamentally from European cultures.

Consider the RCAP's interpretation of history, according to which there are four main periods in the historical relationship between aboriginal peoples and the European newcomers. First was the era of "separate worlds," which lasted until about AD 1500: "In the period before 1500, Aboriginal and non-Aboriginal societies developed in isolation from each other. Differences in physical and social environments inevitably meant differences in culture and forms of social organization. On both sides of the Atlantic, however, national groups with long traditions of governing themselves emerged, organizing themselves into different social and political forms according to their traditions and the needs imposed by their environments."[21]

The second stage was one of "contact and co-operation," a time of "mutual recognition, whereby Aboriginal and non-Aboriginal societies appear, however reluctantly at times, to have determined that the best course of action was to treat the other as a political equal in most important respects."[22] Natives and newcomers traded with each other and made military alliances to go to war against common enemies. The RCAP holds up the Iroquois two-row wampum belt as the great symbol of this period. The two rows mean "we have two different paths, two different peoples."[23]

The third period, beginning at different times in different parts of Canada, was one of "displacement and assimilation." The new-comers imposed a "colonial relationship" upon aboriginal societ-ies,[24] asserting governmental control, taking possession of the land, relegating aboriginal people to reserves, and regulating their lives under the Indian Act. That long nightmare started to end in 1969, when the reaction to the government's White Paper signalled the beginning of the fourth stage, "negotiation and renewal." In this period, which includes the present, aboriginal peoples are reclaim-ing their equality through recognition of their inherent right of self-government. Their governments become a "third order" of the fed-eral system, and they recover land and financial independence as they return in effect to the second stage of contact and cooperation.

In portraying the meeting of equals, the RCAP's version of history implies that the eventual predominance of the European newcomers was due to evil intent and bad faith. But telling the story like this is like trying to stage *Romeo and Juliet* without the romance of the two star-crossed lovers, or *Hamlet* without the death of his father. It leaves out the main thing, namely the civilization gap between the Indians and Inuit, on the one hand, and the Europeans, on the other.

None of the aboriginal societies of Canada were civilized in the sense in which the term is used here. Most advanced were the Iroquoian peoples of southern Quebec and Ontario, who, although they still hunted and fished extensively, also practised food produc-tion in the form of horticulture. They made clearings in the forest, planted corn and beans for ten or twelve years, then moved their villages to new locations after the fertility of the soil was depleted.[25] They did not have a state form of political organization; but with their larger population and semi-sedentary way of life, they had developed political confederacies under the form of rule known as the chiefdom.[26] Given more centuries to develop, they might well have produced an agricultural civilization and an imperial state along the lines of the Aztecs. Although not agricultural, the Indians of coastal British Columbia were also semi-sedentary because of the extraordinary richness of marine resources, especially the riv-erine salmon fishery.[27]

Elsewhere, the natives of Canada were hunter-collectors (agriculture had been practised earlier in some of the western river valleys but had been abandoned because of climate change as well as the adoption of horses and guns, which made buffalo hunting uniquely productive). In the forests of the Canadian Shield, social organization consisted of small bands, and families hunted independently during much of the year. On the great plains, where the buffalo furnished a more concentrated and abundant food resource, there were larger tribal groupings.

The RCAP is right to say that aboriginal peoples organized themselves "into different social and political forms according to their traditions and the needs imposed by their environments"; but that statement omits a significant truth, one pointed out long ago by Diamond Jenness, the most famous of all Canadian anthropologists. "Tools of stone," he wrote, "still formed the basis of all [aboriginal] material culture, and they were no farther advanced economically than the inhabitants of England two thousand years before Christ."[28] The disparity in civilization between the natives and the European colonists was huge, as Jenness described at length:

Let us consider, for a moment, some of the advantages the colonists possessed. They imported with them the seeds of various grains and vegetables, such as wheat, oats, rye, barley, potatoes, and turnips, and they possessed the knowledge of their cultivation. They knew how to irrigate and to fertilize the land, how to rotate their crops. They brought steel axes and saws to clear the ground, ploughs and oxen to break up the soil, scythes to cut the grain, and vehicles to gather in the harvest. Cows, sheep, goats, and poultry provided them both meat and clothing. The newcomers could anchor themselves to any fertile plot of ground, certain that with reasonable industry they could wrest from its few square rods sufficient food to keep starvation from their doors. They could erect substantial buildings of brick or stone, since the same soil that provided their sustenance would provide sustenance also for their children's children; and they could concentrate their homes as a single community, facing the river that linked them during the summer with the motherland.[29]

Striking as it is, this paragraph gives only the barest idea of the colonists' advantages. A complete inventory would also mention the domestication of large animals for carrying people and pulling loads; metallurgy for producing weapons, tools, and implements of all kinds (North American Indians did make some use of native, or elemental, copper for tools and ornaments)[30]; powerful organized states that could send trading and colonizing expeditions to the New World; literacy and record-keeping to bind large populations together; the mathematical, scientific, and engineering knowledge that made transoceanic voyages possible – and much, much more.[31]

It was not a contest between Indian cultures and European civilization, but rather one between Indian cultures and all the civilizations of the Old World taken together. Because the peoples of Europe, Asia, and Africa had been in contact with each other for millennia, European civilization had incorporated within itself the advances of other civilizations past and present, including Babylonian astronomy, Jewish monotheism, Greek philosophy, Roman law, Indian mathematics (the decimal system), and Chinese technology (printing, gunpowder, the compass).

Also part of this pooling process was the disease experience of civilization. Life in dense agricultural communities allowed diseases such as smallpox, influenza, and measles to leap from domesticated animal hosts to become crowd diseases of human beings. By early modern times, all societies of the Old World had acquired some resistance to these diseases, which became lethal when transferred to the inexperienced populations of the New World.[32] All over North and South America, aboriginal populations went into a steep, prolonged, and demoralizing decline that has only been reversed in the twentieth century. Demographic disaster on the aboriginal side multiplied the advantage that civilization conferred upon the European colonists.

The civilization gap shows how ill-suited the RCAP's equality framework is for depicting the contact between natives and new-comers in North America; the frame doesn't fit the picture. Two frames that fit better come from historical experience throughout the world: (1) the displacement of hunter-gatherers by agricultural peoples, and (2) the extension of rule by organized states over state-less societies. The two coincide in the case of Canada, for Canadian natives were both stateless and, for the most part, non-agricultural.

Agriculture was first invented in the Near East about ten thousand years ago. Since then it has expanded relentlessly, both by independent rediscovery and by radiation from established centres. Luigi Cavalli-Sforza calls it "the great trek of the cultivators."[33] It took only about five thousand years for agriculture to reach the northern fringes of continental Europe, the British Isles, and Scandinavia. It used to be thought that only the diffusion of technology was involved, but genetic analysis shows that there must have been a substantial human migration through Asia Minor and the Balkans into the rest of Europe.[34] According to Colin Renfrew, the appropriate model for understanding this migration is neither acculturation and diffusion nor sudden dramatic invasion, but a "wave of advance" in which the cultivators moved gradually but inexorably forward, displacing and absorbing the hunter-collector population.[35] Another great trek was that of the Bantu-speaking peoples, who, having adapted agriculture to tropical conditions about thirty-five hundred years ago in their homeland between Nigeria and Cameroon, spread gradually east and south, displacing and absorbing the aboriginal Khoisan populations.[36] That expansion was still under way when the Bantu collided with the Europeans working their way north from their colonial beachheads on the southern coast of Africa. Seen against this backdrop, the entry of Europeans into North America, as into Australia, was the last act of a great drama – the spread of agriculture around the world. Meanwhile another play was being enacted as organized states extended their sway over stateless societies. The two processes fit together naturally when agricultural peoples organized as states come into contact with small-scale, stateless, hunter-gatherer societies.

RIGHT OR WRONG?[37]

Both of these processes are so prominent in human history that it seems almost beside the point to raise questions about morality. It is like asking whether it is right or wrong that childbirth is painful, or that everyone eventually has to die, or that floods and droughts occur. Moreover, agricultural expansion and state aggrandizement were both happening in the Americas before the Europeans arrived. Fortified with increased food production from horticulture, the Iroquois were pushing hard against their Huron and Algonquian neighbours when the French and English arrived. Further south, the Aztecs and Incas were forcibly incorporating neighbouring peoples into their civilized and growing empires.

Nonetheless, even if no moral defence is needed, one is available within the tradition of Western philosophy. The roots of this defence are at least as old as Thomas More's *Utopia*, published in

1516, just as the colonization of America was beginning. When the island of Utopia became overpopulated, according to More, the authorities would count off

a certain number of people from each town to go and start a colony at the nearest point on the mainland where there's a large area that hasn't been cultivated by the local inhabitants. Such colonies are governed by the Utopians, but the natives are allowed to join in if they want to. When this happens, natives and colonists soon combine to form a single community, with a single way of life, to the great advantage of both parties – for, under Utopian management, land which used to be thought incapable of producing anything for one lot of people produces plenty for two.

If the natives won't do what they're told, they're expelled from the area marked out for annexation. If they try to resist, the Utopians declare war – for they consider war perfectly justifiable, when one country denies another its natural right to derive nourishment from any soil which the original owners are not using themselves, but are merely holding to as a worthless piece of property.[38]

John Locke pushed the argument further in a theory of property specifically designed to justify English colonial policy in the New World.[39] According to Locke, God created the world and gave it to men in common for their sustenance in the state of nature. In this pre-political condition, the world was owned by men in common, but each man had private ownership of his own person: "The labor of his body and the work of his hands, we may say, are properly his."[40] A man could further create private property by mixing his labour with things from the common storehouse of the world – collecting acorns or picking apples, to use Locke's examples. This view of property was a deduction from Locke's principle of equal liberty in the state of nature, "there being nothing more evident than that creatures of the same species and rank, promiscuously born to all the same advantages of nature and the use of the same facilities, should also be equal one amongst another without subordination or subjection."[41]

Also, the institution of private property greatly enhanced the productivity of land: "He who appropriates land to himself by his labor does not lessen but increase the common stock of mankind; for the provisions serving to the support of human life produced by one acre of enclosed and cultivated land are – to speak much within compass – ten times more than those which are yielded by an acre of land of an equal richness lying waste in common."[42] Thus it would have been to the advantage of the Indians to adopt agriculture for themselves, for they were "rich in land and poor in all the comforts of life; whom nature having furnished as liberally as any other people with the materials of plenty, i.e., a fruitful soil, apt to produce in abundance what might serve for food, raiment, and delight, yet for want of improving it by labor have not one-hundredth part of the conveniences we enjoy. And a king of a large and fruitful territory there feeds, lodges, and is clad worse than a day-laborer in England."[43]

The Swiss jurist Emer de Vattel echoed Locke's themes in his treatise on international law, *Le Droit des Gens* (1758).[44] "The whole earth," he wrote, "is destined to furnish sustenance for its inhabitants; but it can not do this unless it be cultivated. Every Nation is therefore bound by the natural law to cultivate the land which has fallen to its share."[45] Nations that live by plunder, as the ancient Germans did, "fail in their duty to themselves, injure their neighbors, and deserve to be exterminated like wild beasts of prey."[46] Living by hunting or herding might have been justifiable when the world's population was smaller, "but now that the human race has multiplied so greatly, it could not subsist if every people wished to live after that fashion. Those who occupy this idle mode of life occupy more land than they would have need of under a system of honest labor, and they may not complain if other more industrious Nations, too confined at home, should come and occupy part of their lands."[47] And again:

We have already pointed out, in speaking of the obligation of cultivating the earth, that these tribes can not take to themselves more land than they have need of or can inhabit and cultivate. Their uncertain occupancy of these vast regions can not be held as a real and lawful taking of possession; and when the Nations of Europe, which are too confined at home, come upon lands which the savages have no special need of and are making no present and continuous use of, they may lawfully take possession of them and establish colonies in them.[48]

Vattel allowed the taking of land that hunter-collectors did not "need" (if they would adopt agriculture), but not total expropriation. He noted at one point that the colonization of North America, "if done within just limits," might be considered "entirely lawful"; and he wrote at another point that "we are not departing from the intentions of nature when we restrict the savages within narrower bounds."[49] Did British colonization in North America exceed its "just limits" and take too much land away from the Indians? Generally speaking, the reserves set aside were large enough that the surviving groups of Indians (admittedly much reduced by disease and frontier warfare) could, and often did, support themselves by adopting the agricultural technology of the day. Today the reserves seem too small because their populations have grown and various aspects of the legal regime adopted for Indians have inhibited the migration from rural to urban locations that almost all other Canadians have undergone; but when first established, they were generally large enough to satisfy Vattel's criterion.

David Gauthier, one of the best-known contemporary American philosophers, has restated Locke and Vattel's line of argument in contemporary language:

Let us grant that, in the state of nature, a group of persons, A, is entitled to appropriate as much land as its members are able to use in any way at all. However, should another group, B, of would-be appropriators appear on the scene, and should this group possess a superior technology to A, then B would be entitled to appropriate, from A, as much as would leave A with land sufficient, using B's superior technology, to maintain at least as many persons as before, with at least as rich an assortment of material goods, and at least as wide a range of opportunities (though perhaps a different range), *provided* B makes its technology effectively available to A.[50]

Gauthier effectively expands the agricultural argument. Much of Canada is unsuited for agriculture, yet is valuable because it contains minerals, timber, and other natural resources essential to a civilized society. Gauthier's formulation does not mention agriculture as such. The contest is really between civilization and savagery, not between agriculture and hunting.

Let me put this line of argument in the simplest terms. Initially, all people, whether hunters or farmers, have an equal right to support themselves from the bounty of the earth. But the hunting mode of life takes up a lot of land, while agriculture, being more productive, causes population to grow and leads to civilization. As their numbers increase, civilized peoples have a right to cultivate the additional land necessary for their support. If the hunters deny them that opportunity by keeping their hunting grounds as a game preserve, they impede the equal access of the farmers to the bounty of the earth. It is wrong for the hunters to insist on maintaining their way of life; rather, they should adopt agriculture and civilization, which would actually make them better off while allowing more people to live. The farmers are justified in taking land from the hunters and defending it as long as they make the arts of civilization available to the hunters.

Aboriginal advocates may dismiss this whole line of thought as self-serving because it was developed by European philosophers and lawyers writing in the period of European imperial expansion and pondering how to justify it. Barbara Arneil, for example, has recently detailed how John Locke's theoretical writings were related to the colonization projects in which he was involved.[51] But all political thinking, not least the aboriginal orthodoxy, arises in a specific historical context and will inevitably express, or be harnessed to serve, some configuration of material interests. Once we are clear about the origin of ideas, we still have to examine them to see if they teach us something that transcends their origin.

Interestingly, Louis Riel, the great Canadian symbol of aboriginal resistance, recognized the force of the argument developed by Locke and Vattel. He said in his treason trial at Regina in 1885 that

civilization has the means of improving life that Indians or half-breeds have not. So when they come in our savage country, in our uncultivated land, they come and help us with their civilization, but we helped them with our lands, so the question comes: Your land, you Cree or you half-breed, your land is worth to-day one-seventh of what it will be when civilization will have opened it? Your country unopened is worth to you only one-seventh of what it will be when opened. I think it is a fair share to acknowledge the genius of civilization to such an extent as to give, when I have seven pairs of socks, six, to keep one.[52]

I find Vattel's argument persuasive, but only up to a point. The fundamental problem with it is that it requires hunter-collectors to give up a way of life to which they are deeply attached. They need their "surplus" lands if they are to live as they have always done. Fencing and plowing the woodlands and prairies will inevitably reduce the quantity of game and inhibit the hunters' access to whatever does survive. So the claim that there is surplus land is valid only from the agricultural, civilized point of view, and I can see no moral justification for telling the hunters that they must give up one way of life and adopt another. On the other hand, I cannot see a moral justification for telling the agriculturalists that they cannot make use of land that, from their point of view, is not being used.

Matters are different where there is already in place an accepted regime of property rights with a sovereign enforcing authority. It would be both immoral and illegal for a modern-day Canadian rancher to let his cattle graze on a neighbouring Indian reserve simply because the residents did not seem to be making use of the pasture. The difference is that the Crown owns this land under Canadian law, reserves it for the beneficial use of an Indian band, and provides the means to punish trespass. However, this combination of explicit property rights and a sovereign enforcing authority is itself an aspect of civilization and thus does not exist where civilization and hunter-collectors collide. I will return to these questions in later chapters on sovereignty and property rights.

As presented thus far, the argument has nothing to do with the state. Farmers would be entitled to appropriate land for agriculture even if they did not have an organized government. But when cultivators are already living under the state form of organization, they will expect the state to enforce their property rights. Inevitably, this will extend the state's rule over hunters who resist appropriation of their hunting grounds for agriculture, and the state will expand along with the agricultural way of life. This is not a justification of state expansion in all circumstances. Vattel, for one, thought that the Spanish conquest of the civilized Aztec and Inca states was a "notorious usurpation."[53] But it works well enough for the case of Canada, where no Indian states existed before the coming of the Europeans.

In 1918, the u.s. State Department commissioned Alpheus Henry Snow to study "the question of aborigines in the law and practice of nations."[54] "Aborigines," Snow reported, "are members of uncivilized tribes which inhabit a region at the time a civilized State extends its sovereignty over the region, and which have so inhabited from time immemorial; and also the uncivilized descendants of such persons dwelling in the region ... The relations of aborigines with each other, with the colonists, and with the colonizing State are necessarily subject to a special régime established by the colonizing State for the purpose of fitting the aborigines for civilization, and opening the resources of the land to the use of the civilized world."[55]

In some instances, colonial states exterminated or enslaved aboriginal inhabitants without any attempt to civilize them. But Snow's description is an accurate description of Canadian policy from the point (reached at different times in different parts of the country) at which agriculture, settlement, and resource extraction started to make the aboriginal way of life impossible. In the RCAP's words, there were three phases "in which first protection, then civilization, and finally assimilation were the transcendant policy goals."[56]

In pursuit of these goals, the Canadian government, with or without treaties, set aside land reserves for Indians, offered agricultural instruction and assistance, provided both basic and industrial education, and facilitated the work of Christian missionaries. The ultimate aim was individual enfranchisement, as stated in the Gradual Civilization Act of 1857. An Indian man over twenty-one years of age who could read and write either English or French, and who was free of debt and of good character, could apply to receive up to fifty acres of land from his reserve. He would hold it as a life estate, after which it would pass to his children in fee simple.[57] Through all the subsequent twists and turns of Indian administration, enfranchisement remained the ultimate goal of Indian policy, until it was challenged in the last thirty years.

Although enfranchisement did not work out as expected, the policy has been successful in a larger sense. The aboriginal population of Canada, as the RCAP points out, is now larger than it was before the arrival of the Europeans.[58] Indians and Inuit have adopted the civilized mode of life. They work, buy and sell, and invest in the economy. They acquire literacy and education, both basic and advanced. They vote and in other ways participate in political decision-making. Obviously all is not well; if it were, I would not be writing this book. But it is important to grasp that not everything has failed. In the largest context, the policy of civilization has succeeded.

IS CIVILIZATION RACIST?

Drawing a distinction between civilized and uncivilized is sure to be denounced as ethnocentric and probably racist. "It is racist," a recent essay states categorically, "to view aboriginal life on the land as inferior to the settler farming culture."[59] Indeed, ethnocentrism and racism abound in history, and denigration of other cultures is often based merely on unfamiliarity. But civilization as explained here is an objectively definable way of life, and societies that adopt it obtain a demonstrable increase in power over nature and over uncivilized societies.

All races in every part of the world have shown the capacity to invent and adopt civilization. However, it is also true that the Old World was about five thousand years ahead of the New World on the path of civilization. Agriculture began much earlier in the ancient Near East than it did in Meso-America or the Andes, and the lead was never overcome. Hence the huge gap in technology, literacy, and social organization between the European newcomers and the neolithic civilizations of Mexico and South America, let alone the horticulturalists and hunters of North America.

According to Jared Diamond, the gap in civilization resulted from differences in the geography and ecology of the two hemispheres. Intensive agriculture depended on the domestication of appropriate plant and animal species, and there were more of both to work with in the Old World. Wild grasses with large seeds were particularly abundant in the ancient Near East, where agriculture was first invented. The Old World had numerous species of large social mammals, such as sheep, goats, horses, pigs, and cattle, that could be domesticated to provide meat, milk, fertilizer, and muscle power for agriculture. In contrast, many of the large social mammals of the New World had been exterminated at the end of the last ice age, leaving only the camelids (guanaco and vicuña) of South America to give rise to domesticated versions (llama and alpaca). There were sheep and goats in the western mountains of North America and bison on the great plains, but both were distant from the areas where agriculture began in the New World.

Smaller size also worked against the New World. "A larger area or population," according to Diamond, "means more potential inventors, more competing societies, more innovations available to adopt – and more pressure to adopt and retain innovations, because societies failing to do so will tend to be eliminated by competing societies."[60] Compounding the disadvantage of smaller size was the north-south geographical layout of the Western hemisphere. Domesticated plants such as maize had to adapt to different climatic and ecological zones as they were carried north and south, thus slowing down the process of diffusion. Such gradients were less of a problem over most of Europe, Asia, and northern Africa. Also, the separation of the large land masses of North and South America by the narrow isthmus of Panama and a thousand miles of jungle and mountains effectively impeded interchange between the Andean and Meso-American civilizations.

Thus, for reasons having nothing to do with race, the European colonists had enormous advantages over the aboriginal inhabitants of Canada. It is also noteworthy that the newcomers wanted and expected the aboriginals to assimilate into their civilization. One can debate the morality and practicality of assimilation, but it certainly was the opposite of belief in racial inferiority, for it assumed that the aboriginals, despite obvious racial differences, could adopt all the practices of civilization – as in fact they have.

CHAPTER 4

The Fiction of
Aboriginal Sovereignty

"Sovereignty" is another political word with multiple meanings and mythic overtones. As with civilization and culture, we have to begin with some etymological history and conceptual clarification.

The word "sovereign" is derived through French from the Latin adjective *superanus,* meaning superior, which in turn comes from the preposition *super,* meaning above. In medieval usage, "sovereign" came to be a synonym for the personal ruler in a monarchical system of government, a usage that still survives in stylized phrases such as "Our Sovereign Lady the Queen." The noun "sovereignty" correspondingly meant the status of being king or queen.

In his book *Six livres de la république* (1576), the French jurist Jean Bodin turned sovereignty into a general concept of political philosophy. "Sovereignty," he wrote, "is the absolute and perpetual power of a commonwealth." And further, "the essence of sovereign majesty and absolute power lies chiefly in making law for subjects on any matter without their consent."[1] For Bodin, sovereignty became an abstraction, the ability to make law and use coercion without being overridden. Bodin saw the sovereign as subordinate to God and natural law, but exempt from positive law *(legibus solutus)*, that is, "absolute," as far as other human authorities were concerned. For Bodin, writing at the height of the religious wars in France, the concept of sovereignty was a way of restoring civil peace by subjecting religious factions to political control.

Thomas Hobbes, during a similar period of religious wars in Britain, brought Bodin's notion of sovereignty to the English-speaking world. Hobbes defined the sovereign as an artificial person "of whose acts a great multitude, by mutual covenants one with another, have made themselves every one the author, to the end he may use the strength and means of them all, as he shall think expedient, for their peace and common defence."[2] After Hobbes, a long series of legal philosophers, including William Blackstone, Jeremy Bentham, John Austin, A.V. Dicey, and Ivor Jennings, made sovereignty in general, and parliamentary sovereignty in particular, the central concept of the British constitution.

Bodin, writing in French, called the political community defined by sovereignty *la république* (a literal translation of the Latin *respublica)*, while Hobbes preferred the term "commonwealth." Today, political scientists and legal theorists would normally use the term "state." The state in modern parlance is a combination of three factors – a settled population living on a fixed territory under a sovereign government.[3] In this context sovereignty has a double meaning. In its internal application, it refers to the highest ruling power in the state, the person or body that has the last say and cannot be overruled by anyone else. In the British tradition, that body is Parliament, which can pass or repeal any law, make and depose kings, call cabinets to account, and pass laws that no court can declare unconstitutional. In its external application, it means freedom from control by outside forces, particularly other states. A state is sovereign in this sense if it can conduct its internal affairs without external interference.

As if all this were not complicated enough, the term "sovereignty" has long been used in a more relaxed sense to apply even to stateless societies as long as they are free from outside control. The American practice of referring to the "tribal sovereignty" of Indians is in this tradition. The phrase does not assume that Indian tribes had organized states or sovereigns in the Hobbesian sense; it means that they lived according to their own customary laws without being ruled by other tribes or imperial states.

Although Bodin and Hobbes thought of sovereignty as a concentrated, unitary power, it can be divided, as it is in Canada. Ever since 1867, the federal Parliament and the provincial legislatures have each had a share of sovereign law-making power assigned by the constitution. More recently, the passage of the Canadian Charter of Rights and Freedoms has enhanced the ability of the courts to strike down both federal and provincial legislation as contrary to the constitution. And the constitution itself can be amended by Parliament and the provincial legislatures acting together under the procedures known as the amending formulas. Sovereignty in this tableau is a hyperabstraction, referring to the putative supremacy of the constitution over the actions of any individual or group. No single person or body wields all the powers adhering to the notion of sovereignty.

Another complication is popular sovereignty. In Switzerland and many American states, voters can legislate directly through referendums. And in all representative systems of government, at least some of the officials who wield sovereign power are elected by voters. Hence there is a limited but real sense in which the whole people can be said to be sovereign, and popular sovereignty is usually taken as the cornerstone of democratic theory.

Sovereignty has become such a tangled concept that it might be better to leave it to the academics and banish it from popular discussion of politics. But that, of course, is impossible, and in fact sovereignty is one of the most current terms in the political marketplace of ideas – especially in Canada.

CLAIMS OF ABORIGINAL SOVEREIGNTY

Claims of aboriginal sovereignty abound in the literature of the last twenty years. Here are three examples:

- The "Treaty and Aboriginal Rights Principles," a founding document of the Assembly of First Nations, states that "all pre-confederation, post-confederation treaties and treaties executed outside the present boundaries of Canada but which apply to the Indian Nations of Canada are international treaty agreements between sovereign nations."[4]
- Three writers from Citizens for Public Justice, an advocacy group in the Dutch Reform tradition, say that the "basic dilemma" for aboriginal people is "sovereignty or assimilation."[5] They clearly come down on the side of sovereignty.
- According to the Royal Commission on Aboriginal Peoples, "Aboriginal nations deny that they ever surrendered their sovereignty."[6]

The rhetoric of sovereignty embraces a wide range of political demands. At one extreme, a claim of sovereignty means an aspiration

of achieving statehood apart from Canada. The best-known exponents of this position are the Mohawks, who, according to Gerald
Alfred, "reject the idea of buying into what are essentially foreign
institutions" by remaining part of Canada: "The people of Kahnawake have allegiance solely to the Mohawk nation, and their view
of the Mohawk nation is one in the fullest sense of the term as it
is used in international law."[7] In 1998 an Ontario Provincial Court
judge in Brantford, Ontario, obligingly removed the Canadian flag
from his courtroom when a Mohawk witness refused to testify in
its presence. "Even though I live in this country ... I don't recognize
your so-called sovereignty because you don't recognize my sovereignty," the witness said.[8] Other Indian groups sometimes take a
similar position. "In 1992," as Mel Smith points out, "the Haida
National Council of the Queen Charlotte Islands declared themselves
to be a sovereign nation and even issued their own passports."[9]

Most aboriginal groups, however, do not talk about the full
status of sovereign statehood. They want their alleged share of
sovereign power to be recognized in the constitution, as is already
true for Parliament and the provincial legislatures. If they had such
a status, they could no longer be overruled by senior governments.
This aspiration is often expressed in terms other than sovereignty,
such as self-determination, jurisdiction, and the inherent right of
self-government. Here are three examples:

- The Dene Declaration of 1975 proclaimed that "while there are
realities we are forced to submit to, such as the existence of a
country called Canada, we insist on the right to self-determination
as a distinct people and the recognition of the Dene Nation."[10]
- In October 1988, when the Lubicon Cree set up a barricade
across the road leading into their land-claim area, they said that
they were ready to "assert jurisdiction," that is, to take control
of the area and keep provincial and federal authorities out.[11]
- In its report, the RCAP endorsed the phrase "inherent right of
self-government" found in the failed Charlottetown Accord. In
both cases, it means a constitutionally entrenched third order of
government, sharing sovereign power with Parliament and the
provincial legislatures. Offering an elaborate legal analysis not
yet tested in the courts, the RCAP argued that the inherent right
of aboriginal self-government is already protected by the words of
s. 35(1) of the Constitution Act of 1982: "The existing aboriginal

and treaty rights of the aboriginal peoples of Canada are hereby recognized and affirmed."[12]

Ron Irwin, minister of Indian affairs in the first Chrétien cabinet, said shortly after the 1993 election that the government was "working steadily towards the implementation of the 'inherent right of self-government' as the cornerstone of a new partnership with aboriginal peoples." He added that the government would act on this premise unless and until there was a contrary court ruling.[13] In August 1995 the federal government released a formal policy paper recognizing the inherent right of aboriginal self-government subject to the Canadian Charter of Rights and Freedoms.[14]

Although the inherent right of aboriginal self-government clearly has much momentum, it still faces obstacles. Even proponents have to admit that "the decisions of Canadian and Commonwealth courts ... have rarely, if ever, upheld aboriginal people's claims to have free-standing, enforceable self-government rights."[15] Moreover, if the right is already in the constitution, why has it been necessary for aboriginal people to try (and fail) several times to entrench it in the form of a constitutional amendment?[16]

Claims couched in terms of self-determination, jurisdiction, and the inherent right of self-government are derivations of sovereignty. Even when advocates of aboriginal rights avoid using the term "sovereignty" to express their current demands, they make clear their belief that Indian nations were at one time sovereign nations of equal status with European nations under international law. Whether, like the Mohawks, they now aspire to sovereign statehood or, like the Assembly of First Nations, they are content to demand a share of Canadian sovereignty, they are united in thinking that their ancestors were unjustifiably deprived of the sovereignty they once possessed. To evaluate this contention, we must examine more closely the historical process by which the European powers asserted sovereignty over the New World.

CLAIMING THE NEW WORLD

From the fourteenth century onward, the rulers of European states sent out voyages of exploration, first to Africa, then to the Americas, Asia, and Oceania. When these explorers happened upon uninhabited islands, such as the Azores or Madeira, they invoked the right of discovery to establish their sovereignty. The European states sorted out their conflicting claims by war or diplomacy among themselves, without considering any claims of aboriginal inhabitants, of whom there were none.

Such simple cases were far less numerous than instances in which newly discovered lands were already inhabited. In these situations, European monarchs and their explorers initially acted on the assumption that they could claim sovereignty to any land not ruled by a Christian prince. A famous papal bull of 4 May 1493 divided the New World between Spain and Portugal, "with this provision however, that ... no right required by any Christian prince, who may be in actual possession of said islands and mainlands ... is hereby to be understood to be withdrawn or taken away."[17]

France and England ignored the papal bull, because its allocation of sovereignty to Spain and Portugal would have made it impossible for them to acquire territory in the New World through discovery and exploration. But in disregarding the pope, they did not uphold the rights of aboriginal inhabitants. All European states were equally insistent on their right to establish sovereignty by discovery. Explorers usually took possession by erecting a large wooden cross or engaging in other ceremonies, often in the presence of natives who could hardly have understood the implications, at least at first.[18]

In principle, the explorers were prepared to claim all territory not ruled by Christian princes, which would have meant almost the whole world outside Europe. In practice, however, they had no way to enforce such claims against the civilized states they encountered in North Africa, the Middle East, India, China, and parts of Indonesia. Many of these states were themselves formidable imperial powers, possessing well-defined territories, large agricultural populations, organized governments, and armies equipped with metal weapons and firearms. When they encountered such opponents, the European explorers pragmatically acquired territory through negotiating treaties of cession rather than invoking the right of discovery.[19]

International law did not really exist when the age of European exploration and colonization began. The first great theorist of international law was a Spanish Dominican priest, Francisco de Vitoria, whose sixteenth-century essays *De Indis* and *De Jure Belli* have much to say about the New World. Faced with the brute fact of the Spanish conquests, Vitoria struggled to find reasons to justify them. By dismissing many commonly given justifications – for example, that the Indians were pagans, or irrational, or slaves by nature, or given to vices such as human sacrifice and cannibalism[20] – he undercut the original rationale of European explorers that they could lay claim to any and all non-Christian lands.

Rather, Vitoria argued that the Indians, like the Spanish, were obliged to submit to the *jus gentium,* the law of nations – that is, to "what natural reason has established among all nations."[21] Hypothetically, the Spanish would have the right to defend themselves and even to overthrow the Indians if the latter did not respect Spanish rights under the law of nations, such as the liberty of travel and trade, or the right to preach the gospel. These were interesting arguments but bore little connection to the historical reality, in which the Spaniards had attacked the Aztecs and Incas without provocation. And why would the Indians be bound by a *jus gentium* of which they had never heard?

But Vitoria also speculated in another direction regarding the differences in level of civilization between Europeans and Indians:

Although the aborigines in question are (as has been said above) not wholly unintelligent, yet they are little short of that condition, and so are unfit to found or administer a lawful State up to the standard required by human and civil claims. Accordingly they have no proper laws nor magistrates, and are not even capable of controlling their family affairs; they are without any literature or arts, not only the liberal arts, but the mechanical arts also; they have no careful agriculture and no artisans; and they lack many other conveniences, yet necessaries of human life. It might, therefore, be maintained that in their [the Indians'] own interests the sovereigns of Spain might undertake the administration of their country, providing them with prefects and governors for their towns, and might even give them new lords, so long as this was clearly for their benefit.[22]

This line of thought reappeared in the work of later theorists of international law as the main justification for the European assertion of sovereignty in the New World. The reworked argument was that the aboriginal inhabitants of the Americas did not possess sovereignty because they were not organized into territorial states with stable governments and thus were not actors under the law of nations. Christian Wolff, one of the leading authorities on the law of nations in the mid-eighteenth century, wrote: "But it is to be noted that we take the name nation with the fixed meaning which we have assigned to it, because of course it denotes a number of men who have united into a civil society, so that therefore *no nation can be conceived of without a civil sovereignty.* For groups of men dwelling together in certain limits but without civil sovereignty are not nations, except that *through carelessness of speech they may be wrongly so called.*"[23] It is not clear whether Wolff regarded the Indian peoples of North America as genuine nations possessed of civil sovereignty or as "groups of men dwelling together in certain limits,"[24] but later writers tended to take the latter position.

Also writing in the eighteenth century, Vattel denied the status of nation to the non-agricultural inhabitants of the Americas, referring to them rather as tribes: "These tribes cannot take to themselves more land than they have need of or can inhabit and cultivate. Their uncertain occupancy of these vast regions cannot be held as a real and lawful taking of possession; and when the Nations of Europe, which are too confined at home, come upon lands which the savages have no special need of and are making no present and continuous use of, they may lawfully take possession of them and establish colonies in them."[25]

The two lines of thought converged in a rationale for the European assertion of sovereignty. According to Wolff, the aboriginal inhabitants did not have sovereignty over territory because they were not organized into civil societies with sovereign governments. According to Vattel, if they did not practise agriculture, they had only an "uncertain occupancy" of the land that did not amount to sovereign possession. In either case, there was nothing to stop the European explorers from asserting sovereignty based on the right of discovery.

Note that Vattel called the Spanish conquest of Mexico and Peru a "notorious usurpation" because these lands were already inhabited by agricultural peoples. Although Wolff did not comment on it, he might well have agreed with Vattel for a different reason, namely that Mexico and Peru were already organized into civil societies with sovereign governments, which precluded the assertion of sovereignty by right of discovery. In any case, here was a powerful new argument, based on philosophical reasoning, to replace the earlier view that only Christian princes had a right to rule. The earlier argument that Christians had a right to govern heathens now gave way to the view that civilized states had a right to extend their sway over uncivilized peoples.

These became virtually standard ideas in international law in the nineteenth and early twentieth centuries. T.J. Lawrence, in a textbook that went through many editions, wrote: "Occupation as a means of acquiring sovereignty and dominion applies only to such territories as are no part of the possessions of any civilized state. It is not necessary that they should be uninhabited. Tracts roamed over by savage tribes have been again and again appropriated, and even the attainment by the original inhabitants of some slight degree of civilization and political coherence has not sufficed to bar the acquisition of their territory by occupancy."[26]

The reader may recognize this justification of "occupancy" as the doctrine of *terra nullius*, which means literally "no one's land." *Terra nullius* is sometimes associated with the belief that European explorers asserted sovereignty in the New World under the mistaken assumption that nobody lived in these "empty, uninhabited lands."[27] This interpretation requires *terra nullius*, "no one's land," to be understood in the sense of uninhabited territory. That is one possibility, but not the only one, as a glance at any reference work shows. One dictionary of international law describes "occupation" in these terms: "The actual taking possession by a State of a territory which is 'terra nullius,' i.e., not under the sovereignty of another subject of international law – either because it is uninhabited or because its native inhabitants are not organized in the form of a State subject of international law, with the intention of acquiring sovereignty over it."[28]

Another work says more concisely that *terra nullius* is the "territory of no one, i.e., territory which is the land of no State."[29] The Europeans knew perfectly well that America was inhabited. When they spoke of *terra nullius*, they meant that the New World did not belong to anyone in the sense that no sovereign power ruled it, and therefore they could assert the sovereignty of their own states. The high-water mark of this doctrine was the Berlin Conference of 1885, which declared that all parts of sub-Saharan Africa were *terrae nullius*.[30] After that meeting, the major European powers quickly proceeded to divide up the continent. The colonization of Africa completed the division of the earth's land surface (with the exception of Antarctica) among states.

Confusion about *terra nullius* has been particularly rampant in Australia, where the widely read books of the historian Henry Reynolds have irretrievably conflated separate issues of inhabitation, property rights, and sovereignty.[31] Even the High Court of Australia has been led astray.[32] In the famous *Mabo* decision of 1992, Justice Brennan attacked the doctrine of *terra nullius*. "It is," he wrote, "contrary both to international standards and to the fundamental values of our common law to entrench a discriminatory rule which, because of the supposed position on the scale of social organization of the indigenous inhabitants of a settled colony, denies them a right to occupy their traditional lands."[33] Yet Justice Brennan, along with others on the *Mabo* court, did not repudiate Britain's claim to sovereignty over Australia; they concluded only that the acquisition of sovereignty had not in itself extinguished aboriginal property rights. But the international-law doctrine of *terra nullius* was never concerned with property rights, only with sovereignty.

The influence of the doctrine of *terra nullius*, even properly understood, has receded considerably in the twentieth century, as shown by the decisions of three international tribunals. The first was a 1925 arbitration over the Island of Palmas, claimed by both the Netherlands and the United States, the latter arguing that it was the successor to Spanish sovereignty based on sixteenth-century voyages of exploration. The arbitrator awarded the island to the Netherlands, holding that while discovery might have conferred an "inchoate" title, "that title must be completed within a reasonable period by the effective occupation of the region claimed to be discovered," which the Spanish had not done.[34] The decision did not directly attack the doctrine of *terra nullius*, but it made it harder to invoke the doctrine by requiring effective possession in addition to discovery in order to establish sovereignty. However, that requirement only comes into play in contested cases where sovereignty had not been securely established earlier. One historian concluded afterwards that "discovery with symbolic taking of possession constituted legal title to terra nullius in North America prior to 1700."[35]

The second case was decided by the International Court of Justice in 1971, when it rejected South Africa's claim to control Namibia as a United Nations trust territory. The court condemned the Berlin Conference: "It was a monstrous blunder and a flagrant injustice to consider Africa south of the Sahara as *terrae nullius,* to be shared out among the Powers for occupation and colonization."[36] The court, however, did not reject the concept of *terra nullius,* only its application in this situation, because it found that before the onset of the slave trade and European colonization "the African peoples had founded states and even empires of a high level of civilization."[37]

The third case, decided in 1975, was a reference from the United Nations General Assembly to the International Court of Justice regarding the Western Sahara. Spain claimed title based on discovery of *terra nullius* beginning in 1884, while Morocco and Mauritania lodged claims based on ancient historical connections with the tribes that inhabited the Sahara. The court rejected all claims and affirmed the local population's right to self-determination. Regarding Spain's claim of *terra nullius,* the historical evidence, in the court's view, "shows that at the time of colonization Western Sahara was inhabited by peoples which, if nomadic, were socially and politically organized in tribes and under chiefs competent to represent them. It also shows that, in colonizing Western Sahara, Spain did not proceed on the basis that it was establishing its sovereignty over *terrae nullius* [but] on the basis of agreements."[38]

Tom Berger, a distinguished Canadian lawyer and advocate of aboriginal causes, wrote that the international court "rejected the idea of *terra nullius*" in the Western Sahara case;[39] but it would be more accurate to say that the court rejected the application of the idea in these particular circumstances (note the very late date, 1884, of alleged discovery). Nonetheless, echoing many calls from aboriginal leaders, the Royal Commission on Aboriginal Peoples has called on Canada "to abandon outmoded doctrines such as *terra nullius* and discovery. We must reject the attitudes of racial and cultural superiority reflected in the concepts, which contributed to European nations' presumptions of sovereignty over Indigenous peoples and lands."[40]

This demand fits logically with the commission's rejection of the distinction between civilized and uncivilized. If that distinction is meaningless, then the doctrine of *terra nullius* has no basis because aboriginal peoples, in the setting of their cultures, would have possessed all the attributes of civilized societies – philosophy, science, law, and, above all, sovereignty. The Americas would have been governed by aboriginal leaders in exactly the same sense as France was ruled by Louis XIV. But if, as I have argued, the distinction between civilized and uncivilized is meaningful, then the doctrine of *terra nullius* comes into play, because sovereignty in the strict sense exists only in the organized states characteristic of civilized societies.

What has yet to be added is a justification for states extending their sovereignty wherever they encounter a vacuum of existing sovereignty. Many writers on international law have not tried to find one, but have simply taken their bearings from state practice. They have reasoned that since states had in fact extended their sovereignty, it must be legitimate to do so. Vattel, however, did offer a justification based on agriculture, as described in the preceding chapter. In his depiction, the assertion of sovereignty was a means to open up previously uncultivated land for those who would cultivate it. The ultimate justification was Lockean, the equal natural right of each person to acquire property by mixing his labour with unused soil. A refusal by hunters to allow cultivation would amount to playing dog in the manger, refusing to let others work the land but not working it oneself. The assertion of sovereignty involved creating and protecting property rights in order to make intensive agriculture possible.

One has to substitute civilization for agriculture in Vattel's argument to reflect the fact that European states asserted their sovereignty over parts of Canada that have no agricultural potential, such as the Canadian Shield, the Arctic tundra, and the Rocky Mountains. In the broader context of civilization, land unsuitable for agriculture can serve other productive purposes such as mining, forestry, tourism, recreation, and national defence. The civilized mode of life includes agriculture but is a much bigger package, in which virtually any feature of the earth's surface can play a useful role.

As I pointed out in the preceding chapter, the difficulty in this whole line of thought is that it requires uncivilized peoples to give up a hunting-gathering mode of life with which they may be quite content. They may not have to give it up completely or all at once, but they know that their children or their children's children will have to complete the transition to civilization. By what right do the civilized require the uncivilized to renounce their ancient way of life?

In Locke's time, it seemed self-evident to almost everyone that whatever caused an increase in population and an improvement in standard of living was not only good in itself but part of God's providential plan for the world. Today, this will still seem plausible to some people, but not to everyone. Large numbers doubt whether God exists or whether he has any plan for the world. Environmentalists assert that there are too many people on the earth and that the material standard of living currently enjoyed by the beneficiaries of Western civilization is unsustainable in the long run (I think that these assertions are empirically wrong, but this is not the place to debate them). The point is simply that the moral justification for European sovereignty stemming from the natural-rights philosophy of Locke and Vattel is no longer universally persuasive.

However, those who do not find Locke and Vattel convincing have to reckon with the following fact: the assertion of European sovereignty in the New World, even if morally unjustified, was historically inevitable. Civilized societies are so much more powerful than uncivilized that it is only a matter of time until the former extend their sway over the latter. Consider, for instance, what would have happened if the European states had initially refrained from asserting their sovereignty but their subjects had privately pursued the alluring opportunities of exploration, trade, mining, forestry, and agriculture in the New World. Private parties and companies would quickly have taken up arms to defend themselves against depredations by both other colonists and the aboriginal inhabitants. The ensuing violence would have drawn in the European sovereigns whether they had originally wanted to be involved or not. There is plenty of evidence in support of this conclusion in the history of the United States, where many of the early colonial ventures were private. In order not to assert sovereignty, the European states would have had to take drastic and continuing measures to prevent any of their subjects from reaching the New World – not a realistic possibility, given the governing capacities of early modern states.

If one eschews attempts at moral justification, the appropriate concept in international law is not *terra nullius* or discovery but prescription, that is, long-continued possession. Vattel wrote: "In view of the peace of Nations, the safety of States, and the welfare of the human race, it is not to be allowed that the property, sovereignty, and other rights of Nations should remain uncertain, open to question, and always furnishing cause for bloody wars. Hence, as between Nations, prescription founded upon length of time must be admitted as a valid and incontestable title."[41] A modern authority writes in the same vein: "Prescription ... is a portmanteau concept that comprehends both a possession of which the origin is unclear or disputed, and an adverse possession which is in origin demonstrably unlawful. For prescription, therefore, the possession must be long-continued, undisturbed, and it must be unambiguously attributable to a claim to act as sovereign."[42]

State practice, interpretive works, and decisions of international tribunals unanimously agree that long-continued possession and effective control, combined with declarations of sovereignty, eventually confer title by prescription. The length of time required varies according to circumstances – for example, whether any protests or challenges are lodged – but there can be no doubt that prescription has conferred title to the European discoverers and their successor states over the hundreds of years that they have controlled the New World. Maybe it was wrong for Cortez and Pizarro to overthrow the Aztec and the Inca regimes. Maybe it was wrong for John Cabot, Jacques Cartier, and all the other explorers to claim sovereignty for Britain and France. Nonetheless, Canada, the United States, and all the other states of the Americas exist and their sovereignty is recognized throughout the world. In a free country like Canada, aboriginal leaders can talk all they want about their own inherent sovereignty, but the expression is only a rhetorical turn of phrase. It may produce domestic political results by playing on guilt or compassion, but it has no effect in international law or, as shown below, in domestic law.

THE ANGLO-AMERICAN LEGAL TRADITION

For over three hundred years, all British, Canadian, and American authorities – legislative, executive, and judicial – have been unanimous in upholding their sovereignty in the New World. Often it has been done by simple assertion and action, without any argumentation; sometimes arguments based on civilization and prescription have also been adduced. Below are some examples.

• In 1670, Charles II granted to the Hudson's Bay Company ownership of, and a trading monopoly in, all the lands drained by the rivers flowing into Hudson Bay. The charter was explicit that this grant of property rights stemmed from the sovereignty of the Crown: "And further we do by these presents for us, our heirs and successors, make, create and constitute the said governor and company for the time being and their successors the true and absolute lords and proprietors of the same territory, limits and places aforesaid and of all other the premises, saving always the faith, allegiance, and sovereign dominion due to us, our heirs and successors."[43]

• After acquiring Canada from France through the Seven Years' War and the Treaty of Paris, King George III was explicit about sovereignty in the Royal Proclamation of 1763, again without feeling a need to give reasons: "And we do further declare it to be our Royal Will and Pleasure, for the present as aforesaid, to reserve under our Sovereignty, Protection, and Dominion, for the use of the said Indians, all the Lands and Territories not included within the Limits of Our Said Three New governments."[44]

• In *Johnson v. M'Intosh* (1823), John Marshall, the chief justice of the Supreme Court of the United States, began to develop the theory of sovereignty that still largely prevails in American and Canadian courts. He laid the foundations on prescription and conquest rather than on civilization: "We will not enter into the controversy, whether agriculturalists, merchants and manufacturers, have a right, on abstract principles, to expel hunters from the territory they possess, or to contract their limits. Conquest gives a title which the courts of the conqueror cannot deny, whatever the private and speculative opinions of individuals may be, respecting the original justice of the claim which has been successfully asserted."[45]

We will return later to some of the complexities in Marshall's view of the relationship between Indians and the American state. Here it is sufficient to point out that he took American sovereignty over Indian nations for granted in all his judgments.[46] Since Marshall's day, the American Supreme Court has repeatedly reaffirmed that Congress is competent to legislate in any way whatsoever regarding Indians, because it is sovereign over them.[47]

Still classic in Canadian law is the *St Catherine's Milling v. The Queen* case, decided by the Judicial Committee of the Privy Council in 1888. Lord Watson's decision stemmed directly from the Royal Proclamation of 1763: "There has been no change since the year 1763 ... Their possession, such as it was, can only be ascribed to the general provisions made by the royal proclamation in favour of all Indian tribes then living under the sovereignty and protection of the British Crown ... The lands reserved are expressly stated to be 'parts of our dominions and territories; and it is declared to be the will and pleasure of the sovereign that, 'for the present,' they shall be reserved for the use of the Indians."[48]

The assertion of sovereignty has continued in Canadian jurisprudence down to the present, even in the Supreme Court's 1997 *Delgamuukw* decision, perhaps the most favourable ever rendered to Indian litigants. The Gitksan and Wet'suwet'en Indians of British Columbia began by claiming that they had "jurisdiction," that is, the ability to make law in their traditional territory; but the lower courts rejected that claim, after which the Supreme Court of Canada allowed them to shift their argument to aboriginal rights and title.[49] At no stage did the plaintiffs successfully defend a sovereignty argument. Chief Justice Antonio Lamer ended his opinion in *Delgamuukw* by quoting from his earlier judgment in *Van der Peet,* that the goal of negotiations was "the reconciliation of the pre-existence of aboriginal societies with the sovereignty of the Crown."[50]

AMERICAN TRIBAL SOVEREIGNTY

The relaxed use of the term "sovereignty" to describe the governmental powers of Indian tribes is non-controversial in the United States. A striking example is the book *Sovereign Nations or Reservations?* by Terry L. Anderson, an economist committed to property rights and free markets – ideas generally considered to lie on the conservative side of the political spectrum. Yet Anderson concludes that "the U.S. government has recognized the sovereignty of Indian nations. This recognition of Indian sovereignty has laid the foundation for self-determination that can be exploited by Indian nations wanting to escape the trap of reservation status."[51]

The intellectual foundations of American Indian tribal sovereignty were laid by Chief Justice John Marshall in several early-nineteenth-century decisions. In *Johnson v. M'Intosh,* referred to above, he held that Indians' "rights to complete sovereignty, as independent nations, were necessarily diminished" because the European powers had asserted their own sovereignty over the New World.[52] In *Cherokee Nation v. Georgia,* he coined the famous phrase "domestic dependent nations" to describe the status of American Indians.[53]

Marshall's decisions gave rise to the doctrine that Indian tribes, although subject to American sovereignty, possess a residual sovereignty stemming from their prior independence from external control. As separate political communities within the United States, they exercise internal autonomy, subject to federal legislation. The American Supreme Court has repeatedly upheld the right of Congress to legislate as it chooses with respect to Indian matters. The court said in 1978, "Congress has plenary authority to legislate for the Indian tribes in all matters, including their forms of government."[54]

One recent work says, "Tribes still maintain sovereign powers, although they have been eroded by time and the United States government." These, "with some exceptions, are not delegated powers, granted by express acts of Congress, but are inherent powers of a limited sovereignty that have never been extinguished."[55] Another work puts it this way: "An Indian tribe is a distinct political community. Congress has the authority to limit or even abolish tribal powers, and thus tribes are 'limited' sovereignties. But absent Congressional action, a tribe retains its inherent right of self-government, and no state may impose its laws on the reservation."[56] Extinguishment of Indian rights, however, is always possible by an act of Congress signed by the president. Americans thus accept the application of the term "sovereignty" to Indians because it is understood that such sovereignty is limited. It does not make Indian tribes candidates for sovereign statehood in the international realm, nor does it confer a position of constitutional entrenchment beyond the reach of democratic processes as expressed in acts of Congress.

The discourse on sovereignty in the United States differs in several important ways from that in Canada. There is a long-standing American tradition, going back to colonial times, of speaking of the states as sovereign. Anyone who has ever watched a presidential nominating convention has seen the spokesman of a state delegation rise to say something like, "The great sovereign state of Alabama casts its votes for the next President of the United States!"[57] Nobody takes the use of the word "sovereign" in this context as a claim of the right to exercise supreme, unfettered authority. In Canada, only Quebec separatists speak of the sovereignty of the province in which they live.

If Americans were to reflect upon sovereignty, they would conclude that the only concept that fits their system is popular sovereignty.

Their constitution begins with the words "We the People" and contains the Tenth Amendment, which says, "The powers not delegated to the United States by the Constitution, or prohibited by it to the States, are reserved to the States respectively, or to the people." In contrast, the Crown in Canada is the ancient source and symbol of sovereignty, and legal theorists stress the concept of parliamentary sovereignty in the British tradition. Neither the Crown nor parliamentary sovereignty is the same as popular sovereignty. In the Canadian frame of reference, sovereignty belongs to a person or body of people who actively governs. This makes sovereignty potentially more dangerous, or at least activist, in Canada than in the United States, where sovereignty is seen as inhering in the whole people, who cannot use it on a day-to-day basis.

Finally, there is no important separatist movement in the United States using sovereignty as a catchword. There are, to be sure, separatist movements, such as the Nation of Islam and the Aryan Nations, but they are not serious threats to the territorial integrity of the United States. Moreover, none of these fringe separatist movements have given sovereignty a central place in their political vocabulary. Contrast that to the Canadian situation, where the large and powerful separatist movement in Quebec, which obviously jeopardizes the future of Canada, has always talked about sovereignty, as in the famous phrase "sovereignty-association." This backdrop makes the aboriginal rhetoric of sovereignty much more threatening in Canada than in the United States.

THE INHERENT RIGHT OF SELF-GOVERNMENT

The term "sovereignty" can be used freely in the United States to describe aboriginal governments because the qualifications implicitly attached to it – particularly the supremacy of Congress – make it non-threatening. In Canada, however, the word is far more ominous, and so aboriginal leaders have learned to use other terms, especially self-determination and the inherent right of self-government, which both sound less expansive. But as shown in the RCAP's proposals for aboriginal self-government, what Canadian aboriginals mean by these terms is actually more far-reaching than what American Indians mean by sovereignty.

One difference relates to constitutional entrenchment. According to the RCAP, the aboriginal right of self-government is already entrenched in section 35(1) of the Constitution Act of 1982; although not explicitly mentioned, self-government is one of those "existing aboriginal and treaty rights" protected by that section. If this view is accepted (and it has not been tested in the courts), aboriginal government cannot be changed except by constitutional amendment, whereas in the United States, Indian tribal government can be changed by Congress through normal legislation.

A second difference has to do with legislative jurisdiction. In the United States, Congress can override anything decided by an Indian tribal government, but Parliament would not have the same plenary power under the RCAP scheme, under which "the inherent right of self-government has a substantial degree of immunity from federal and provincial legislative acts, except where, in the case of federal legislation, it can be justified under a strict constitutional standard."[58] According to RCAP, aboriginal governments have both core and peripheral jurisdiction: "core areas of jurisdiction, which include all matters that are of vital concern for the life and welfare of a particular Aboriginal people, its culture and identity, do not have a major impact on adjacent jurisdictions, and are not otherwise the object of transcendent federal or provincial concern; and peripheral areas of jurisdiction, which make up the remainder."[59] Aboriginal governments are supreme within their core jurisdiction; if they choose to legislate, "any inconsistent federal or provincial legislation is automatically displaced," although federal law "may take precedence" if there is "a compelling and substantial need ... consistent with the Crown's basic fiduciary responsibilities to Aboriginal peoples."[60]

What this would mean in practice is anybody's guess. However, it certainly implies that Parliament could not override aboriginal governments without passing certain tests that the courts would devise and enforce – a very different situation from the plenary power of Congress in the United States. In short, the claim to possess an inherent right of self-government, as that phrase is understood in Canada today, is an assertion of sovereignty contrary to the history, jurisprudence, and national interest of Canada.

CHAPTER 5

Bands, Tribes, or Nations?

One of my most prized possessions is a baseball cap with the words "Lubicon Lake Band" on the front. It was a present from my friend Barry Cooper, who bought it at a rally when the Lubicon and their supporters were trying to disrupt the 1988 Calgary Winter Olympics. It is an invaluable artifact from the archaeology of knowledge. Today the Lubicon, like other Indian bands in Canada, refer to themselves as a nation, indeed a "First Nation." Winning wide public acceptance of this terminology has been one of the most striking victories of the aboriginal political movement, reinforcing their assertions of sovereignty and the inherent right of self-government. But my hat is graphic evidence of how recent this development is; less than fifteen years ago, the Lubicon were calling themselves a band. To understand what has happened, we must again examine the history of a word – "nation."

NATION: THE HISTORY OF A WORD

The word "nation" is derived from the Latin word *natio*, which in turn was formed from the verb *nasci*, meaning "to be born." In classical Latin, *natio* could mean the process of being born and it could also refer to groups united by some inherited characteristic. In practice, it was usually used to designate lower-status groups, such as resident aliens living in port cities. The normal word for a higher-status group was *gens*, originally referring to the patrician clans of Rome, to which only the aristocrats belonged. Later the meaning of *gens* was extended to include foreign peoples, as in the expression *ius gentium*, normally rendered into English as "the law of nations."[1] *Natio* was not an important part of the Roman political vocabulary, whose main words to designate political communities were *civitas* (city-state), *imperium* (empire), *respublica* (republic, commonwealth), *populus* (people), *plebs* (common people), and *gentes* (patrician clans).

This would hold true for hundreds of years in medieval Latin and in the vernacular languages as they emerged. The word *natio* (and its derivatives such as *nation* and *nazione)* appeared, but not in a political context. To cite one example, medieval universities distinguished "nations" of students according to their birth in various regions of the country. That archaic terminology is still employed at the universities of Glasgow and Aberdeen when the rector is elected.[2]

In early modern times, "nation," along with terms such as "country," "commonwealth," and "state," came to be used to designate the political community. But at first it had no particular significance or talismanic characteristics. For example, the English Bill of Rights of 1689, one of the most important documents in the evolution of representative government, was enacted by Parliament "being now assembled into a full and free representative of this nation."[3] That is the only occurrence of the word "nation" in the text, and it is definitely in the background.

Compare that to a later democratic document, Abraham Lincoln's Gettysburg Address of 1863, in which the term "nation" appears five times in 250 words and in highly evocative ways: "Fourscore and seven years ago our fathers brought forth on this continent, a new nation, conceived in liberty, and dedicated to the proposition that all men are created equal ... we here highly resolve that these dead shall not have died in vain – that this nation, under God, shall have a new birth of freedom."[4]

The word "nation" is not to be found in the three great documents of the American Revolution – the Declaration of Independence (1776), the Constitution (1787), and the Bill of Rights (1789) – but it is definitely front and centre in the documents of the French Revolution (1789). Consider the famous pamphlet of the Abbé Sieyès, *What Is the Third Estate?* "The Third Estate embraces everything belonging to the nation, and anything that is not of the Third cannot be regarded as being of the nation. In every free nation, and every nation should be free, there is only one way of ending differences concerning the constitution. Not by turning to the notables but to the nation itself. The nation exists before all, it is the origin of everything. Its will is always legal, it is the law itself."[5] Consider also the Declaration of the Rights of Man and of the Citizen, 27 August 1789, by which the Constituent Assembly turned itself into the National Assembly: "The nation is essentially the source of all sovereignty; nor can any individual, or any body of men, be entitled to any authority which is not expressly derived from it."[6]

The evolution of language has given the word "nation" a double meaning recognized by all students of the subject. In the first sense, it refers to a "cultural/ancestral or ethnic group,"[7] that is, a people sharing some combination of race, language, religion, history, and culture. This usage incorporates the original idea of *natio* as birth because it groups people by characteristics they are born with or absorb from their parents, family, and community as they grow up.

But the term "nation" is also often applied to "the political/ territorial group. In the clearest cases such groups lack both common culture and common ancestry or any illusion thereof."[8] In this political sense, we normally call Switzerland a nation even though its people speak four different languages and are religiously divided between Roman Catholics and Protestants, and likewise the United States, even though its people are composed of many races and ethnic groups. In both cases, overarching loyalty to the governmental system produces a political community that can be called a nation. George Etienne Cartier said the same thing about Canada when he called the new confederation a "political nationality."[9] He meant that the Canadian political community could be considered a nation, even though it embraced two major linguistic and religious groups. Interestingly, however, the Canadian founders shied away from using the term "nation" at an official level. They constructed Canada as a self-governing "Dominion" within the British Empire, based on the (perhaps tacit) insight that the ambiguity of the term "nation" easily leads to battles over its application.

From the semantic point of view, the underlying problem is mutual interference between the two conceptually distinct but practically interwoven meanings of nation. It is all very well to say that one will speak of a nation in the cultural/ancestral sense without making political claims, but since the same word is commonly used to designate political communities, listeners are bound to hear political overtones in what is said. In the world of the late twentieth century, calling any cultural/ancestral group a nation is automatically associated with political demands for decentralization, autonomy, self-government, or sovereign independence.

In modern Canadian history, Pierre Trudeau understood this better than anyone else. As prime minister and leader of the Liberal Party, he refused to use the *deux nations* terminology that became popular in Quebec in the 1960s and was even adopted for a time by Robert Stanfield as leader of the Progressive Conservatives. Trudeau took measures to define Canada as bilingual and multicultural, and indeed entrenched those characteristics in the constitution; but he recognized the existence of only one nation – Canada as a whole – that could claim sovereignty. He opposed all other phrases of this kind, interpreting "distinct society," for example, as code for two nations – correctly in my view.

ABORIGINAL NATIONHOOD

The English explorers, traders, and colonists in the New World needed words to describe its inhabitants. "Indian," even though based on the misconception that the explorers had reached the East Indies, became the generic term for anyone and everyone, while words from aboriginal languages were borrowed to refer to specific peoples. But there was also a need for a common noun to refer to aboriginal communities, as opposed to individuals. The two terms that emerged to satisfy this need were "nation" and "tribe."

"Tribe" is the English version of the Latin *tribus*, which in its original Roman usage referred to the three great divisions of the Roman patricians, each of which was supposed to be descended from a different ancestor. The number was later extended to thirty and then to thirty-five to include all the common people, represented politically by "tribunes." Later usage took the term outside the Roman context and applied it, for example, to the Twelve Tribes of Israel, each of whom was supposed to be descended from one of the sons of Jacob.[10]

Eighteenth-century documents commonly referred to Indians as members of tribes, as in the treaty of 1717 made in the Massachusetts Bay Colony ("We, the Subscribers, being Sachems and Chief men of the several Tribes of Indians")[11] or the Micmac Treaty of

1752 ("That the said Tribe shall use their utmost Endeavours to bring in the other Indians to Renew and Ratify this Peace").[12] Yet one also finds the term "nation," as in the beginning of the Royal Proclamation of 1763: "And whereas it is just and reasonable, and essential to our Interest, and the Security of our Colonies, that the several Nations or Tribes of Indians with whom We are connected, and who live under our protection, should not be molested."[13] There was a passing reference to Indian nations in the first American constitution, the Articles of Confederation of 1781, but the Constitution of 1787 used the phrase "Indian tribes."[14] In the early nineteenth century, the Selkirk Treaty was signed in the Red River Valley with "the undersigned chiefs and warriors of the Chippeway or Sauteaux Nation and of the Killistine or Cree Nation."[15] It seems that both "nation" and "tribe" were acceptable terms in this early period and were used more or less interchangeably.

Also in the early nineteenth century, the American chief justice John Marshall, although he occasionally used the word "tribe," usually referred to Indians as nations. He coined the phrase "domestic dependent nations,"[16] as noted earlier, and laid some stress on the word "nation":

The very term "nation," so generally applied to them, means "a people distinct from others." The Constitution, by declaring treaties already made, as well as those to be made, to be the supreme law of the land, has adopted and sanctioned the previous treaties with the Indian nations, and consequently admits their rank among those powers who are capable of making treaties. The words "treaty" and "nation" are words of our own language, selected in our diplomatic and legislative proceedings, by ourselves, having each a definite and well understood meaning. We have applied them to Indians, as we have applied them to the other nations of the earth. They are applied to all in the same sense.[17]

This sounds unambiguous, yet Marshall also wrote, in explaining his phrase "domestic dependent nations": "They occupy a territory to which we assert a title independent of their will, which must take effect in point of possession when their right of possession ceases. Meanwhile they are in a state of pupilage. Their relation to the United States resembles that of a ward to his guardian." Therefore, concluded Marshall, when he denied the Cherokee people a judicial remedy for their grievances against the state of Georgia, "the framers of our constitution had not the Indian tribes in view, when they opened the Courts of the union to controversies between a state, or the citizens thereof, and foreign states."[18]

Marshall's decisions were the high-water mark in American jurisprudence of references to Indian nations. From that point on the concept of tribe quickly became standard and continues to predominate in official usage.[19] Even American advocates of Indian self-government generally use the same vocabulary. In 1980 Barsh and Henderson published their well-known book *The Road*, subtitling it *Indian Tribes and Political Liberty*.[20] Likewise, the American Civil Liberties Union's authoritative reference work on Indian law is entitled *The Rights of Indians and Tribes*. The author notes that "the term 'nation' usually refers to a government independent from any other government, possessing the power of absolute dominion over its territory and people. Technically, Indian tribes are no longer nations because their governmental authority has been restricted by the United States government. Some tribal governments, however, continue to call themselves 'nations' rather than 'tribes.' This designation reflects the belief, shared by a number of people, that the United States has no right to exercise any power or authority over Indian tribes."[21] Examples of tribes now calling themselves nations range from the Navajo, with nearly a quarter of a million members, to the tiny Skull Valley band of Goshutes in central Utah, with barely a hundred members.[22]

In Canada the term "tribe" also became commonplace in the nineteenth century. It appeared in several pre-Confederation statutes;[23] in the numbered treaties, 1871–77;[24] and in the opinion of the Judicial Committee of the Privy Council in the seminal *St Catherine's Milling* case, 1888.[25] The word "nation" largely disappeared from statutes and court decisions, although it continued to appear occasionally in other usages – sometimes in reference to multitribal confederacies, such as the Six Nations of Ontario or the Blackfoot Nation of Alberta,[26] sometimes as an approximate synonym for tribe.[27]

The Indian Act, 1876, introduced a new element into the discourse by specifying the "band" as the effective unit of organization under the law.[28] Bands had always existed as loose subtribal, familial groupings, leading a separate existence at times but also coming together with other bands for hunting, warfare, and festivals. Now the Indian Act transformed these loose groupings into rigidly defined communities complete with membership lists, assigned reserves, and institutions of local government. From this time onward, "band" became the standard term for any Indian group having a legal, corporate existence, while "tribe" referred to larger, mostly linguistic, groupings scattered across separate reserves and no longer capable of collective action except through the cooperation of their constituent bands.

Yet, at least in British Columbia, the terminology of nationhood survived to some degree throughout the twentieth century. In 1916 that province's Royal Commission on Indian Affairs referred in their report to a "visit to the home of the ancient Nishga nation."[29] In 1960 George Manuel, testifying on behalf of the Interior Tribes of British Columbia before the Parliamentary Joint Committee on Indian Affairs, called upon the government to help Indians become "self-supporting nations."[30] In 1969 the British Columbia Supreme Court heard the *Calder* case, which became the most important aboriginal-rights case in modern Canadian law prior to the 1997 *Delgamuukw* decision. The plaintiffs were the "Nishga Indian Tribe" joined with several bands, four of whom styled themselves the "Nishga Nation."[31] In his 1974 book *The Fourth World*, George Manuel called his people the "Shuswap Nation" and commented in a note: "'Nation' refers to any group who traditionally thought of themselves as one people and governed themselves accordingly with a common language, territory, and social structure, e.g., the Shuswap Nation. A 'band' is a group who commonly lived and worked together as a unit, or who are presently constituted as a band under the Indian Act ... Many Indian groups in the United States refer to themselves as a 'tribe,' and the term is often in the general sense interchangeable with 'nation.'"[32] Manuel's explanation seems to summarize the state of usage in the early 1970s: "nation" and "tribe" were more or less interchangeable terms for Indian peoples, and the choice of words did not signal a specific political theory.

This changed radically in 1975 with the adoption of the "Dene Declaration," which opened with this assertion of nationhood: "We the Dene of the Northwest Territories insist on the right to be regarded by ourselves and the world as a nation. Our struggle is for the recognition of the Dene Nation by the Government and peoples of Canada and the peoples and governments of the world." Borrowing George Manuel's concept of the "Fourth World," the declaration depicted the Dene as a colonized nation deprived by Canada of self-determination. "The Dene find themselves as part of a country. That country is Canada. But the Government of Canada is not the government of the Dene ... And while there are realities we are forced to submit to, such as the existence of a country called Canada, we insist on the right to self-determination as a distinct people and recognition of the Dene Nation ... What we seek then is independence and self-determination within the country of Canada."[33]

The word "nation," appearing thirteen times in the Dene Declaration, took on talismanic significance, representing a political theory in which native nations stood on the same plane as colonial empires. The nations of the Third World having achieved sovereign independence, it now remained for the nations of the Fourth World – those encapsulated within, not just ruled by, colonial states – to assert their right of self-determination. For the Dene, this meant not independence as a sovereign state but a kind of partnership status, which they called "self-determination within the country of Canada."

The concept of nationhood quickly spread to the entire aboriginal movement after the Parti Québécois won the Quebec provincial election in 1976. When Prime Minister Trudeau's response to the PQ victory was to restart the constitutional process, aboriginal leaders demanded to be included as one of the "founding peoples" or "founding nations," on equal terms with the English and French. This was partly a defensive manœuvre, born of fear that aboriginal and treaty rights might be dealt away in constitutional reforms negotiated by others; but it was also an offensive strategy, an attempt to gain more leverage in the political process by assuming the status of "nation," which clearly trumps "tribe" in terms of respect and political power.

The attempt to enter the constitutional process led to the invention of the inspired phrase "First Nations," which first appeared in public in late April 1980, when the National Indian Brotherhood (NIB) hosted a "First Nations' Constitutional Conference" in Ottawa. The conference, attended by about 375 chiefs and 2,000 other delegates,[34] lasted four days and was addressed by Prime Minister Trudeau as well as other cabinet members. It passed a resolution "to unify Canada's 570 Chiefs into one organized assembly."[35] Although it was not clear at the time, this would lead within two years to the demise of the National Indian Brotherhood. At the NIB meeting in August 1980, when Del Riley was elected president, a Council of Chiefs was chosen. Riley commented, "That's the first step on the way out for the NIB as we know it."[36] The transformation was completed on 21 April 1982, when the NIB voted to become the Assembly of First Nations.[37]

The change was partly organizational. The National Indian Brotherhood had been based on provincial and territorial Indian organizations, whereas the voting members of the Assembly of First Nations were the chiefs of all the Indian bands. But the name change was also highly symbolic. The "nation" in the National Indian Brotherhood was Canada, representing the view that Indians were an interest group within the larger nation-state. In contrast, the "nations" in the Assembly of First Nations were the Indian peoples themselves, thus generalizing the Dene Declaration's assertion of nationhood.[38] Moreover, calling them "First Nations" brought in the theme of aboriginality, laying claim to privilege in virtue of prior occupation. Around the same time, aboriginals were also calling themselves "founding nations" or "founding peoples,"[39] but that was not such a powerful statement as "First Nations," since there would be at least three founding nations in Canada but only one set of First Nations. In that sense, "First Nations" resembled the slogan "Original People" (or "Original Peoples") that is sometimes still heard. But "First Nations" is crisper; it requires the pronunciation of only three syllables as compared to six for "Original People"; and "nation" is a stronger, more precise political word than "people." In the Darwinian struggle for survival of political slogans, "First Nations" was the fittest.[40]

In Ottawa in early December 1980, another large gathering of First Nations adopted the Declaration of the First Nations:

We the Original Peoples of this land know the Creator put us here.
The Creator gave us laws that govern all our relationships to live in harmony with nature and mankind.
The laws of the Creator defined our rights and responsibilities.
The Creator gave us our spiritual beliefs, our languages, our culture, and a place on Mother Earth which provides us with all our needs.
We have maintained our freedom, our languages, and our traditions from time immemorial.
We continue to exercise the rights and fulfill the responsibilities and obligations given to us by the Creator for the land upon which we were placed.

The Creator has given us the right to govern ourselves and the right to self-determination.

The rights and responsibilities given to us by the Creator cannot be altered or taken away by any other Nation.[41]

The president and vice-president of the National Indian Brotherhood took the declaration to Governor-General Ed Schreyer, who tactfully expressed Ottawa's reluctance at that time to recognize aboriginal nationhood: "I know you speak of nations somewhat differently than we do, but we've already had a difficult time with some of the people in Quebec with words like 'nation' and 'sovereignty.'"[42]

The patriation of the constitution in 1982 was more a failure than a success from the viewpoint of aboriginal politicians. They did not succeed in getting their talismanic terms – nation and sovereignty – into the constitution, nor were they ever treated as anything other than one of many interest groups in the constitutional process, and their political and legal attempts to block patriation in Britain failed completely. They had to be content with getting three sections into the Constitution Act of 1982: section 25 prevented the Charter of Rights and Freedoms from overriding aboriginal and treaty rights; section 35 entrenched "the existing aboriginal and treaty rights" of the Indian, Inuit, and Metis peoples; and section 37 mandated a constitutional conference to deal with aboriginal issues. But through the process of the constitution's patriation, their new term, "First Nations," with all its implicit assumptions about sovereignty and nationhood, rapidly became standard usage in Canada – an invaluable asset that helped them achieve later political victories such as the appointment of the Royal Commission on Aboriginal Affairs and their participation in the Charlottetown Accord negotiations.

The new terminology received a boost in 1983 from the report of the Special Parliamentary Committee on Indian Self-Government, chaired by Liberal MP Keith Penner. In recommending a wholesale transfer of jurisdiction to Indian governments, the Penner Committee adopted the First Nations terminology throughout its report, explaining in a footnote, "We are using the term 'nation' to refer to a group of people who possess a common language and culture and who identify with each other as belonging to a common political entity. It is not intended to carry separatist connotations. Throughout our report we use the term 'Indian First Nations' (IFNs) to refer to the entities that would be exercising self-government."[43] From the Penner Report onward, all Canadian federal governments, both Liberal and Conservative, have declared their support for aboriginal self-government and have taken steps in that direction, even if not always as far and as fast as would satisfy aboriginal leaders.

Of course, it takes time for a new item of vocabulary to become entrenched in popular usage. Paul Tennant reports that "'first nation' was not a term yet in common use among British Columbia Indians" in 1988, when they established a provincial coordinating forum called the First Nations Congress.[44] But acceptance of the term, if gradual, has been steady. At the end of the 1990s, its use at the official level is almost invariable. One can still say "Indian" in informal conversation, but it is close to becoming a taboo word in print.

I saw a striking example of this when I visited the restored village of Fort Steele in British Columbia. The exhibits emphasize the gold and silver mining industries of the late nineteenth century, but at the entry to the park stands a painted sign describing the prior occupation of the land by aboriginal people. The word "Indians" had recently been painted out and replaced by the word "natives," which conveniently has the same number of letters. I'm sure "First Nations" would have been used had it fitted into that space. In any case, "Indian" now teeters on the verge of obsolescence, just as "black," which replaced "negro," is giving way to "African-Canadian."

PROBLEMS OF THE TERMINOLOGY

Widespread acceptance of a political vocabulary, even to the point of entrenching it in legislation,[45] does not mean that the intellectual problems associated with the new terminology disappear. Who exactly are the First Nations? The Penner Committee encountered this problem at the outset: "The Assembly of First Nations suggested that the Committee think, at least initially, of each individual Indian band as a 'First Nation,' although some bands may amalgamate and others may choose to split into two or more units."[46] In practice, today, First Nations are individual Indian bands. The Assembly of First Nations has an organizational structure in which the constituent elements are bands and the voting delegates at national meetings are band chiefs.

There are many complexities, however. A relatively simple case is the Stoney Nation in Alberta, which consists of three bands sharing three inhabited reserves. For all practical purposes, this is a single community, and it is usually called the Stoney Nation, not the Stoney First Nation. Although there is no consistency, the term "Nation," rather than "First Nation," is often used for larger groupings of many bands, such as the Cree Nation or Nisga'a Nation. Paul Tennant says that such larger groupings are sometimes called "tribal nations,"[47] but that phraseology has not been widely adopted, perhaps because of the primitive connotations of the adjective "tribal." In any case, there is a fundamental conceptual problem. Why should bands, which are artifacts of the Indian Act, have the prestige of being First Nations, with all the powerful connotations of aboriginality, while much larger and older historic groupings are merely Nations?

Another conundrum is that Metis leaders now refer to their people as the Metis Nation. It may seem to make some sense for Indians to be First Nations and the Metis a Nation, since by definition the Indian presence had to be chronologically prior to the Metis presence; but do the Metis qualify for nationhood when, as latecomers on the aboriginal scene, they never had their own territory? In fact, they hunted, trapped, and traded throughout territories in northern Ontario and western Canada claimed by Indian nations such as the Blackfoot and Sioux, who resented their presence and sometimes tried to drive them out.

Perhaps only an academic like me would worry about such conceptual quibbles, but a serious practical issue is widely recognized in the aboriginal community. The nation, whatever else it may be, should be a unit of government, but most First Nations are so small that they hardly seem viable as governments. In October 1999, there were 625 Indian bands in Canada with a total status Indian population of about 610,000.[48] The mean size of a band was thus about 1,000, and the median was even smaller. As of 1993, 70 per cent of bands held less than 1,000 people, and only 10 per cent were bigger than 2,000. And these already tiny figures give a misleading impression of how many people actually reside on reserves, because 42 per cent of registered Indians live off-reserve.[49]

The RCAP recognized that the right of self-government cannot sensibly be "vested in small local communities that are incapable of exercising the powers and fulfilling the responsibilities of an autonomous governmental unit," and that "at least several thousand people" need to be involved, "given the range of modern governmental responsibilities."[50] It was the RCAP's opinion that aboriginal communities should consolidate themselves into about sixty to eighty "Aboriginal nations."[51] A few of these might be individual Indian bands, such as the Tsuu T'ina (Sarcee), who have over a thousand band members, one reserve, and no nearby linguistic relatives; but most would be groups of First Nations associated by similar languages and cultures and historic ties. Such Aboriginal nations might span more than one province, although convenience would make them coincide with provincial boundaries in many cases. There would also probably be several Metis and Inuit nations, because these are also diverse aggregations, even if they are identified in the constitution as peoples.

There is something to be said for the RCAP's point of view, but it has an obvious weakness: the committee perceives Canada as a multinational state but is unable to specify for certain who the nations are, or how and when they will be identified. In the meantime, 625 First Nations already enjoy legal existence under the Indian Act, have a powerful pan-Canadian organization in the AFN, and play politics vigorously in pursuit of their own self-interest. The situation is a bit reminiscent of Arab nationalism in the 1950s and 1960s. It was obvious to everyone that the boundaries of Iraq, Syria, Egypt, and other Middle Eastern states were colonial vestiges and that Arabs were in a sense one nation, even though they had long been ruled by other empires. Charismatic leaders such as Egypt's President Nasser preached unification, and a few small steps were actually taken, but in the end the self-interest of already existing states prevailed. It remains to be seen whether the Indian bands now calling themselves First Nations, with their governmental machinery already in place, will ever coalesce into the larger Aboriginal nations recommended by the RCAP.

A final question concerns the interpretation of First Nations symbolism. When the Dene first began to speak of themselves as a nation, Peter Russell, one of Canada's most thoughtful political scientists, argued that this was cultural rather than political nationalism. The Dene, he said, would be satisfied with survival as a distinct ethnic community, legislative recognition of their property rights, and "devolution of governmental authority to their communal organizations."[52] Russell saw "no legal obstacle to recognition of the Dene claim" in "the letter of our constitutional law."[53] But that hardly seems true in retrospect, after seeing explicit constitutional amendments on aboriginal rights in 1982, aboriginal opposition to the Meech Lake Accord, elaborate provisions for a "third order of government" in the failed Charlottetown Accord, and the even more extensive recommendations for constitutional change put forward by the RCAP. Perhaps the demands of aboriginal nationalism can be accommodated, but clearly not within the existing constitutional framework.

The young Cree leader Harold Cardinal, who had become famous for his opposition to the federal government's *White Paper* of 1969, criticized the "tainted" Dene Declaration as "an intrusion of left-wing thinking that is perhaps much closer to the academic community in Toronto than it is to the Dene."[54] Like Russell, Cardinal wanted Indian nationalism to be cultural rather than political. "A declaration of nationhood by a group of traditional Indians is substantially and fundamentally different from a declaration of nationhood by a group of Quebec separatists. The nationhood that our elders talk about would be similar to the nationhood of the Jews." Cardinal wanted "a tribal definition of nationhood," one "based upon the relationship between the people and the Creator." Such an understanding of nationality, he felt, would be less threatening to federal officials, who were "perhaps overly sensitive to the connotation of the term *nation* in relation to the separatist movement in Quebec."[55]

A few years later, University of Lethbridge scholars Menno Boldt and J. Anthony Long offered a related critique, arguing that Indians were indeed nations in the cultural sense, but that sovereignty and statehood were alien to their tribal traditions, which did not include a hierarchical organization of power. To pursue sovereignty now would destroy their authentic traditions and culture.[56] Again, a perceptive insight, but largely beside the point. Aboriginal nationalism in practice has oriented itself resolutely towards achievement of political power. If the movement's leaders speak less of sovereignty than they did in the early 1980s, it is because they have learned that the "inherent right of self-government" can serve the same purposes. The goal is still to obtain a constitutionally entrenched share of sovereign power in the Canadian state – or, for a much smaller, though not insignificant minority, to create sovereign nation-states separate from Canada in the international realm.[57]

METIS NATIONALISM

Metis nationalism has its own history, distinct from that of Indian nationalism. The idea of a "Metis Nation" goes back to 1815, when the officials of the North West Company, caught up in their fur trade war against the Hudson's Bay Company, encouraged the Red River Metis to attack the Selkirk settlers. The Nor'Westers told the Metis that, as a "New Nation" and the true "Lords of the Soil," they should drive out the agricultural colonists that the HBC had imported from Scotland and settled along the Red River. According to the historian A.S. Morton, "this belief of the half breeds that they were a nation, that as the Indian population, depleted by smallpox and drawn off to the more distant posts for their livelihood, left the land vacant, the Métis inherited their vast domain through the mother blood in their veins, held them together as one at every juncture at which they revolted against the domination of the 'whites.'"[58]

Louis Riel became the heir and main exponent of this nascent Metis nationalism, although he made little of it in the Manitoba uprising of 1869–70, apart from authorizing publication of a newspaper called *The New Nation;* at that point he was trying to represent all the inhabitants of the Red River colony, whites as well as Metis. In 1873–74, however, Riel spent much time in Quebec and was powerfully influenced by the ecclesiastical ideology known as Ultramontanism. The Ultras pictured French Canadians as a nation called to carry out the divine mission of spreading the Roman Catholic religion in North America. Initially, Riel saw the French Metis as "a branch of the French-Canadian tree," extending the work of evangelization into the Canadian North-West.[59] Later, after he started to call himself the "Prophet of the New World," he depicted the Metis as a veritable Chosen People, the successors to the French Canadians.[60] He wrote to a French-Canadian cousin: "The French-Canadian nation has received from God the wonderful mission of continuing the great works of France on this side of the ocean ... When the French-Canadian nation will have done its work and will be afflicted with the infirmities of old age, its mission must pass to other hands ... We are working to make the French-Canadian Metis people sufficiently great to be worthy to receive the heritage of Lower Canada."[61]

In Riel's mind, the Metis were no longer just a branch on the French-Canadian tree; he wanted French and French-Canadian immigrants to Manitoba and the North-West to assimilate into the new Metis nation. As he put it in a poem entitled "Le peuple Métis-Canadien-français":

> Métis et Canadiens ensemble
> Français, si nos trois éléments
> S'amalgament bien, il me semble
> Que nous serons un jour plus grands.[62]

> [Metis and French Canadians together
> Are French – if our three elements
> Mingle well, it seems to me
> That we will be greater one day.]

Riel's national feeling was not for mixed-race people in general but solely for the French Catholic element that owed its origins to the Montreal-based fur trade. He regarded as relatives the equally large English Protestant group of mixed-race people in the North-West stemming from the Hudson's Bay Company fur trade, but he did not consider them part of the same nation.

Towards the end of his life, Riel conceived a grandiose scheme of *métissage* in the North-West. He wanted to promote the immigration of various European nationalities by setting aside specific areas for specific groups – a New Poland, a New Italy, and so on. He expected the new immigrants to intermarry with the Indians, thus "solving" the Indian problem by absorbing them into a new family of Metis nations led by *la nation métisse-candienne-française*. Riel, however, never pushed his nationalism to the point of wanting a Metis nation-state. Like his Ultramontane mentors in Quebec, he thought the interests of his people could be served within a multinational state. When he soured on Canada, he turned to thoughts of American annexation and ultimately of a merger between the American republic and the British Empire. Although he twice took up arms against Canada and declared a provisional government, these tactics were intended to assert Metis rights, not to promote separatism in the strict sense.

Today, only historians are aware of the details of Riel's thinking. Yet he has been transmuted into the great symbol of a new kind of Metis nationalism, which, at least potentially, includes all people of partially Indian ancestry, whether Catholic or Protestant, anglophone or francophone, western or eastern. This new Metis nationalism developed gradually out of the pan-aboriginal movement of the late 1960s.

In 1968 William Wuttunee's National Indian Council, which had tried to represent all people of native ancestry, split into the National Indian Brotherhood, representing status Indians, and the Canadian Metis Society (later the Native Council of Canada, or NCC), representing Metis and non-status Indians.[63] The NCC took part in the patriation debate of the early 1980s without using nationalist language to describe the Metis.[64] Such terminology started to creep in with the formation of the Metis National Council in 1983, when the plains Metis split away from the non-status Indians.[65]

In 1992 the Metis National Council succeeded in negotiating the Metis National Accord (MNA) as an attachment to the Charlottetown Accord: "Whereas in the Northwest of Canada the Metis Nation emerged as a unique Nation with its own language, culture and forms of self-government; And whereas historically the Metis Nation has sought agreements with Canada to protect its land and other rights."[66] The MNA would have converted the Metis into a constitutionally recognized aboriginal people on the model of the Indians, with a registry of members, self-government, land base, and transfer payments to support the new machinery of government. However, the referendum defeat of the Charlottetown Accord put the scheme on hold.

The RCAP distinguished the "Metis Nation" (the descendants of Metis employed in the fur trade in northern Ontario and western Canada) from the "other Metis" in eastern Canada, such as the people of mixed Inuit-white ancestry in Labrador or other mixed-race groups in the Maritimes, Quebec, and Ontario.[67] Eventually, thought the RCAP, there could be several Metis nations as the other mixed-race groups become aware of their identity and claim national status.

Although Indians and Metis have both advanced their cause with nationalist terminology in the last fifteen years, their nationalisms differ in one important respect. In the Indian movement, the nations are bands (First Nations) that already have a land base in the form of reserves. They hope to get more land through treaty-entitlement negotiations (Ontario and the Prairies) or aboriginal-claims settlements (British Columbia), but they already have some land to serve as a focus of identity. The Metis, in contrast, have very little land of their own other than the Metis settlements of northern Alberta. Some villages in the prairie provinces and in northern Ontario are largely Metis in population, but in legal terms they are rural municipalities under provincial jurisdiction.

These objective differences colour the two types of nationalism. First Nations nationalists emphasize autonomy (self-government) on existing territorial holdings even as they strive to increase those territories. Metis nationalists, while they would like to acquire even the most minimal land base, will always have to deal with a population spread across the villages, towns, and cities of Canada. Metis nationalists, therefore, want to create non-territorial forms of self-government for this dispersed population. Thus they must emphasize the single Metis Nation, whereas First Nations activists emphasize their particular identities at the band level.

PROBLEMS

It is difficult to reconcile both Indian and Metis nationalism with standard notions of the nation. The historian Philip White, after an extensive survey of the literature of nationalism, identifies five criteria that Americans normally use (and that Canadians could use as well) "in making their own subjective judgments as to whether they should or should not employ the term nationality in referring to a particular group ... 1) civilization, 2) significance, 3) territory, 4) solidarity, and 5) sovereignty."[68] Aboriginal nationalism runs into difficulties on all five counts.

1. *Civilization.* White writes that "groups deemed uncivilized tend to be called tribes, even though they meet all or nearly all the other conditions for recognition as a nationality."[69] Canadian aboriginal people are now civilized, but they project the concept of nationhood back into the past, claiming to have always been nations. "It

is true," says White, "that the word nation was once applied to primitive groups as in the 'Five Nations' of the Iroquois Indians of North America, but that use has died out, and it would now appear eccentric to designate as nationalities such groups as the eighteenth-century Iroquois."[70]

What may seem like a conceptual quibble represents a much deeper philosophical and political conflict. In claiming to be nations, aboriginal peoples reject the distinction between civilization and savagery and the political implications arising from it. They thus implicitly (and sometimes explicitly) challenge the legitimacy of the Canadian state, whose sovereignty is based on the rights of discovery and prescription and the doctrine of *terra nullius*.

2. *Significance.* "Historically," says White, "people have preferred to reserve the term nationality for groups which they consider important, and to deny it to groups too few in numbers or possessed of too small a territory to be deemed significant."[71] However, he also notes that usage is relaxing. The United Nations, for example, has admitted some states whose populations are extremely small. The 181 member states of the UN now include six with populations less than a hundred thousand: Andorra, Antigua and Barbuda, Dominica, Grenada, St Kitts and Nevis, and the Seychelles (all of them islands, except the historic principality of Andorra).

Aboriginal nationalism in Canada goes an order of magnitude further. The world's population of about six billion people is represented in the United Nations by 181 member states, whereas Canada's 610,000 status Indians claim to consist of 625 First Nations. Even if they follow the RCAP's advice to consolidate themselves into seventy or eighty "Aboriginal nations," most of the resulting nations would be no more populous than a small town and certainly much smaller than even the smallest member of the United Nations.

3. *Territory.* White admits that "during the heyday of the cultural/ ancestral concept in the nineteenth and early twentieth centuries," non-territorial cultural groups such as Jews and Gypsies were sometimes referred to as nations. In the twentieth century, however, Gypsies, who have no land base, are no longer called a nation; and those Jews who have acquired a territory now have the national designation "Israeli," while "Jew" remains a religious or ethnocultural

label.[72] In the United States, attempts to refashion blacks and Hispanics as nations have never succeeded. The Nation of Islam has exercised some influence in black politics but has never come close to mobilizing the majority, or even a significant minority, of the black population behind itself.

Indian reserves and similar lands administered on behalf of Indians already make up an area about the size of Vancouver Island.[73] It has been estimated that, "with further land settlements on the way, Aboriginal land holdings will continue to increase and ... First Nations will own or control one-third of the total land mass of Canada by the year 2000."[74] (This estimate includes huge areas in Nunavut, Yukon, and the Northwest Territories that aboriginals will not own outright but over which they will have various kinds of co-management rights.) Yet two problems stand in the way of seeing this as national territory in the ordinary sense. First, most aboriginal land is held in trust by the Crown. Aboriginal people have the beneficial use of it, but they have neither full ownership rights nor complete political control. Depending on the interpretation given to self-government, they may have a share of sovereignty; but so do the Canadian provinces, and they do not claim to be nations and would not be recognized as such. Second, the aboriginal land base is an archipelago of thousands of non-contiguous parcels across all provinces and territories belonging to hundreds of First Nations and other poorly defined "Aboriginal nations." These "nations" are viable only through the massive and continuing financial support of the federal government.

4. *Solidarity.* For a nation to exist, there must be a widespread consciousness of national identity and a degree of cohesion and commitment sufficient to permit collective action. Aboriginal peoples in Canada meet this test at the local level of First Nations but not at higher levels. The pan-Canadian scene is a shifting kaleidoscope of status Indian, non-status Indian, Metis, and Inuit organizations occasionally making common cause but just as often in conflict with one another. Lack of higher-level solidarity reflects the territorial dispersion of aboriginal people. The truly solidary communities are too small to be viable nations, while the larger aggregates lack sufficient solidarity to be politically effective.

5. *Sovereignty.* White's general observation certainly applies to aboriginal politics in Canada: "Because the prestige of a territorial

group is so closely tied to sovereignty, those who sympathize with a particular group's aspirations for it are quick to discover its existence and slow to acknowledge its loss. Antagonists reverse the pattern. As with solidarity, however, each interested observer makes his own judgment as to whether or not a group has sovereignty and, in time, a consensus usually appears."[75] The Canadian consensus seems clear enough. Canadians are willing, indeed eager, to devolve substantial self-governing power upon aboriginal communities and to protect their rights in the constitution. They are not willing to endorse a clearly stated theory of aboriginal sovereignty, but they will accept a murky concept, such as the inherent right of self-government, that seems to preserve the integrity of the Canadian state. Outside of Canada, there is no effective movement to recognize aboriginal sovereignty in any way that would detract from Canadian sovereignty. Canada remains a recognized sovereign power in the international sphere. Other nations have no desire to meddle in Canada's internal distribution of sovereignty among provincial, local, and aboriginal governments; they will continue to deal with Canada as a sovereign power.

These five considerations help explain the otherwise paradoxical way in which Canada has rejected Quebec nationalism while embracing aboriginal nationalism. Quebec politicians routinely call their province a nation, but neither the constitution, nor federal legislation, nor the statements of federal politicians recognize the nationhood of Quebec. In fact, official Canada goes to great lengths to concoct phrases such as "distinct society" or "unique characteristics" in order to avoid speaking of Quebec as a nation. Why? Because Québécois nationalism meshes perfectly with White's five criteria. The people of Quebec are, and have always been, civilized; at seven million, their population is relatively numerous; they occupy and govern a large, contiguous territory; they have high solidarity, at least among francophones, who make up over 80 per cent of the whole; and they have not only a share of sovereignty within the federal system but also an arguable claim to sovereignty in the international sense. In short, Quebec nationalism has the potential to destroy Canada, and so Canadians have generally reacted by refusing even to recognize the concept of a Quebec nation.

Contrast that to the aboriginal situation. Aboriginal peoples in Canada project the concept of nation backwards into a pre-civilized past; they have tiny popoulations; they do not control a contiguous territory; they are internally divided among dozens or hundreds of different collective identities; and they receive support only from scattered intellectuals for their assertions of sovereignty. Aboriginal nationalism can disrupt Canadian politics, but it cannot threaten the existence of the Canadian state in the same way as Québécois nationalism does. Is this why the Penner Committee in 1983, and Canadians in general soon after, rushed to accept the First Nations terminology? Pierre Trudeau was prime minister at the time; yet he, who had always refused to speak of *deux nations,* even though the Progressive Conservatives and New Democrats both accepted that terminology in the 1960s, made no objection when his MPs began to speak of six hundred nations in Canada. Two nations are a threat, but six hundred are an inconvenience.

Widespread acceptance of First Nations terminology helped aboriginal peoples win political victories in the 1980s and 1990s, but neologisms quickly lose their force. Consider the history of feminism. When the word "gender" was introduced into political debate in the early 1970s, it represented the theory that differences between men and women are not natural but result from social conditioning. Twenty-five years later, the word "gender" has passed into ordinary usage and lost its special meaning; it is now just a synonym for "sex" and is routinely used by speakers who are not aware of the theory behind it. In the same way, phrases such as "First Nations" are quickly becoming routinized and losing their special meaning. Words such as "Indian" and "band" have come to seem vaguely derogatory, even though they are embedded in the constitution and legislation; and so Canadians, wishing to be polite, say "First Nations" instead. But changing the word does not change the reality. Calling Indian bands First Nations does not change Canada into a genuine multinational state because the objective attributes of Indian bands are far from what nations are generally understood to be.

CHAPTER 6

The Inherent Problems of
Aboriginal Self-Government

"White people have organized crime; we've got chief and council."
– Dan Burnstick, Cree comedian, in
"The Difference between White People and Us Guys"[1]

Under normal conditions, Canadians hear little about politics on Indian reserves. Reporters seldom venture onto reserves and may be physically ejected if they try. Meetings are often closed and sometimes held off reserve, even in foreign countries. Occasionally, however, when a reserve is in crisis, one faction may resort to the media, and then the public will get some information. That happened among the Stoney Nation west of Calgary in 1997–98.

The Stoneys are a branch of the Assiniboine or Sioux people. They are governed by a council of twelve plus three chiefs, elected every two years (they have three chiefs because they consist of three bands). With a population of about thirty-three hundred they have four reserves in the foothills of the Rockies. By far the biggest, about forty thousand hectares, is the Morley reserve on the highway to Banff, seventy kilometres west of Calgary.

The Morley reserve sits on several pools of natural gas, from which the tribe draws annual royalties of about $13 million, approximately $4,000 per resident. Royalties were even higher in the 1980s, peaking at about $40 million a year.[2] The Stoneys also get about $23 million a year in federal transfers, mostly from the Department of Indian Affairs, while band-owned businesses bring in additional money. Total revenues are estimated at $50 million,

---

Note: For earlier versions of this chapter, see Flanagan, "Last Immigrants" and "Inherent Problems."

or about $16,000 for each man, woman, and child. That's an astonishing amount of money, far above anyone's definition of the poverty line. In fact, it's higher than the mean income of Canadian families. With this much money coming in, the Stoneys should be well off.

But money hasn't bought happiness. The first public indication that something was wrong was a rash of clear-cutting on the forested parts of the Morley reserve. Within a few months in 1994, 20 per cent of the reserve's pine and spruce was cut and hauled to British Columbia for milling. It was an election year, and in an apparent bid for electoral support, the band council encouraged families that exercise loosely defined customary rights over land and timber to make their own deals with off-reserve loggers. The Department of Indian Affairs stepped in to stop the pillage in early 1995, leaving the land littered with logging slash and unsold fallen timber, and the courts clogged with lawsuits alleging illegal sales, broken contracts, and neglect of administrative responsibility.[3]

Things then went from bad to worse. In 1997 the department appointed Coopers & Lybrand as financial trustee for the Stoney Nation because the Stoney had run up a deficit of $5.6 million in the previous year; another accounting firm, KPMG, was hired to carry out a forensic audit.[4] An Indian Affairs memo written in early 1998 said that "the magnitude and complexities of the allegations have far exceeded anyone's expectations,"[5] and the two accounting firms billed $1.8 million for services rendered in a period under a year.[6] However, the budget has been gradually brought back towards balance, with zero deficit scheduled for the start of the fiscal year, 1 April 1999. A band election held in December 1998 replaced two of three chiefs and seven of twelve councillors with new members supposedly committed to fiscal responsibility, and so maybe the budget will stay balanced for a while.[7] Throughout these events, dissidents leaked fascinating allegations to the media. None of the information has been proved in court, but neither has anything been effectively contradicted.

• The three chiefs were paid more than $450,000 in 1997. A chief's basic salary was $46,000, but each got additional payments for attending meetings and serving on committees, as well as generous expense accounts.[8] All this was tax-free.

- Chief John Snow, who had been in office from 1968 to 1992, was re-elected in 1996. He quickly fired thirty-nine band employees and gave four of his children senior jobs. Considering the logging fiasco that occurred while he was out of power, this may have been a progressive move.
- Another chief continued to receive welfare cheques after being elected and also used band funds to engage a nanny for her children. She hired a number of her relatives to work in the welfare department, but after the reserve went into trusteeship they were fired, allegedly for also receiving welfare payments while working.[9] In early 1998 the province threatened to take over child protection on the reserve because Stoney welfare workers weren't coming to work. A provincial spokesman said child welfare had been "off the rails" ever since the tribe took control of it in the early 1990s.[10] In November 1998 the Alberta Family and Social Services threatened to take back control if the problems were not fixed soon.[11]
- The same chief chose Phoenix, Arizona, to hold a budget meeting attended by a dozen band members, including several from her immediate family.[12]

Meanwhile, social indicators are dreadful. There were twelve unnatural deaths by suicide, accident, violent crime, or drug overdose in 1997. Two-thirds of residents are said to be on welfare (although, given the lax administration, some welfare recipients may also hold jobs with the band). The Stoneys' social service agency has about 130 children in care – an astonishing number for a community of 3,300 people.[13] A sympathetic doctor in nearby Cochrane, who treats many Stoneys in her practice, has tried to set up a food bank. "We need cash for bannock," she told a reporter.[14] But Chief John Snow's wife is not so soft-hearted. "All they want is bingo money. They are not really starving," she told reporters while her husband lay in a cardiology ward in a Calgary hospital.[15] Four buildings, including the Morley community centre, were burned to the ground in one night of arson in early 1998; the damage to the community centre was estimated at $350,000.[16]

There is abundant evidence that the Stoney situation is unusual only in its extreme concentration of bad news. Fiscal mismanagement is commonplace on Canadian Indian reserves. As of late 1998, the Department of Indian Affairs estimated that it would have to step in with "remedial management plans" for 20 to 25 per cent of Indian bands. The problem is quite generalized; "a dozen indebted bands straighten out their finances each year as another 12 sink into the red."[17] In the middle of 1998, "15 of 43 First Nations in Alberta [were] on a remedial fiscal plan, after audits showed their deficits exceeded eight per cent of total revenues."[18]

In April 1999 the auditor general's annual report again upbraided the federal government for exercising inadequate control over the billions of dollars transferred each year to Indians: "The department is not taking adequate steps to ensure that allegations of wrongdoing, including complaints and disputes related to funding arrangements, are appropriately resolved."[19] The following are two specific examples: the Gitxsan Health Authority, representing Indian people in central British Columbia, had invested (and lost) $300,000 of "surplus" funds in the Calgary stock market;[20] and a Saulteaux Indian band in Saskatchewan with eight hundred members spent $600,000 on travel last year, more than the Saskatchewan cabinet. The chief alone spent $176,000.[21]

Fiscal irresponsiblity is only the tip of a much larger iceberg of political pathology. Two recent examples from Alberta can be cited as evidence.

The first concerns the Tsuu T'ina Indians near Calgary. Jane Stewart, the minister of Indian affairs, invited Indians to write to her office in confidence about maladministration on their reserves. Bruce Starlight, a resident of the Tsuu T'ina (Sarcee) reserve near Calgary and a former member of the band council, took up her offer and wrote a letter alleging financial improprieties on the part of Chief Roy Whitney, who had been a federal Liberal candidate in the 1993 election. The confidential letter to the minister was leaked to the band council, which thoughtfully paid for Whitney to launch a defamation suit against Starlight. After considerable delay, the minister expressed regret that her office had not kept the letter confidential and offered to help Starlight with his legal bills. It was later revealed that the band is a regular contributor to the Liberal Party of Canada. Such contributions are legal, but is it appropriate for political parties to be getting money appropriated by Parliament for provision of basic services in aboriginal communities?[22]

The Samson First Nation provides the second example. Located near Hobbema, it is one of the wealthiest Indian bands in Canada, with accumulated trust funds once holding over $400 million from oil and gas royalties. This First Nation is suing the federal Crown for over a billion more, claiming long-term mismanagement of its resources as well as non-fulfilment of treaty obligations. In August 1997 its offices were occupied for five days by dissidents demanding an external investigation of tribal finances. They claimed that the chief and council were corruptly using public money for themselves and their relatives. "The chief's daughter runs social services. The chief's daughter determines who gets the cheque," said one protester, who also claimed to have been fired from his job on the reserve after he started the public protests.[23] Six hundred of the band's forty-three hundred members signed a petition calling for an investigation.

In October 1998 the *Globe and Mail* published a long piece of investigative journalism whose heading summarized the situation: "The money pit: an Indian band's story. Taxpayers pour millions of dollars into the Samson Cree Reserve. That's good for the well-connected few. But most people there live in abject poverty."[24] Nothing had changed when the newspaper did a follow-up story in April 1999. Indeed, the band had recently withdrawn $50 million from its trust account to cover a budget deficit, and this had followed a $16 million withdrawal for the same reason the previous September. Before approving the latest withdrawal, Ottawa required the band to bring in external accountants to restore financial order.[25] As with the Stoneys, social indicators are depressing. Hobbema has the highest automobile-accident rate in Alberta, an almost unbelievable forty times higher than Edmonton's.[26] Band members, especially young people, use their share of royalties to buy high-powered trucks. Too many drive them too fast, too often under the influence of alcohol and other drugs. It's the worst kind of stereotype – a true one.

There has been a veritable flood of writing on aboriginal self-government in the last two decades, culminating in the RCAP *Report*.[27] Although some cautionary notes have been sounded,[28] almost all of this literature is laudatory. The scholar Helen Buckley, in an otherwise excellent book full of penetrating insights about the failure of past policies, writes of "the magic of self-government," which means "more people will be working; aspirations and self-confidence will rise; the costs of welfare, social services, and the rest will go down."[29] The skeptic is reminded of Lucien Bouchard's famous statement in the 1995 referendum campaign: "A Yes has magical meaning because with a wave of a wand it will change the whole situation. The day after sovereignty there will be no more federalists, no more sovereignists. There will only be Quebeckers."[30] Aboriginal self-government may indeed bring some benefits; yet it is beset with serious and inherent problems whose effects are becoming increasingly visible as more money and power are devolved upon the chiefs and councils who govern Indian reserves.

The problem is not that Indian leaders are especially venal, although many are. Politicians of all races manifest venality when they get the chance to pursue their private interests without constraint. The problem is that aboriginal governments in Canada are beset with structural features that encourage rather than constrain venality, and that these structural features are so deeply engrained as to be inherent.

INSTITUTIONS

According to Menno Boldt, "Indian leaders tend to view self-government in terms of taking over the [Department of Indian Affairs'] authority and structures on their reserves." He is critical of this approach, pointing out that institutional structures have their own logic and that a mere change of personnel "is no guarantee that the entrenched norms of paternalism, authoritarianism, self-interest, and self-aggrandizement by office-holders will be eliminated."[31] In Boldt's view, if self-government is to be worth having, Indians will have to revive the communal patterns of their past and jettison the formal, bureaucratic institutions imposed by the Indian Act.

The diagnosis is acute. Up to the 1960s, Indian agents, subject to administrative control by the Department of Indian Affairs, exercised a remarkable fusion of legislative, executive, and judicial powers over the residents of reserves. Those powers have now been largely transferred to chiefs and band councils, even as the department has withdrawn much of its administrative supervision. Unfortunately, however, Boldt's solution is utopian. Pre-contact Indian forms of governance did not possess the formal institutions characterizing modern states – written laws, bureaucracies, competitive elections, courts and police, and so on; and it is unrealistic to imagine that the informal approach to governance could be revived in contemporary Canada. The governance of pre-contact aboriginal people was suited to their hunting-gathering way of life with its band or tribal form of social organization (the horticultural Iroquoian societies had more elaborate chiefdoms, but not full-fledged state structures). Contemporary aboriginal people, are integrated into the broader Canadian society. They are literate and educated, own property (even if property rights on reserves are poorly specified), work for wages and salaries, supply their needs through market transactions rather than through self-provision, and deal with state agencies in a multitude of ways.

Because of this integration, aboriginal communities will not be able to revive their ancient systems of informal governance. Their own cultures, now closely integrated with the general Canadian culture, require formal government. Members of aboriginal communities have to protect their own property rights and guarantee the market transactions in which they engage. Moreover, dealing with the all-encompassing Canadian society requires formal government. Aboriginal communities have to account for transfer payments from Ottawa; even when they develop internal institutions of criminal justice, they have to provide information about offenders to the Canadian justice system to prevent double jeopardy; and so on.

The present reality on Indian reserves is that elected chiefs and councils collectively exercise the kind of formal authority once exercised by Indian agents. That will not change, no matter how the titles are revised. State institutions are here to stay, for aboriginals as well as for everyone else. In itself, this does not mean that aboriginal self-government is unworkable or harmful; it merely means that, like other forms of government, it will never fulfil millenarian expectations about the withering away of the state. But there are further questions about how well aboriginal self-government can work in practice.

SIZE

As described in the preceding chapter, aboriginal communities are very small. In the literature, the problems that small size poses for self-government are usually noted under two headings: (1) shortage of financial resources and (2) shortage of skilled personnel.[32] Indeed, these are serious difficulties. How is a community of a few hundred people, located far from major centres of population, supposed to provide residents with the amenities of modern life?

One obvious solution is for communities to work together to offer services otherwise beyond their means. Bands can pool their efforts in tribal governments to provide expensive services.[33] Another commonly used approach is for an aboriginal government to contract with a nearby city or rural municipality, or with the provincial government, for services such as water and sewerage, fire protection, policing, and education.[34]

Although effective up to a point, these strategies of pooling and cooperation are not a panacea. Several bands might work together as a tribe, but most tribal groupings in Canada are still extremely small and thus limited in their ability to provide services to their members. Cooperation with other tribes is possible but raises additional problems of cultural conflict. One of the main purposes of aboriginal self-government is supposed to be cultural preservation and revitalization. Some governmental services, such as sewage disposal and road maintenance, are culturally neutral; but others, such as policing, child protection, and education, are culturally sensitive. Working through a multitribal consortium cannot help but pose challenges of cultural integrity. The same is true of cooperation with non-aboriginal governments in culturally sensitive fields.

Retaining skilled personnel in aboriginal communities may be particularly difficult. The numbers of highly educated aboriginals are steadily increasing; sociologist Rick Ponting concludes that the "First Nations' post-secondary enrolment rate of 6.5% of persons aged 17–34 is closing in on the rate of 10.4% for all of Canadian society."[35] But even if the flow is increasing, the stock of highly educated aboriginals will take decades to reach Canadian norms; and as long as that discrepancy exists, aboriginals with advanced education will be in demand, with attractive opportunities off reserve. Many may prefer to work in Vancouver, Calgary, Toronto, and Ottawa rather than use their skills in the communities where they grew up, even though they continue to retain band membership. Is aboriginal government really *self*-government when, even though the elected officials are band members, the technostructure of administrators, accountants, and other professionals consists largely of non-aboriginals? That's a rhetorical question with no simple answer, but it illustrates a problem unlikely to go away in the lifetime of those now living.

Another problem of size, much less well discussed in the literature, is that of factionalism. Political scientist Roger Gibbins, inspired by James Madison's tenth essay in *The Federalist,* points out that "individual rights and freedoms are best protected within larger, more heterogeneous communities where it is more difficult to articulate a majority will and where a multitude of conflicting and competing interests fragment and immobilize the majority."[36] In the older but still powerful language of Madison: "Extend the sphere, and you take in a greater variety of parties and interests: you make it less probable that a majority of the whole have a common motive to invade the rights of other citizens."[37]

The empirical literature on aboriginal politics suggests that kinship, if not the only factor, is a key one. The Hawthorn Commission, in studying the politics of thirty-four bands of different sizes in the 1960s, found that the influence of kinship was hard to pin down on small reserves because almost everyone was related to everyone else. In such small settings, personal ties and friendship were extremely important. But members of larger bands openly recognized kinship as the main principle of politics, particularly in cases, such as the Blood reserve in Alberta, where the legal band is really a tribe composed of multiple lineages. Another kind of diversity, similar in political effect, arises on reserves where some members are descended from Metis who took treaty and may not be regarded by others as genuine Indians.[38]

In field work done on a large Manitoba Saulteaux reserve in the 1970s, an anthropologist found about twenty-five informal "bunches," each with membership of about five to ten and a varying number of followers. Kinship seemed to be the main, though not the only, factor in the composition of these bunches. Politics on the reserve was pluralistic. Candidates could get elected by pulling together the support of several bunches, but alignments were fluid and temporary, with no permanent majority coalition. Residents saw distribution of Indian Affairs benefits as the main purpose of politics. The looseness of the coalitional structure tended to result in egalitarian outcomes, because "every distribution dissatisfies a majority of the community members."[39]

A study of the Okanagan Nation in the 1980s revealed that "in the absence of formal political parties there are informal campaigns [for chief] involving kin and friendship networks."[40] Tom Pocklington, who carried out a public-opinion survey in two of the Alberta Metis settlements, found large majorities agreeing with the proposition that "if you're looking for something like a job on the settlement or a new house, it helps to be related to a council member." He also found wide agreement about who the leading and favoured families were on both settlements, although he was unable to document the actual practice of nepotism.[41]

In his research on politics on the Blood and Peigan reserves in Alberta, J. Anthony Long found that extended kin groups "run slates of candidates during each election. Sponsorship of candidates usually occurs in informal kin group caucuses, where decisions are made as to who should run for council or the chieftanship."[42] These kin-sponsored candidates are motivated by the prospect of economic gain for themselves and their relatives. As we know from revelations about the Stoney reserve, sources of such gain include

- salaries for holding elected office
- extra honoraria for elected officials in aboriginal governments to attend meetings or sit on committees
- poorly monitored expense allowances
- appointment of family members and political supporters to positions on the band payroll
- preferential access to welfare funds
- assignment of valuable on-reserve property rights, such as housing, agricultural land, and timber licences.

Strater Crowfoot, who was chief of the Siksika (Blackfoot) Nation for eight years, confirms that the family is "a pivotal unit in reserve politics." He calls nepotism the "sustaining discourse" of politics on the reserve. Relatives routinely approach those in power for financial assistance. Opposing factions interpret decisions in nepotistic terms and plan to decide the same way when they come to power. "After the election where I was defeated," writes Crowfoot, "one voter said: 'The Crowfoots are no longer in charge; it's my family's turn.'" Crowfoot gives the impression that this nepotistic style of politics is ubiquitous in aboriginal governments.[43]

Religion can also be a source of factionalism, with lines drawn between Christians and traditionalists, or between different Christian denominations. On one northern Ontario reserve in the 1970s, the Anglicans moved to a new location *en masse,* leaving the Roman Catholics behind.[44] Religion, of course, is likely to be tightly interwoven with kinship. It is similar in that respect to place of residence, which can also be a political factor where there are multiple nodes of settlement on a large reserve, or where a band or tribe occupies several reserves. There are also economic lines of cleavage on reserves between those who have *de facto* property rights over housing, land, and natural resources and those who are shut out. Again, these factions are interlaced with kinship because property rights are passed on through inheritance from generation to generation.

As more aboriginal people pursue formal education and acquire highly remunerative employment, a somewhat different class cleavage between haves and have-nots is also emerging, but it is strongly affected by the tendency of more prosperous Indians to live off reserve.[45] Even the activists in the aboriginal political movement, unless they are band chiefs, tend to live in towns and cities, where they work as lawyers, professors, administrators, and consultants. Time will tell whether this new, largely urban aboriginal middle class will remain involved in band politics.

All politics is factional. As Madison wrote, "the latent causes of faction are thus sown in the nature of man; and we see them everywhere brought into different degrees of activity, according to the different circumstances of civil society."[46] But whereas factionalism in Canadian politics operates on a large scale and in a formalized way involving competition between linguistic, regional, and economic organizations, factionalism in aboriginal politics operates on a small scale and in an informal way involving competition between kin groups and friendship networks. This familial style of politics often involves a high degree of patronage and nepotism, as winning factions take advantage of the majority position easily obtained in such tiny polities.

Roger Gibbins suggests that the Charter of Rights and Freedoms will help defend residents of aboriginal communities against the bad effects of majority factionalism.[47] In practice, however, the Charter is unlikely to be of much help because it does not protect property, and factionalism in an aboriginal community typically involves property rights – nepotistic hiring practices, misuse of expense accounts, denial of housing or welfare, reassignment of land or timber, and so on. Recourse to the Canadian courts outside the Charter may be possible but is likely to be worthwhile only in cases of aggravated loss, because the legal system is so expensive to use. Moving off the reserve is often the only remedy available to those who lose factional fights.

SCOPE

Aboriginal governments deal with a remarkably wide range of issues. One listing, shorter than most, mentions six broad categories:

1. *cultural preservation* – the maintenance of traditional lifestyle, language and culture;
2. *cultural adaptation* – assisting a culture and community to change so that it and the individuals within it can interact effectively with the economy and lifestyle of the non-native society;
3. *service delivery* – the economic and effective provision to the community, in a form adapted to and suitable to its needs and circumstances, of services such as health, welfare, education, justice;
4. *economic development* – the active involvement of the self-governing unit in projects and activities which improve the well-being of individuals and the community;
5. *resources and environmental management* – aboriginal populations who maintain a traditional lifestyle will need some control over the resources of their land base; and
6. *law enforcement* – the relationship of the aboriginal peoples to the law and the judicial system is a major issue at present and will continue to be for most self-governing units.[48]

This list combines functions of all three levels of Canadian government and, indeed, includes some that no government in Canada undertakes. Local governments deliver services to Canadian residents (utilities, police and fire protection), albeit within a framework of provincial funding and supervision. The provinces and the federal government share responsibility for law enforcement, environmental protection, and resource management. In a market economy, government plays an important but limited role in economic development, maintaining the indispensable framework of a sound currency, civil law, vital statistics, and so on. And in a liberal democracy such as Canada, governments are involved in cultural preservation and adaptation only at the margins.

John Stuart Mill wrote that "every additional function undertaken by the government, is a fresh occupation imposed upon a body already overcharged with duties."[49] When aboriginal governments, with their small size, limited resources, and shortage of skilled personnel, undertake such an ambitious agenda, there are bound to be many failures of competence. One example is the Manitoba child welfare experiment, in which five Indian agencies took over child protection for Indian people in the province. "The Manitoba agencies," according to two otherwise sympathetic authors, "failed in their delivery of child welfare services."[50] The number of children in care went up dramatically even as it fell in all other provinces. Reported incidents of sexual and physical abuse multiplied as children were placed in Indian foster homes. Finally, the suicide of a thirteen-year-old boy forced a judicial inquiry followed by a legislative inquiry. Although the initiatives of aboriginal self-government may sometimes succeed where the initiatives of senior governments have failed, the practical difficulties of resourcing and competence at the ground level will continue to be enormous, no matter what deals are struck at the symbolic level of constitutional politics.

The scope of aboriginal self-government on reserves means that the local public sector is enormously overdeveloped in comparison to other Canadian communities of similar size. The difference is evident in the role of elected politicians. The Stoney reserve has three chiefs and twelve councillors, all drawing full-time salaries. The Stoneys are a slightly exceptional case because they consist of three bands living together; an ordinary band of the same size would have one chief and twelve councillors. But that is still a lot of full-time politicians compared to a typical Canadian town of the same size, whose elected mayor and council would retain their day jobs and meet perhaps for one evening a couple of times a month. For example, in Grand Forks, British Columbia, which has a population of thirty-eight hundred, the mayor is paid only $15,000 a year and the councillors $8,300 (taxable).[51]

The difference is even more striking at the administrative level. The typical Canadian town of three thousand people might have a full-time secretary-treasurer to manage the budget, a planning officer to look after land-development issues, and maybe one or two other employees. A school board will look after the schools, the RCMP or provincial police will enforce the law, and the province will administer social services, while many functions will be contracted out to the private sector. The typical reserve, in contrast, will have an overall manager and support staff, an education department to run the school, a welfare department to administer social assistance, a housing department to manage all the homes

owned by the band, an economic-development department, and
several other branches of government to look after roads, sanita-
tion, and other functions. The band's public sector will have dozens
of full-time employees, indeed hundreds if the reserve is wealthy.

These are all important tasks that need to be done by someone.
The difference is that, under aboriginal self-government, they are
pulled together into a single governmental structure dwarfing the
society it purports to serve, whereas in the outside world these
functions are dispersed among a welter of levels of government,
independent boards and agencies, and private-sector entrepreneurs.
Aboriginal government is not devoid of independent boards and
agencies, but political authority is incomparably more focused on
a single entity – the band council – than is true in the outside world.
This concentration of authority means that a small group of officials has control over, or at least a say in, the disposition of large
volumes of money passing through the community. Thus the potential rewards for holding office in an aboriginal government are
larger than those for being, say, city councillor, mayor of a small
town, or reeve of a municipal township. Chiefs and councillors
have far greater opportunity to appoint their relatives and supporters to jobs, to sign contracts with well-connected businesses, and
to manipulate the assignment of property rights. It is a fertile field
for factionalism.

FUNDING

Aboriginal governments depend heavily on fiscal transfers from the
federal government. By far the largest paymaster is the Department
of Indian Affairs, but other departments also have significant aboriginal programs. Federal spending from all departments on status Indians and Inuit was estimated at $5.9 billion in the fiscal year 1994/
95,[52] and $6.3 billion in 1997/98.[53] Aboriginal spending was main-
tained and even increased slightly after 1995, at a time when the
Chrétien government was reducing almost all other line items in the
federal budget. In addition, band governments receive transfers for
particular purposes from provincial and municipal governments, as
well as private foundations, that may be important in specific cases,
although they are nowhere near the total of federal spending.

Most bands raise relatively little money on their own. Section 87
of the Indian Act exempts land and personal property on Indian

reserves from federal and provincial taxation.[54] Section 83(1), added in 1985, allows a band council to levy property taxes on the reserve.[55] As of 1995, fifty-four councils had created property-tax regimes, leading to about $17 million in collections; but in practice this new power has been used mainly to tax non-Indians who lease reserve property.[56] It is still generally true that Indians on reserve do not tax themselves and are not taxed by any other government. The Nisga'a Agreement provides for the exemption from sales tax to be phased out over eight years, and from income tax over twelve years; but even at the end of this process, most Nisga'a residents will pay little tax because much of their income will continue to be received in non-taxable, in-kind benefits such as free housing, education, and medical care.[57]

Aboriginal governments also generate revenue by running businesses. There are long-standing, traditional enterprises such as farming, ranching, and lumbering as well as many new ventures such as shopping malls, golf courses, housing developments, gambling casinos, hotels, and financial institutions. Businesses provide cash flow and jobs, but it is often hard to know whether they are truly profitable when they are backed by revenues from government programs, land-claims settlements, or oil and gas royalties.

Fiscal transfers, land-claims settlements, and natural-resource rents all have a common characteristic – they are not earned in the usual sense of the term. Fiscal transfers and land-claims settlements can be enhanced politically through strategic litigation and negotiation, but that is quite different from generating income by working for an employer or investing one's own resources. Natural-resource rents arise largely from the good luck of being situated on top of a hydrocarbon reservoir. In the past, the energy companies negotiated a deal through Indian Oil and Gas Canada, explored the reserve, built pipeline connectors, pumped out the oil and gas, and paid royalties. For most people in the community, the net effect was the same as an increase in the fiscal transfer from Ottawa because the money came without the need to work for it, although some residents might subsequently have found employment in enterprises generated by the royalty cash flow. There is now a tendency for companies to become partners with the band government and to include some jobs and industrial training as part of any deal;[58] time will tell how much difference this makes in the impact of resource revenues upon reserve communities.

This predominance of external, unearned funding reinforces the factional character of aboriginal politics. A useful perspective on this linkage comes from the research on so-called neopatrimonial, or rentier, states in the Third World, particularly the Middle East.[59] In the historical literature, regimes featuring a "fusion of sovereignty and ownership"[60] are known as "patrimonial" states. Examples would include the ancient empires of the Middle East as well as the Russian Empire after it emerged from Mongol rule in the fifteenth century. Patrimonial states were characterized by autocratic rulers claiming not only the right to govern, but also ownership rights over all aspects of their subjects' lives. Private property may have had some customary basis in practice but did not exist in legal theory, according to which the ruler was also the owner of the realm.

Contemporary neopatrimonial states, of which the purest examples are the Gulf sheikhdoms, exhibit a similar fusion of property and sovereignty. They differ from the classical patrimonial type chiefly in their dependence on foreign technology, which yields the oil revenues that sustain these states. Another relevant case is the Palestine Liberation Front, supported by a combination of grants from sympathetic Muslim states and foreign aid from the United Nations and Western powers. Some other Middle Eastern states have also had semi-rentier status, at least at certain times. For example, foreign grants constituted between 25 and 55 per cent of national government expenditures in Jordan in the late 1970s and early 1980s, though they afterwards fell considerably.[61]

The rentier state exhibits a specific pattern of political economy. The government, as the principal recipient of external rents, redistributes them throughout the society by means of outright grants to citizens, contracts with privileged businesses, and state employment. "The whole economy," say the leading authorities on this subject, "is arranged as a hierarchy of layers of rentiers with the state or the government at the top of the pyramid, acting as the ultimate support of all other rentiers in the economy." The result is an allocation state, "an *état providence*, distributing favours and benefits to its population."[62] The Pharaohs of ancient Egypt or the tsars of seventeenth-century Russia would feel at home.

Neopatrimonial politics tends to be secretive, factional, and familial. The purpose of political action is to get more favours from those in power. Concepts like democracy and the rule of law can hardly establish a foothold because subjects, not having to pay for the activities of government, do not see it as an emanation of themselves. Because there is no private property in the Western sense, there is no limit to the public sphere. The population tends to develop a rentier mentality: "Reward – income or wealth – is not related to work and risk bearing, rather to chance or situation. For a rentier, reward becomes a windfall gain, an *isolated* fact, situational or accidental as against the conventional outlook where reward is integrated in a *process* as the end result of a long, systematic and organised production circuit. The contradiction between production and rentier ethics is, thus, glaring."[63] It does not take much imagination to perceive similarities between neopatrimonial economies and the political economy of Canadian aboriginal communities.

Many Indian spokesmen claim that immunity from taxation is a perpetual condition – an aboriginal right, a treaty right, or, as lawyer Alan Pratt says, "a fundamental component of the special relationship" between aboriginal peoples and the Crown.[64] A common sentiment is that federal transfer payments "are reparations for previous wrongs ... We are still sovereign if we rely on government funding because it's owed to us as rent."[65] Canadian taxpayers, however, are unlikely to accept this forever, and a few perceptive commentators have pointed out that self-taxation is essential to good government. Allan Maslove and Carolyn Dittburner put it well: "there can be no effective representation without taxation."[66] The RCAP has recommended that members of self-governing aboriginal communities pay taxes to their own governments, though not to the federal or provincial governments; aboriginal governments should then reimburse provincial governments directly for any services provided, thus avoiding the necessity of paying tax to the latter.[67]

Any degree of aboriginal taxation should be encouraged as a step towards more open and accountable government at the community level. Nonetheless, all who have made a serious study of the fiscal aspects of self-government proposals agree that "for the most part, the sources of funding will remain the same under self-government arrangements."[68] This is as true of the Metis settlements as it is of Indian reserves.[69] Even with a maximum degree of self-funding through taxation, aboriginal governments will continue to depend chiefly on government transfers, supplemented by resource revenues and occasional land-claims settlements. The rentier aspects of aboriginal governments in Canada are unlikely to change very much in the foreseeable future.

Indeed, the proposals now under discussion may well intensify the aboriginal rentier state. Advocates of self-government emphasize that as high a proportion as possible of fiscal transfers should take the form of unconditional grants.[70] Over 80 per cent of Indian Affairs transfers are already "devolved to Indian bands or tribal councils for self-administration" under several different funding frameworks. In recent years, the auditor general has complained twice about lack of accountability for expenditures, both to local aboriginal communities and to Parliament through the responsibility of the minister.[71] Further devolution might well make this lack of accountability worse rather than better.

IMPLICATIONS

None of the problems described above is likely to change in the foreseeable future. There is no shortage of visionary reform proposals, but there is a countervailing abundance of fiscal constraints and political veto points. Aboriginal communities will continue to be small, impoverished, supported by fiscal transfers, and mostly governed by elected chiefs and councils trying to carry out an extraordinarily wide range of functions. The contest for advantage of extended kin groups will continue to be the motor of internal politics.

In this tableau, we must think realistically about what constitutes responsible public policy. Politicians would do well to adopt the medical maxim *primum non nocere*, "first of all, do no harm." Simply transferring more money and power to local aboriginal governments is likely to increase the abuses of familial factionalism. More accountability in the management of public funds is urgently needed. Many small reforms might help move the system in this direction: more publication of information, better auditing, more-open meetings, more systematic media coverage, and development of a professional and politically neutral aboriginal public service.

Some steps of this kind are being taken. The University of Victoria runs a special program to train Indians in local public administration. The Banff Centre for Management sponsors an Aboriginal Leadership and Self-Government Program. Embarrassed by bad publicity, the Assembly of First Nations and the Department of Indian Affairs have discussed how to improve accountability in financial administration, and in March 1998 the AFN signed an agreement with the Certified General Accountants Association to improve training and standards of practice on reserves.[72] These are all useful initiatives, but their impact will be limited because they leave the basic incentive structure intact. As long as reserves are small, impoverished, overgoverned, and supported by external money, they will be prey to factionalism, nepotism, and waste.

Perhaps the single most constructive reform that could be made at this time would be for the members of aboriginal communities to begin taxing themselves in support of their own governments. No negotiations, no constitutional amendment, no legislation would be required to take this step; the power is already present in section 83.(1) of the Indian Act. In most cases, the amount of money raised would be small, but the effect would be important. Aboriginal voters would have a greater stake in the doings of their own governments if these governments were spending their own voters' money. Out of this might grow greater political account-ability at the local level.

More accountable band governments might finally start to deal with the deficiencies of property rights on reserves. The passage of Bill C-49 in 1999 has given them at least some of the tools they need. The bill allows band councils, subject to community referen-dum, to promulgate comprehensive land codes regulating occu-pancy and use of reserve lands and resources, inheritance, and division of assets in case of divorce. Only fourteen bands have entered the framework agreement at this point, but others may fol-low. Enlightened bands now have the opportunity to create property rights that work for their people's benefit in a modern economy.

Housing would be a good place to begin. It is no secret that there is a chronic shortage of good-quality housing on Indian reserves. A 1996 federal study found that 65 per cent of reserve housing lacked bathroom facilities, was in need of major structural repair, or was overcrowded according to the national occupancy standard (more than two people per bedroom, to oversimplify a bit).[73] Surprisingly, the housing stock on reserves is much newer than the Canadian average. As of 1991, 52 per cent of homes on Indian reserves had been built within the last ten years, as compared to 22 per cent for all of Canada. Ironically, homes on reserves are in much worse repair: 39 per cent needed major repair in 1991, as against only 8 per cent in all of Canada.[74] Drive through almost any reserve and you will see derelict houses with windows broken, doors askew, holes in the walls and roof. Sadly, many of those homes will be inhabited.

Observers who attribute these problems to remote location, low incomes, and poor quality of construction overlook the most important factor: "Almost all of the housing on reserves is provided by the federal government, and because individual title is severely limited, most homes are not owned by individuals but by the band."[75] Bands assign housing to individuals, typically charging little or no rent. Sometimes the band even pays all utilities. The result of such public ownership of housing is no better than it was in the Soviet Union under communism or in the vast public housing projects of American inner cities. Lacking pride of ownership, tenants neglect maintenance. Without the incentive of ownership, there is chronic under-investment in housing. Private funds are not mobilized, and the band never seems to have enough to meet its needs.

The band government's monopoly of housing is potentially, and sometimes actually, a serious threat to individual rights. A notorious example is the resource-rich Sawridge band in northern Alberta, controlled by the twenty-six surviving relatives of the late Senator Walter Twinn. These people, the only ones living on the reserve, have elected the chief and band council, who refuse to build any more housing, thereby preventing approximately two hundred other would-be band members from moving onto the reserve. Thus the Twinn family keeps control of a business empire whose worth has been estimated at $85 million.[76]

Privatization of on-reserve housing is urgently needed, but legal hurdles must first be overcome. As long as the Indian Act protects real and personal property on reserves from attachment, banks and trust companies will not give conventional mortgages to would-be owners. But there are ways around this dilemma. For example, the band government could secure loans or even become a lender, because the Indian Act allows it to attach property for non-payment of debts. If 1 per cent of the intelligence and industry that has been applied to land claims had been invested in this issue, the problems might have been overcome long ago and residents of Indian reserves, like other Canadians, could enjoy the benefits and shoulder the burdens of home ownership.

Another common problem is that the good agricultural land on reserves – and there is a fair amount of it – is often not farmed by residents of the reserves. "On reserves in Ontario, only about 4800 ha or 6 percent of arable land of fair to good quality was under cultivation in 1987."[77] On the prairies, one can drive across reserves where almost all the land, while cultivated, is rented to neighbouring farmers and ranchers. As one example, about 60 per cent of the twenty thousand cultivated acres (eight thousand hectares) on the John Smith reserve near Prince Albert, Saskatchewan – considered one of the best-run reserves in that province – was rented to white farmers in 1989.[78] The underlying problem is that the sudivision of members' rights to use portions of the reserve has produced uneconomically small landholdings that can neither be sold nor farmed with profit, leaving rental as the only rational option.[79]

Similar problems in European history were often "solved" by forced emigration, as happened to my own family. In 1847, in the midst of the Irish potato famine, my great-great-grandfather, like a million other Irishmen, had to leave his six-acre farm and flee to America in order to escape starvation. A more humane solution for Indian reserves might be to formalize customary property rights and allow band members to sell their land, either to other band members or to the band government, to produce viable farms and ranches.

Also, the design of First Nations' governments can be improved by drawing on the results of the so-called Harvard Project in the United States. Those researchers studied a wide variety of tribal governments and their relative success or failure in promoting economic development. They found that the most successful tribal governments were characterized by a separation of powers, with an independent judiciary and a strong chief executive elected for a term longer than two years and not dependent on the council.[80] This offers valuable lessons for our aboriginal governments; here band councils are elected for terms that are too short, and they wield powers that are too great over land, housing, education, welfare payments, and investment decisions. The Harvard Project also found that successful tribal governments maintained a stable regime of property rights to encourage investment and that they kept elected politicians away from day-to-day involvement in business enterprises.[81] Again, valuable lessons for Canada.

It is treacherous to generalize about the American situation because a third of the 554 recognized tribes are now operating gambling casinos, some of which are fabulously profitable. A few bands that combine a small population with a location close to a metropolitan area have been able to provide all their members with high incomes out of gambling revenue.[82] Yet unemployment in "Indian Country," as the Americans call it, is more than 30 per cent, compared to less than 5 per cent in the overall population, and the average income of those who do work is well below American norms. Social pathologies such as alcoholism, suicide, and child abuse are reported to be more common among native Americans than among any other American ethnic group.[83] The evidence from both Canada and the United States suggests that aboriginal communities that keep their distance from the larger society can do better or worse for themselves (and it is vital that they do as well as possible), but there is little evidence that they can bring the bulk of their people up to the general standard of living.

Aboriginal people are gradually being integrated into Canadian society. Integration does not mean that they give up all aspects of their native culture and identity, only that they live and work in the larger society, not in aboriginal communities. Forty-two per cent of registered Indians live off reserve; this proportion has been increasing for decades and will soon exceed 50 per cent. And that is just registered Indians. There are additional hundreds of thousands of people (no one is sure how many) of partly Indian ancestry who call themselves Metis, non-status Indians, or just Canadians. Registered Indians living on reserves are a steadily decreasing minority of the entire aboriginal population.

As more and more aboriginal people move into the wider society, one must question whether there is any way of winding down the anomalous and dysfunctional reserve system. Frankly, I doubt it. Various schemes of allotting reserve land and enfranchising individual Indians have been tried before in both the United States and Canada, with little success. There is no sign that contemporary residents want their reserves to be dissolved; and Canada, through the treaty and reserve system, has encouraged the survival of aboriginal communities as collective entities for more than a century. The movement towards self-government will continue because it has been accepted by most of the Canadian political elite and represents the unanimous demand of the aboriginal political class.

Indeed, it serves the interests of the latter group very well because they administer the reserves, run the business enterprises, litigate and negotiate with government, and fill positions in the Department of Indian Affairs and other agencies that deal with aboriginal communities. They are directly rewarded with increasing transfers of public money with no strings attached.

Meanwhile, living conditions in most First Nations reserves will continue to stagnate or even deteriorate for those outside the power structure. Population growth will intensify the shortage of jobs, housing, and other amenities, so that more and more aboriginal people will seek new lives in Canadian cities. In spite of the rhetoric of self-government, the reserves will grow less and less relevant to a majority of aboriginal people in Canada. Indians will become, in effect, a new immigrant ethnic group in our already pluralistic society. Their places of origin will be geographically closer than Hong Kong or the Punjab, but their social distance from the world of the reserves may be even greater.

Under the circumstances, the course of wisdom may be to leave reserves much as they are while these long-term processes take effect. Government should help the reserves to run as honestly and efficiently as possible, but should not flood them with even more money, which would encourage further unsustainable growth in the numbers of residents. I leave the last word to Stoney Nation councillor Tina Fox, commenting on cuts to social services required to balance the tribal budget: "We may have to encourage our young to work off the reserve."[84]

Would that be such a bad thing? The Stoney reserve sits in the middle of one of the most dynamic areas of the Canadian economy. Seventy kilometres to the east lies the perpetual boomtown of Calgary. Thirty years ago 330,000 people lived in Calgary; now there are over 800,000, at least one-sixth of whom belong to visible minorities. The unemployment rate is less than 6 per cent. Fifty kilometres to the west lies Banff, with its chronic labour shortage. Young people come from all over the world and find jobs there immediately.

Canadian Indians now call themselves the "First Nations" to embody their claim to an aboriginal right of self-government. Yet they were also the first immigrants because their ancestors, like the ancestors of everyone else in North America, moved here from the Old World. Now they are en route to becoming the last immigrants, the latest group to take advantage of the opportunities that Canadian society offers.

This process of adjustment takes place at the level of individuals and families, not nations. Government is often the biggest obstacle, whether it is the paternalistic regime of the Department of Indian affairs or the "self-government" of chiefs and band council. John Stuart Mill had in mind the advent of democracy when he wrote that "the 'people' who exercise the power are not always the same people [as] those over whom it is exercised; and the 'self-government' spoken of is not the government of each by himself, but of each by all the rest."[85] Nonetheless, his words apply just as well to the contemporary phenomenon of aboriginal self-government. The true progress of aboriginal people will depend upon emancipation from political control, whether exercised by federal bureaucrats or their own politicians.

CHAPTER 7

In Search of Property

INDIGENOUS PROPERTY RIGHTS

An old and recurrent fantasy about American aboriginal peoples is that they had no conception of property. Christopher Columbus got the impression that "in that which one had, all took a share, especially of eatable things."[1] The Baron de La Hontan, who had served as a soldier and explorer in the New World, wrote in 1703 in *New Voyages to North America:* "The *Savages* are utter Strangers to distinctions of property, for what belongs to one is equally another's."[2]

The same misconception crops up in our own day in the speech allegedly given by Chief Seattle in 1854 but actually composed by a Texas writer in 1971, popularized in a made-for-TV movie the following year and quoted with approval by American vice-president Albert Gore in his environmentalist book *Earth in the Balance.*[3] Seattle is made to say, "The earth does not belong to man; man belongs to the earth,"[4] and "the President in Washington sends word that he wishes to buy our land. Buy our land! But how can you buy or sell the sky? The land?"[5] While it is true that Indians did not have the specific notion of selling land, they understood other aspects of property, especially the right to exclude others from what they considered to be their own lands.[6]

The discussion about Indian conceptions of property is both confused and ideologically charged. Aboriginal advocates portray Indians as proto-socialists and natural environmentalists; yet they also typically deny the distinction between savagery and civilization, so they have to maintain that Indian cultures incorporated all the institutions of civilization, including philosophy, science, law, and government; and since institutions of property are found in all civilizations, native partisans cannot deny that Indians had property without making them seem like savages. On the other hand, advocates of free-market capitalism, such as the American economists Terry Anderson and Bruce Benson,[7] believe that Indians cannot make progress in the contemporary world without reliance on property rights and economic competition (a view that I share). But this conviction leads them to overemphasize the extent of property rights prior to contact with European civilization. They want to demonstrate the strength of indigenous traditions of property in order to show that Indians can and should become successful participants in the contemporary market economy. Somewhere in these swirling ideological crosscurrents lies the historical truth about aboriginal institutions of property.

The economist Harold Demsetz canonically expressed the modern understanding of property in his article "Toward a Theory of Property Rights," published in 1968. Demsetz described property as a "bundle of rights"[8] that "develop to internalize externalities when the gains of internalization become larger than the cost of internalization."[9] In this vein, the historian Richard Pipes writes that "for property to arise, two conditions have to be met: an object has to be desirable and available in limited quantities."[10] Like everything else in economics, property involves trade-offs of costs and benefits dependent upon environmental conditions as well as the state of technological development.

A full-fledged system of private property in land is expensive to operate. It requires techniques of measuring land and marking boundaries; administrative methods, usually involving writing, for recording titles and transfers; a legal code to define property rights with some precision; and a judicial system to settle disputes. No society will evolve such elaborate and expensive institutions unless the value of land is great enough to make it worthwhile. At a minimum, this means the society must have arrived at the intensive agriculture stage, so that the same piece of land can be farmed indefinitely without its productivity being destroyed. The population must also be dense enough that good agricultural land is in short supply; otherwise the costs would far outweigh the benefits of a system of real property.

In this perspective, property is not a single institution but an infinitely variable set of rights conferring control over things and people in different circumstances.[11] The exact mix in the bundle of property rights will depend crucially upon population density, the distribution of resources in the environment, and the level of technological advancement of the society.[12] No society, no matter how simple its way of life, will be without some rules of property; but the rules become more formalized and complex as societies grow larger, more technologically sophisticated, and more dependent upon the division of labour. There cannot have been a single indigenous conception of property, for the ecological and cultural settings of Indians were quite varied. Consider four major groups: the hunters of the plains, the hunters of the forests, the horticulturalists of the Great Lakes and St Lawrence valley, and the fishers of the Pacific coast.

The Hunters of the Plains

After obtaining horses from the Spanish in the eighteenth century, the Indians of the Great Plains began to exploit the buffalo as their main food resource. Because the buffalo ranged so widely, laying claim to small areas of land would have been pointless. Moreover, buffalo hunting was best carried out by large groups to chase the herd, slaughter the animals, and preserve the meat as pemmican. Under these conditions, tribes or nations had large but overlapping hunting territories. A party of Cree might ride for days in Blackfoot territory without encountering any Blackfoot. If they met, they might fight, or they might establish friendly relations and the Blackfoot might allow the Cree to hunt without opposition. Perhaps more than anything else, it is the fluidity of the prairie situation that has given rise to the stereotype that Indians had no conception of owning the land.

But even if the Plains Indians did not have real property, they had institutions of personal property, as anthropologists have found to be true of all societies, even the simplest.[13] What Bruce Benson writes of the Comanche is generally applicable to all the buffalo-hunting tribes:

Private ownership was firmly established for such things as horses, tools for hunting and gathering, food, weapons, materials used in the construction of mobile shelters, clothing, and various kinds of body ornaments that were used for religious ceremonies and other activities. Cooperative production (group raids to take horses from enemy tribes or group hunts) did not imply communal ownership. The product of such cooperative activities was divided among participants according to their contributed effort. Individuals might share such things as food at times, but they did so out of generosity. Food could be given but not taken because it was private property not communal property.[14]

The Hunters of the Forests

The forest hunters of North America also practised private property in personal possessions, but they faced a different situation in hunting and land use. Hunting in a forest usually means stalking or trapping animals one by one rather than exploiting a herd, as on the prairies. Hence forest hunters tend to work individually or in small groups rather than in large tribal aggregations, except for some kinds of fishing, when spawning runs produce herd-like densities of prey.

The intensive involvement of the Ojibwa in the fur trade has generated much scholarly interest in their institutions of property. Although some earlier researchers thought that the Ojibwa had had a form of private ownership of hunting and trapping territories in pre-contact times, it is now generally accepted that such forms of ownership arose later in the fur trade period.[15] Beaver had always been hunted as a food item, but the demand from fur traders greatly augmented its value, along with that of the other furs that Europeans found fashionable. As the Indians increased their trapping effort, the number of fur-bearing animals tended to fall, further increasing their market value. It thus became reasonable for individuals to assert exclusive rights to trap in specific areas, to stabilize economic returns over time. Indian trappers asserted not a full ownership of the land, but exclusive rights to harvest certain species of animals in defined territories. Even though not originally part of their culture, such rights were well entrenched by the time the forest-dwelling Indians signed land-surrender treaties in the nineteenth and early twentieth centuries.

The Horticulturalists of the Great Lakes and St Lawrence Valley

Canada's eastern horticulturalists, such as the Iroquois and Hurons, had still another form of property rights in land. Anthropologist Bruce Trigger describes Huron farming:

The planting, care, and harvesting of crops were women's tasks ... One of the most arduous horticultural tasks was the clearing of the fields. The transformation of forest into clearing was men's work ... Armed with stone axes, the men cut down the smaller trees ... then girdled the larger ones and stripped off some of their branches [which] were burned at the base of the larger trees to kill them. The women then planted their crops between the stumps ... Huron horticultural practices forced them to relocate their settlements at intervals which varied between ten and thirty years ... the pressure on land does not appear to have been great enough to induce particular communities to occupy a number of specified sites in rotation.

Teams of men working together could clear as much land as they wanted or were able, and this land remained in the possession of their extended families as long as the women of these families wished to cultivate it. Once abandoned, however, a field could be used by anyone who wished to do so. It is unclear to what degree each woman regarded the corn, beans, and squash she planted as her property, or the women living in a single longhouse considered all the food they produced to be their collective possession.[16]

Although time has obscured the details, the general picture is that of temporary ownership of agricultural land by extended families. Absence of machinery and draft animals meant that farming had to be a collective enterprise involving human muscle power, and lack of animal manure (the Indians did use ashes for fertilizer) meant that fields had to be abandoned periodically. Under the circumstances, permanent ownership of specified lots would have been senseless.

The Fishers of the Pacific Coast

The greatest proliferation of property rights in what is now Canada occurred in the fishing societies of the Pacific coast. According to the anthropologist Leland Donald, "ideas of property and ownership were highly developed throughout the culture area. Almost everything could be and often was owned. From the indigenous point of view this included not only resource loci and material goods but also noncorporeal property such as songs, myths, and knowledge of various types."[17] There was no farming, except occasional growing of tobacco, but the predictability of the salmon runs generated land ownership at specific sites. Salmon were abundant and easy to catch at certain places; and those places, along with weirs, traps, platforms, and smokehouses, belonged to families. These rights could be transferred through lease, sale, or inheritance, often witnessed publicly at potlatch celebrations.[18] An egalitarian mythology has grown up around the potlatch because property was given away at these ritual celebrations, but such festivals of lavish gift-giving could exist only because property rights were strong.

Rare among hunting-gathering peoples, the coastal Indians also practised slavery on a large scale. Hunter-collectors seldom hold slaves because it is uneconomic in their way of life. You can't send a slave out to track a deer or trap a beaver because he will escape, and there is not much for slaves to do in camp. But in the sedentary fishing culture of the west coast, slaves could be put to work processing fish and cutting timber. An economic asset, slaves were eagerly sought in war and were afterwards subject to inheritance, gift, and sale. They were reduced to the status of property and deprived of all human rights and dignity, sometimes even put to death in a demonstration of the owner's power. Although Governor Simcoe had prohibited the importation of slaves into Canada in 1793 and slavery itself was legally abolished throughout the British Empire in 1834, it continued to exist in fact among the Indians of British Columbia as late as the 1880s. It even plays some role today because coastal Indians still consider descent from slaves a stigma.[19]

The example of the west coast Indians shows that property has nothing to do with race; under the right circumstances Indian peoples could and did develop complex institutions of individual property. However, such complexity and individualism were exceptional among the aboriginal inhabitants of Canada prior to colonial settlement. The fur trade encouraged the growth of individual property rights among some forest-dwelling peoples. Elsewhere, Canadian Indians, though they held personal property as individuals and families, owned land collectively as tribes, with no real distinction between ownership and political control and no mechanisms of transfer except abandonment or defeat in war.

THE ROYAL PROCLAMATION OF 1763

Property rights were not entirely independent of the rights of the sovereign in the early years of European exploration of North America. According to both French and English legal theory of the sixteenth century, the king, as political sovereign, held the underlying title to all land in the realm, and all landowners held their estates as grants from the Crown. Even if the practical reality was gradually turning into mercantile capitalism, the understanding of the social order was still expressed in feudal terms, as illustrated by the phrase "ownership in fee simple." The word "fee," derived from a now-obsolete Germanic word for cattle, is closely related to the root that also appears in "feudal." The modern conception of property as a bundle of individual rights, to be enforced and respected by, but conceptually distinct from, government, is a later development of liberal capitalism.

The sixteenth-century explorers, both French and English, travelled with royal charters authorizing them to claim newly discovered lands for their respective monarchs, to establish settlements, to subdue the natives by force if necessary, to spread the Christian religion, and to carry on trade.[20] At this early stage, the European powers could hardly envision displacing the aboriginal population of North America. What they had in mind was to plant colonies to trade in whatever profitable commodities they might discover.

The French established colonial governments in Acadia and New France, and made war and peace with native nations in the course of elaborating a vast fur-trading network. They considered themselves masters of the land and took whatever they needed for military forts, trading posts, villages, and farms. Royal grants conferred upon French noblemen title to large seigneuries along the St Lawrence River. The French paid no compensation to the prior inhabitants for the taking of their property rights nor engaged in formal negotiations for the surrender of land. In reality, however, this was less highhanded than it sounds because the French presence in these vast territories was so thin. Except in parts of Acadia and the St Lawrence valley, there was little agricultural settlement. Also, in many areas of New France the indigenous population was so reduced through warfare and disease that the Indians simply withdrew from the lands used by the French. It was as if a new and better armed tribe had pushed its way in, seizing some land for itself and touching off a round of warfare and relocation among the earlier tribes. The new tribe claimed sovereign authority over all other tribes, but in practice it dealt with the Indians more through diplomacy than conquest.

English colonization started in much the same way and indeed continued in that vein until 1870 in the Hudson's Bay Company's territories of Rupert's Land. But along the Atlantic seaboard, agriculture meant population growth and hence an ever-growing demand for land. There was little effective imperial supervision in the seventeenth and early eighteenth centuries, so the English colonists acquired land from the Indians in every conceivable way. Once the colonies were planted, they often expanded when the natives withdrew after being defeated in warfare. There were also land purchases, both by colonial authorities and by private individuals, although the former did not approve of the latter buying land and repeatedly tried to stop the practice.[21] Land acquisition was driven by events and necessity, not by any overall theory, although the prohibition of private purchase lent credence to the idea that whatever property rights the Indians possessed did not amount to ownership in fee simple.

The first attempt to impose a coherent perspective came with the Royal Proclamation of 7 October 1763, by which the British government organized the New World colonies it had acquired from France through the Seven Years' War and the Treaty of Paris. The proclamation attempted to reserve the land west of the Appalachians as "Hunting Grounds" for "the several Nations or Tribes of Indians, with whom We are connected, and who live under Our Protection." They were not to "be molested or disturbed in the Possession of such Parts of Our Dominions and Territories as, not having been ceded to, or purchased by us, are reserved to them." Colonial governors were enjoined from issuing survey warrants or land patents in the Indian territory. Any white men living in the Indian country were called upon "forthwith to remove themselves." Because "great Frauds and Abuses have been committed in purchasing Lands of the Indians," the proclamation forbade any further purchases by private persons. However, "if, at any Time, any of the said Indians should be inclined to dispose of the said lands, the same shall be purchased only for Us, in Our Name, at some publick Meeting or Assembly of the said Indians to be held for that Purpose by the Governor or Commander in Chief of Our Colonies respectively, within which they shall lie."[22]

The Proclamation of 1763, issued as a royal proclamation without approval or debate in Parliament, and indeed without consultation with the people in the New World that it purported to affect, was a monument to monarchy and imperialism. The cabinet did not ask the English colonists whether they would consent to remain east of the Appalachians, nor did it ask the Indians whether they wished to be prohibited from selling their hunting grounds to anyone except colonial governors, although afterwards, in 1764, the proclamation was presented to, and accepted by, a large assembly of Indians at Niagara.[23]

The proclamation was also mercantilist in inspiration. One reason for attempting to reserve the interior of North America for the Indians was to force the seaboard colonists to keep up their trade with the mother country. Henry Ellis, the chief adviser of Lord Egremont, secretary of state for the Southern Department, wrote that there had to be a western boundary to keep the colonists from "planting themselves in the Heart of America, out of reach of Government, and where, from the great Difficulty of procuring European Commodities, they would be compelled to commence Manufactures to the infinite prejudice of Britain."[24]

It is not surprising that the proclamation, as a monarchist, imperialist, and mercantilist document penned at the dawn of our democratic, nationalist, and capitalist era, failed in its primary objective of creating a huge native land reserve in the heart of America. Its attempt to confine the colonists was one of the main factors leading to the American Revolution and Britain's loss of control over the American interior and the Indians residing there. But despite its practical failure, the proclamation deeply affected our thinking about aboriginal property rights, for the administrative measures it describes presuppose certain views on the subject:

- Indians have property rights of some sort. The Proclamation uses terms such as "Possession" and "Lands of the Indians."
- These rights are not the same as full ownership in fee simple but are connected with the traditional use of the land. The proclamation speaks of Indian lands as "their Hunting Grounds."
- Indian property rights are collective or communal rather than individual. The proclamation is silent about any kind of ownership in severalty and further specifies that henceforth Indian title can only be given up "at some publick Meeting or Assembly of the said Indians to be held for that Purpose."
- Regardless of what has happened in the past, Indian property rights should henceforth be surrendered voluntarily, by cession or purchase.
- Indians are subject to British sovereignty. If the Crown is able unilaterally to set aside a reserve for Indians and announce the conditions under which they can surrender their property rights,

the Crown can also adjust the boundaries, change the procedure for surrender, or modify their property rights in other ways. The proclamation was an act of sovereignty protecting Indian property rights against depredations by colonists or colonial authorities; it did not limit the sovereign authority of the Crown.

FORMULATION OF A JUDICIAL DOCTRINE

In 1888 the Judicial Committee of the Privy Council (JCPC), the highest court of appeal in the British Empire, formalized the implicit theory of the Royal Proclamation of 1763 when it decided the case of *St Catherine's Milling and Lumber Company v. The Queen*.[25]

Since Confederation, Ontario and Canada had been in dispute about the province's western boundary. In 1878 arbitrators fixed the boundary at the northwest angle of the Lake of the Woods, and in 1884 the JCPC upheld that decision. But Sir John A. Macdonald would not give up. He held that even if Ontario had won the boundary arbitration, the federal government owned all the public lands and natural resources in the area of Treaty 3, which it had signed in 1873. To validate this theory, the Dominion government in 1883 issued a timber-cutting licence to the St Catherine's Milling Company. The Ontario government brought suit the following year to eject the company and claimed damages for trespass, arguing that it was the owner of public lands and natural resources under section 109 of the British North America Act, 1867. The case reached the JCPC in 1888 after having been heard initially in the Ontario Court of Chancery and subsequently in the Ontario Court of Appeal and the Supreme Court of Canada. Ontario won decisively at each of the four trials. Although the case led to an authoritative definition of Indian property rights, Indians were not involved in it and probably did not even know about it. Judicial interpretation might have been different if the aboriginal peoples had had a chance to state their own understanding of property before the courts.

Chancellor John Boyd, head of the Ontario Court of Chancery, held at trial that the Royal Proclamation was no longer valid, having been repealed by the Quebec Act of 1774. The JCPC overturned that ruling but otherwise accepted Boyd's minimalist characterization of Indian property rights. Boyd had written:

The Colonial policy of Great Britain as it regards the claims and treatment of the aboriginal populations in America, has been from the first uniform and well-defined. Indian peoples were found scattered wide-cast over the continent, having, as a characteristic no fixed abodes, but moving as the exigencies of living demanded. As heathens and barbarians it was not thought that they had any proprietary title to the soil, nor any such claim thereto as to interfere with the plantations, and the general prosecution of colonization. They were treated "justly and graciously," as Lord Bacon advised, but no legal ownership of the land was ever attributed to them.[26]

The JCPC found different words to express more or less the same perception. It held that "the tenure of the Indians was a personal and usufructuary right, dependent upon the good will of the Sovereign."[27] Calling the Indian title a personal right distinguished it from property rights as normally understood in common law. The Indian title, as a personal right, was not a form of ownership of the land but a right of Indian persons to carry out certain activities. The activities were summarized by the word "usufruct," derived from Roman law, where it meant the right to use and dispose of the produce of a piece of land without being able to sell the land or bequeath it to an heir. The view of the JCPC was that the Royal Proclamation of 1763 had confirmed the Indians' right to hunt, trap, fish, pick berries, and so forth, but had not recognized Indian ownership of the land. The Indians' usufructuary rights were a burden or easement on the title, but the Indians did not hold the title themselves. "There has been all along vested in the Crown a substantial and paramount estate, underlying the Indian title, which became a plenum dominium [full ownership] whenever that title was surrendered or otherwise extinguished."[28]

With respect to the dispute at hand, the Indians could not have conveyed lands and resources by treaty to the federal government because they had not really owned them. What they had done was to renounce their usufructuary rights of hunting and fishing in return for the various benefits itemized in the treaty. Since the Crown had been the real owner all along, the land and resources now belonged to the province, according to the general formula for public lands under section 109 of the BNA Act. In the words of the decision, the provinces had a right "to a beneficial interest in these lands, available to them as a source of revenue whenever the estate of the Crown is disencumbered of the Indian title."[29]

As final courts of appeal are supposed to do, the JCPC provided legal certainty, at least in the context of Ontario and the three Prairie provinces, where Canada had negotiated land-surrender treaties. *St Catherine's Milling* gave a legal rationale for that process: the Indians had never owned the land, but their usufructuary rights were a burden on the title, which could be cleared through surrender of aboriginal title in exchange for treaty benefits. In British Columbia, however, historical differences turned that certainty into uncertainty.

In the years 1850–54, James Douglas, the first governor of the Vancouver Island colony, made fourteen land purchases on southern Vancouver Island totalling 358 square miles (916 square kilometres). He then shifted to a different policy, signing no more treaties but unilaterally setting aside small reserves, averaging about ten acres (four hectares) per family and corresponding more or less to existing Indian villages. This seems niggardly in comparison to Canada's treatment of Indians in Ontario or on the prairies, but there was a compensating factor. Douglas treated British Columbia's Indians as British subjects endowed with full civil and political rights, including the right to vote and to pre-empt vacant Crown land (similar to homesteading). Perhaps Douglas's personal history – he had come from the Caribbean, was of partially black ancestry, and had married a Metis woman – conditioned his new policy of rapid assimilation of Indians into white society on terms of legal equality.[30]

Douglas's approach, however, did not survive his retirement in 1864. The new governor and legislature took away the Indians' rights to vote and to pre-empt land, leaving them with undersized reserves, no treaties, and no recognition of their aboriginal title. When British Columbia entered Confederation in 1871, the Canadian authorities apparently did not realize how much the new province's treatment of Indians differed from the Ontario standard that would soon be applied on the prairies. Thus Canada agreed to the following clause – no. 13 – in the Terms of Union: "The charge of the Indians and the trusteeship and management of the lands reserved for their use and benefit, shall be assumed by the Dominion Government, and a policy as liberal as that hitherto pursued by the British Columbia Government shall be continued by the Dominion Government after the Union."[31] After the Canadian authorities realized what was happening in British Columbia, they worked with some success over the years to enlarge the reserves; but provincial politicians refused to adopt the land-surrender treaty model, arguing that they had unilaterally extinguished aboriginal title by the implications of their colonial and (later) provincial legislation.

The judges who heard the *St Catherine's Milling* case, from Chancellor Boyd to the members of the JCPC, viewed Indians as nomads, hunting and gathering to sustain life, but not otherwise attaching themselves to the land. This may have described the lowest common denominator of aboriginal economies, but it was not an adequate account of the fur-trade-era trapping rights of the Ojibwa, the horticultural land use of the Mohawk and Hurons, or the fishing practices of the West Coast Indians. Fatefully, it was in British Columbia, where aboriginal property rights were most highly evolved, that governments proceeded unilaterally, without recognizing those rights or compensating their loss. This set the stage for the legal struggles over aboriginal rights now being played out in British Columbia.

THE LAMER DOCTRINE

The unsettled legal situation in British Columbia has given rise to an important series of modern judicial decisions.[32] The earliest was *White and Bob* (1964), in which the British Columbia Court of Appeal held that the Douglas land-purchase agreements should be interpreted as treaties. Another important case was *Calder* (1973), in which the Nisga'a people tried to obtain a declaratory judgment that their aboriginal title had never been extinguished. The Supreme Court of Canada split 3–3–1 on this issue. Three held that it had been extinguished by provincial actions, three held that it had not, and one refused to address the issue on the technical ground that the Nisga'a had not obtained standing to sue the province. In *Sparrow* (1990), the Supreme Court held that the aboriginal right to fish for food, never having been extinguished in British Columbia, was now protected by section 35(1) of the Constitution Act, 1982 ("The existing aboriginal and treaty rights of the aboriginal peoples of Canada are hereby recognized and affirmed.")

The capstone in this series of British Columbia cases is *Delgamuukw*, decided by the Supreme Court of Canada on 11 December 1997. The litigation commenced in 1984, when counsel for the Gitksan and Wet'suwet'en peoples (neighbours of the Nisga'a) filed a statement of claim for jurisdiction over, and ownership of, twenty-two thousand square miles (fifty-six thousand square kilo-metres) of traditional territory. This was a maximal demand for sovereignty and outright ownership, but the plaintiffs amended their pleadings in the course of the hearings to lesser claims for self-government and aboriginal title.

The trial was conducted by Allan McEachern, chief justice of the Supreme Court of British Columbia. The hearings occupied 374 days spread over three years; the evidence and transcripts amounted to tens of thousands of pages; and the government of Canada paid $8 million to the lawyers representing the Indian plaintiffs.[33] In his 1991 decision, the chief justice upheld British Columbia's position that extinguishment of aboriginal title had occurred through pro-vincial policies of making fee-simple grants and generally treating lands formerly inhabited by Indians as available for settlement. As had some of the justices in *Calder*, Chief Justice McEachern relied for legal authority upon a series of American Supreme Court decisions ultimately going back to *Johnson v. M'Intosh*; in that decision, John Marshall, chief justice of the u.s. Supreme Court, had written that Indian title could be extinguished "by treaty, by the sword, by purchase, *by the exercise of complete dominion adverse to the right of occupancy,* or otherwise [emphasis added]."[34] Chief Justice McEachern also described aboriginal rights as usufructuary, in terms drawn from the *St Catherine's Milling* decision: "It seems to me, with respect, that the Privy Council got it right when it described the aboriginal interest as a personal right rather than a proprietary one."[35]

When this hugely controversial decision was appealed, the newly elected NDP government of the province, trying to appear less con-frontational, discharged the lawyers who had won a sweeping vic-tory at trial and engaged a new legal team. The British Columbia Court of Appeal took the unusual step of appointing the discharged lawyers as "friends of the court" so that there would be someone present to argue the original position that had persuaded Chief Jus-tice McEachern. In the event, the Court of Appeal overturned the chief justice's ruling on the issue of extinguishment but agreed with him on the nature of aboriginal title as a limited, personal, non-proprietary interest in land: "The Court found no ownership rights, no rights to inherent self-government, no expansive definition of aboriginal rights or title, and what limited aboriginal rights it did find [did] not include the right to engage in commercial practices."[36]

Upon further appeal, the Supreme Court of Canada agreed with the Court of Appeal that extinguishment had not taken place, holding that, because section 91(24) of the Constitution Act, 1867, gives Parliament jurisdiction over Indians and lands reserved for Indians, only the federal government can extinguish aboriginal title. Clarity was achieved on that point, but unfortunately not on very much else. The Supreme Court made no ruling on the Indians' substantive claim for aboriginal title and self-government, arguing that the law had evolved so quickly in the 1990s that the arguments and evidence submitted at trial no longer provided a proper basis for decision. Also, said the court, the trial judge had erred in his weighing of the oral traditions offered as testimony. Thus, the aboriginal title of the Gitskan and Wet'suwet'en has still not been established. The court has held that their title (if it ever existed) has not been extinguished but that the plaintiffs will have to prove their title to specific lands. The absence of a decision on the merits has frustrated the hopes of the aboriginal litigants. Chief Herb George, one of the main strategists on the native side, now says, "Twenty-four years working on *Delgamuukw,* and when I go home, nothing has changed!"[37]

What makes the *Delgamuukw* decision particularly important is a long disquisition by Chief Justice Lamer, writing for the majority, on aboriginal rights and title. It pulls together ideas from several previous judgments to form a framework intended to guide lower courts in future cases. While it is coherent and systematic, the disquisition is also highly abstract. Because the court left most of the practical issues in *Delgamuukw* undecided, the theoretical analysis of the chief justice lacks empirical reference points. Common-law courts usually let principles emerge from the resolution of specific conflicts, but here the procedure was reversed. The court laid down a set of principles, but it is hard to say what they will mean in practice.[38]

For our purposes, Lamer's distinction between aboriginal rights and aboriginal title is crucial. He posits a spectrum of aboriginal rights "with respect to their degree of connection with the land." At one end are cultural practices, such as songs, dances, and ceremonies, not specifically tied to the land. In the middle are "site-specific" activities, "which, out of necessity, take place on land and indeed, might be intimately related to a certain piece of land." Examples include hunting and fishing on certain sites and performance of religious ceremonies at sacred places. At the other end of the spectrum is aboriginal title, which "is a *right to the land* itself [emphasis in original]."[39]

In other words, aboriginal title is a specific kind of aboriginal right. All aboriginal rights are constitutionally protected, but only aboriginal title implies ownership of the land. If, for example, Indian plaintiffs could produce convincing historical evidence about catching salmon at a particular spot on the riverbank, that would establish their aboriginal right to continue fishing there or to receive compensation if they were prohibited from fishing there, but it would not confer ownership of the riverbank. The right to fish would be an easement on the Crown's title, not a title in its own right. Aborginal rights, as described by Lamer, fit comfortably into the framework of *St Catherine's Milling* – usufructuary rights worthy of recognition and protection, but not conferring ownership as such.

Aboriginal title, on the other hand, sounds like a more robust property right and as such is a new departure. Lamer characterizes it in these terms: "Aboriginal title encompasses the right to use the land held pursuant to that title for a variety of purposes, which need not be aspects of those aboriginal practices, cultures and traditions which are integral to distinctive aboriginal cultures."[40] Described that way, aboriginal title seems to be a full-fledged ownership right that justifies the shouts of jubilation and doom (depending on the shouters' point of view) heard in British Columbia when the decision was released. Remember, however, that not one square inch of British Columbia has yet been held to fall under aboriginal title, and it is unclear how much ever will.

Aboriginal title, according to the Lamer doctrine, must be based upon proof of occupancy when British sovereignty was asserted – 1846 in the case of British Columbia.[41] Quite apart from the difficulties of proving occupancy 150 years ago, the chief justice did not specify the type and density of occupation necessary to validate aboriginal title. His discussion of site-specific aboriginal rights implies that more than hunting, fishing, trapping, and berry-picking is required to prove title, but how much more? On a restrictive view, Indians in British Columbia may not be able to prove aboriginal title to much more than their ancient village sites, which for the most part they already possess as reserve land. All one can say with certainty is that aboriginal-title litigation will be a bonanza for lawyers, historians, and anthropologists because such cases demand huge amounts of evidence about past land use. Also, there is bound to be an increasing tendency for multiple Indian nations to launch overlapping and conflicting claims to aboriginal title.

The Lamer doctrine, furthermore, specifies four characteristics of aboriginal title that limit it substantially as a form of property right:

1. *Aboriginal title is communal.* "It is a collective right to land held by all members of an aboriginal nation. Decisions with respect to that land are also made by that community."[42]
2. *It is inalienable except to the Crown.* That means that aboriginal people cannot sell their land to the highest bidder; they can only deal with the federal government. It also means that they cannot offer their lands and resources as security for loans.
3. *There is an "inherent limit" to aboriginal title.* "Lands held pursuant to aboriginal title cannot be used in a manner that is irreconcilable with the nature of the attachment to the land which forms the basis of the group's claim to aboriginal title."[43] To cite Lamer's examples, aboriginal owners cannot strip-mine their hunting grounds or turn their sacred places into parking lots.[44] This principle could be restrictive for aboriginal lands located near towns and cities, where the best use might be shopping centres, golf courses, industrial parks, and so on. If these limitations turn out to be substantial, aboriginal title in practice may be closer to the "personal and usufructuary right" of *St Catherine's Milling* than appears at first glance.[45]
4. *Governments, both federal and provincial, may infringe aboriginal title, though compensation may be required.* Lamer envisions very broad grounds for such infringement:

In my opinion, the development of agriculture, forestry, mining, and hydroelectric power, the general economic development of the interior of British Columbia, protection of the environment or endangered species, the building of infrastructure and the settlement of foreign populations to support those aims, are the kinds of objectives that are consistent with this purpose and, in principle, can justify the infringement of aboriginal title. Whether a particular measure or government act can be explained by reference to one of those objectives, however, is ultimately a question of fact that will have to be examined on a case-by-case basis.[46]

Infringement cannot be unilateral and cavalier because "there is always a duty of consultation."[47] Lamer, however, does not make clear the degree of consultation required. He speaks of a spectrum running from mere discussion to full consent, without explaining how to locate any particular project on this spectrum. He speaks in similarly abstract terms of a spectrum of compensation for infringement. "Fair compensation will ordinarily be required when aboriginal title is infringed. The amount of compensation payable will vary with the nature of the particular aboriginal title affected and with the nature and severity of the infringement and the extent to which aboriginal interests were accommodated."[48] Once again it will be a bonanza for lawyers and consultants, as every demand for consultation and compensation will have to be adjudicated on a case-by-case basis.

ASSESSMENT

Delgamuukw is such a far-reaching and multifaceted decision, and so recently delivered, that it is hard to offer an overall assessment in a few pages. Nonetheless, here are a few comments tailored to the particular concerns of this book.

While it is beneficial to have the legal question of extinguishment in British Columbia settled, in a practical sense it does not make much difference. This is because the provincial government had already admitted that modern treaties were necessary and had embarked in 1993 upon a course of tripartite negotiations with First Nations and the federal government. Debates over extinguishment may move now to Quebec and the Atlantic provinces, where the seventeenth- and eighteenth-century treaties of submission do not mention surrender of Indian title to the land. *Delgamuukw*'s principle of federal extinguishment will not apply straightforwardly in eastern Canada, where the issue is complicated by the transition from French to British sovereignty. I would not presume to predict the outcome of the litigation that, I think, is certain to arise sooner or later.

Second, the Lamer doctrine makes an intellectual advance beyond the *St Catherine's Milling* case. As noted earlier, the JCPC recognized only the lowest common denominator of usufructuary rights. Lamer's spectrum of aboriginal rights, including site-specific usufructuary practices as well as the ownership right of aboriginal title, can recognize the variety of property rights that had emerged in different aboriginal cultures. In particular, it may offer a better fit than *St Catherine's Milling* ever could with the relatively sedentary culture of the West Coast Indians.

Unfortunately, however, the Lamer doctrine defines aboriginal title as collective without considering any argument to the contrary. There is in fact considerable historical evidence that aboriginal property rights were, if not individual in the modern sense, held by families rather than by the community at large. The anthropologist Adrian Tanner concludes that "the model of aboriginal title laid out in *Delgamuukw* ... exclusively involving a collective right, one that can be sold, although only to the Crown, thus already represents a major transformation and simplification of not only prehistoric aboriginal practice, but also of some practices of aboriginal people that have continued to the present."[49]

The Lamer doctrine, moreover, by typecasting aboriginal title as collective, makes its own application in a modern market economy difficult. Even if the courts in British Columbia were to award substantial tracts of land under the heading of aboriginal title, the owners would have to manage those lands through internal political processes. Communal ownership is an awkward instrument in a dynamic market economy. Profitable opportunities are likely to pass before all the meetings and votes necessary to make a decision can be held. Prospective business partners may not be absolutely deterred, but they will perceive higher risk and cost and will have to adjust their terms accordingly.

Similarly, the principle of inalienability except to the Crown limits the usefulness of aboriginal title. It will prohibit the owners not only from selling any of their lands but also from mortgaging them to raise investment capital. It raises all of the same problems that have plagued Canada's Indian reserves in the past, where the principle of inalienability has also applied. Similarly, Lamer's "inherent limit" on the use of land held under aboriginal title restricts its economic usefulness. Land is most valuable when it can be put to its most profitable use. Potential restrictions on use that in particular cases can be articulated only by the courts cannot help but detract from economic value by introducing uncertainty.

A market economy has to be undergirded by a set of rules about ownership that make efficient exchanges possible. It took centuries for English property law to progress from feudal notions of entailment to the modern conception of ownership in fee simple. Property law now unites the owner with the decision-maker and facilitates all sorts of transactions, including subdivision, sale, mortgage, and inheritance, thereby allowing land and natural resources to find their most efficient, highest-value usage. Collective, inalienable title, on the other hand, will tend to render land and resources legally immobile. Michael Warby's comments about Aboriginal property rights in Australia are equally applicable here: "It is not possible to achieve industrial-age life expectancies in an industrial-age society with hunter-gatherer notions of illness, causality and nutrition. Similarly, it is not possible to achieve industrial-age standards of living with hunter-gatherer notions of asset management or social organization. In particular, the choice of communal, inalienable title is the choice of poverty: as the experience of the command economies have shown very clearly."[50]

In the Canadian context, Chief Justice Lamer's theory of infringement is the sword that cuts the Gordian knot of communal, inalienable, aboriginal title. Government can legally do the things that the aboriginal owners cannot, as long as it engages in appropriate consultation and pays appropriate compensation, both subject to judicial review. This notion of infringement may save the day in a practical sense, but as legal theorist Kent McNeil points out, its logical status is questionable. Aboriginal title, as part of aboriginal rights, is constitutionally protected under section 35(1) of the Constitution Act, 1982. In fact, aboriginal title is the only kind of property right to enjoy constitutional protection in Canada. "Since when," asks McNeil, "can constitutional rights be overridden for the economic benefit of other Canadians who do not have equivalent rights? Isn't this turning the Constitution on its head by allowing interests that are not constitutional to trump rights that are?"[51] He has a point. The criticism is particularly relevant since Chief Justice Lamer relied on McNeil's publications at several key points in his opinion.

There are problems of economic efficiency as well as logic. Only government can infringe aboriginal title. That is, the blockages imposed by one collectivist institution – aboriginal title – can be overcome only by another collectivist institution – government. In this scenario, politics is likely to trump economic rationality as elected officials use the power of government to make allocative decisions that ought to emerge from market transactions.

These are all serious issues, but they may be dwarfed in significance by the legal uncertainty *Delgamuukw* has created. In spite of its attempt at conceptual sophistication, the Lamer doctrine leaves most of the pressing practical issues unsettled. As one critic has said, *Delgamuukw* "undermined everything but settled nothing."[52] How much of British Columbia is subject to aboriginal title and site-specific aboriginal rights? How will aboriginal title and rights be proved? How much consultation and compensation will be required in cases of infringement? The only answer to these vital questions is that the courts will have to decide through further litigation. It is a lawyer's dream but an entrepreneur's nightmare.

Sadly, Canada's aboriginal people seem as far as ever from attaining a workable system of property rights. The treaties and the Indian Act have conspired to imprison them within a regime of collective rights that fit badly with the needs of a market economy. Now the Supreme Court of Canada, while asserting and redefining aboriginal property rights, has carved their collective and inalienable character in judicial stone. If there is anything for which Canadians should feel guilty, it is that our government, laws, and courts have kept Indians outside the world of individual property rather than encouraging them to step inside.

CHAPTER 8

Treaties, Agreements, and Land Surrenders

The 1969 Vienna Convention on the Law of Treaties defined a treaty as "an international agreement concluded between States in written form."[1] This understanding has been more or less the same for centuries. In 1758 Vattel wrote that a treaty was "a compact entered into by sovereigns for the welfare of the State."[2] Behind these modern definitions lies a much longer tradition of statecraft going back through the Romans and Greeks to the covenants entered into by the Egyptian, Babylonian, and Hittite empires of the ancient Middle East.

Statehood and sovereignty are essential concepts here. Only states – that is, political systems with fixed territories under the control of a sovereign power – can enter into the agreements recognized as treaties in international law. And treaties must be approved by the highest power in the state, the sovereign, whether sovereignty is exercised by an individual or a committee. It is the interlocking of statehood and sovereignty that makes treaties an enforceable part of international law. Because the state has fixed boundaries, one knows where the treaty will apply; and because the sovereign is the highest authority, one knows whose task it is to ensure that the treaty is respected. Treaties, in other words, are an aspect of the state system.

To see this more clearly, imagine a world without states, a world populated by tribes of hunter-collectors. The chiefs of these tribes exercise a kind of authority, but they do not have long-lasting control over specific territories; and their tribes are subject to fission and fusion as families and clans exit, merge, and form new entities. Under such conditions, there could be agreements between tribes not to make war against each other or agreements to join in war against a third party; but these would be more like personal pledges, without the long-term stability expected of treaties as defined by the Vienna Convention.

From this perspective, it is clear that the many agreements made over the centuries between Indians, on the one hand, and Great Britain or Canada, on the other, are not treaties in the international sense. They could not be, because, as shown earlier in this book, Indians were not organized into states and did not possess sovereignty in the technical sense. Great Britain and then Canada, as the successor state to Britain, have always upheld their own sovereignty by right of discovery and prescription, and they have both regarded Indian tribes as subject peoples.

Canadian courts have come to the same conclusion. In the *Sioui* (1990) case, the Supreme Court of Canada held "that a treaty with the Indians is unique, that it is an agreement *sui generis* which is neither created nor terminated according to the rules of international law."[3] In decisions made before 1982 Canadian courts ruled that the provisions of Indian treaties could be changed by federal legislation.[4] This could not have been true of an international treaty, in which all parties must agree to changes and unilateral action means abrogation. However, since 1982, treaty rights are "recognized and affirmed" in the Canadian constitution,[5] which raises novel questions about the ability of a simple act of Parliament to override treaties.

Contemporary exponents of the aboriginal orthodoxy insist that Indian treaties are "nation to nation." Since such statements directly contradict Canadian law, they are best understood as claims that Canada should be restructured as a multinational state held together by treaty federalism. But they also rest upon a view of history. In the RCAP's words, "in entering into treaties with Indian nations in the past, the Crown recognized the nationhood of its treaty partners."[6] It is necessary, therefore, to take a closer look at the Indian agreements now known as treaties, even though many of them were not called that when they were made.

BEFORE THE ROYAL PROCLAMATION OF 1763

All politically organized human societies that come into contact with one another develop relationships of conflict and cooperation, and against that backdrop their leaders sometimes make agreements with one another. Therefore, among even the simplest societies, there is a functional equivalent to "international relations," and North American Indians were no exception. Agreements involving the Iroquois were particularly numerous and are being intensively researched by modern scholars.[7]

When the Dutch, English, and French entered North America in the early seventeenth century, their military and political leaders made agreements with Indian tribes for all sorts of purposes, such as war and peace, exchange of prisoners, trade, and use of land. Some of these early agreements are lost to memory, while others are briefly mentioned or even recounted at length in documents of the period such as the *Jesuit Relations;* but even when described in writing by observers, the agreements themselves were oral in character. It is now fashionable to call them treaties, but they did not have that status in the minds of the European colonists or the authorities in their mother countries. As they understood it, treaties were written agreements solemnly ratified by sovereign heads of states; these, in contrast, were verbal agreements made by colonial commanders and governors with the chiefs of native tribes. They were to be respected while they lasted, but they were not of the same order as, say, a treaty between the king of France and the king of England.

Starting in the 1680s, there was a century of stop-and-start warfare between the French colonists and English settlers and their Indian allies in Acadia, New France, and northern New England. Sometimes the fighting was an extension of European wars between France and Great Britain; sometimes it broke out spontaneously over local issues on the American frontier. Whatever the case, it was bloody, protracted, and expensive for all concerned.

After major bouts of fighting, written peace agreements were entered into between the British authorities and various Indian tribes in the region. The first one was signed at Pemmaquid, Maine, in 1693 with the Abenaki, whose homeland, to describe it in contemporary terms, lay in Maine and eastern Quebec. The last was signed in 1779 with the Micmac of what is now northern New Brunswick. In between came other agreements, in 1713, 1717, 1725, 1728, 1749, 1752, and 1760. It is difficult to say exactly how many agreements were concluded, for they often involved renewal of earlier agreements or the acceptance by one tribe of a compact negotiated previously with another tribe. The precise boundaries of the lands affected are also unclear because none of the documents contained anything but vague geographical references cutting across several (sometimes contested) colonial boundaries.

There is at the present time no authoritative listing of early agreements or treaties that might apply to the Maritime provinces and Quebec. In its 1990 *Sioui* decision, the Supreme Court of Canada held that a one-paragraph note of safe conduct issued to the Hurons of Lorette by General Murray on 5 September 1760 constituted a treaty and allows the present-day descendants of the Hurons to camp, cut trees, and make fires for ceremonial purposes in the provincial parks of Quebec.[8] It is impossible to say what "treaties" the courts may discover in future decisions. The RCAP, for example, speaks of "written treaties ... between the French and the Haudenosaunee [Iroquois] in 1624, 1645 and 1653."[9] Further litigation may give sanction to these and other "treaties," thus entrenching them in the constitution.

W.E. Daugherty's 1981 study of agreements in the Maritimes characterized them in the following terms:

Most of the treaties began with the words "Articles of Peace and Submission," hardly an indication of agreement signed between two equal powers for mutual benefit.

Indeed, it is dubious whether they may be construed as treaties at all ... Perhaps it is more accurate to consider these agreements, called treaties, to be a cross between a document of surrender and an armed truce, with the Indians making most of the concessions with an occasional quid pro quo from the British ... The treaties were the outcome of a period of intense warfare. Designed for the immediate purpose of obtaining peace, clearing the way for colonization and as diplomatic tools to destroy French power, they were not intended to, nor do they, provide the basis for aboriginal entitlement in the Maritimes.[10]

As Daugherty emphasizes, all of these covenants were negotiated to bring an end to periods of fighting. The Indian signatories typically proffered their submission to the British monarch, expressed regret for past acts of warfare, and promised to keep the peace in the future. In the same vein, they promised to release prisoners of war, turn over criminals whom the British wanted to prosecute, and abide by British law.

These were not land-surrender agreements. Most of them said nothing at all about land, although the agreements of 1713, 1717, and 1725 did specify that the English could continue to enjoy their settlements in Massachusetts and New Hampshire. Governor Dummer's Treaty of 1725, which made peace with Indians of both New England and Nova Scotia, also contained a limited statement about Indian land rights in Massachusetts: "Saving unto the Penobscot, Naridgwalk and other Tribes within His Majesty's province aforesaid and their natural Descendants respectively all their lands, Liberties and properties not by them convey'd or sold to or possessed by any of the English Subjects as aforesaid. As also the privilege of fishing, hunting, and fowling as formerly."[11] This repeated a similar guarantee in the agreement of 1713 made with the Abenaki of New England; the Indian tribes of Nova Scotia do not seem to have been included.[12]

Several of the treaties also provided for the establishment of trade relations between the Indians and the English – not surprising, because much of the fighting between the English and the French had been for the express purpose of denying the Indian trade in furs and fish to the other. These trade clauses have been the subject of much recent litigation designed to expand them into guarantees of aboriginal control over natural resources. One important case is *Regina v. Paul,* decided by the New Brunswick Court of Appeal on 22 April 1998. Thomas Peter Paul, a Micmac Indian, was charged in 1995 with cutting bird's-eye maple trees on Crown lands and removing them without having a licence and without paying any stumpage fees. Because of the pattern in the wood grain, bird's-eye maple logs can be worth thousands of dollars apiece. If, like Paul, you are looking exclusively for them, you have to slash many maple trees with your chainsaw to find the ones you want, thus compounding the loss to the Crown and to the lumber company holding the licence for the area.

Judge Arsenault of the New Brunswick Provincial Court acquitted Paul at trial, finding that a right to trade, including a limited right to cut timber on Crown land, was protected by the treaty of 1752 as well as by "Doucette's Promises" or the "Mascarene Treaty," which was the extension of Dummer's Treaty of 1725 to the Indians of Nova Scotia. At that time, Major Paul Mascarene promised the Nova Scotia Indians that they would "not be molested in their persons, hunting, fishing, and planting grounds, nor in any other [of] their lawful occasions."[13] Judge Arsenault found that these early agreements had never been terminated and that the phrase "lawful occasions" included cutting trees on a limited scale, though probably not extensive clearcutting.

On appeal, Justice Turnbull of the New Brunswick Court of Queen's Bench upheld the acquittal, but for a different reason. Rejecting Judge Arsenault's theory that New Brunswick Indians had a treaty right to trade, he conducted his own research and concluded that Dummer's Treaty had confirmed Indian land rights in the province: "Governments must accept that Dummer's Treaty was understood to protect Indian Land and recognize the Indians' primacy when enacting legislation if it [*sic*] intends to enact laws affecting treaty rights. At the present time Indians have the right to cut trees on all Crown land."[14]

Upon further appeal, the New Brunswick Court of Appeal ordered a conviction for Paul and rejected both theories that the lower courts had developed to justify acquittal. The Court of Appeal agreed with Justice Turnbull's critique of Judge Arsenault's trade theory, but it dismissed Justice Turnbull's land-rights theory because he had developed it through his own research without giving the parties an opportunity to argue the issue in court: "Thus ... a case that was acknowledged by Justice Turnbull ... to have been argued 'on the basis of a treaty right to trade' was transformed by him into one premised upon aboriginal title. This transition occurred without giving notice to the parties and without affording counsel the opportunity to address the issues with written or oral argument or to dispute the documents or the inferences drawn from them or to present evidence of any kind."[15] The judges also pointed out that two earlier decisions of the New Brunswick Court of Appeal had ruled that Dummer's Treaty applied only to the Massachusetts Bay area and not to New Brunswick. The Supreme Court of Canada declined to hear a further appeal.[16]

Shortly before this book went to press, the Supreme Court rendered an even more important decision in the *Donald Marshall* case. I will discuss it only briefly, for its implications are still far from clear. Donald Marshall (famous in another context for having been wrongfully convicted of murder and then exonerated) is a Micmac Indian from Nova Scotia. He was convicted by the lower courts of catching eels out of season and without a licence. On 17 September 1999, however, the Supreme Court reversed that conviction with a novel reading of the "truck house" clauses in the Passamaquody and Micmac agreements of 1760–61. A truck house was a trading post established by the British authorities, and these clauses, like similar clauses in the other Maritime treaties, were promises by the Indians to trade with the British rather than the French: "And I do further engage that we will not traffic, barter or exchange any commodities in any manner but with such persons or the managers of such truck houses as shall be appointed or established by His Majesty's Governor at Fort Cumberland or elsewhere in Nova Scotia or Acadia."[17]

The Supreme Court reasoned that if the British were offering to trade with the Indians, the latter must have had the right to collect fish, furs, and other produce of the land and exchange it at the truck house. Judicial legerdemain then converted this two-century-old practice into a modern right to derive a "moderate livelihood" from hunting and fishing without regard to the licence laws, bag limits, and seasonal restrictions that all other citizens must follow.[18]

The decision quickly plunged the Atlantic lobster-fishing industry into chaos. Indians started taking lobsters in Miramichi Bay even though the season was closed for spawning, and Acadian fishermen, fearing this out-of-season fishing might jeopardize the lobster population and ruin their own spring season, took to the water to disable the traps set by Indian fishermen. Amidst intensive national media coverage, several more incidents of vandalism and violence broke out along the coasts of New Brunswick and Nova Scotia. As of late October 1999, Indian and white fishermen are meeting with politicians, officials, and a federally appointed arbitrator, trying to reach agreement on many difficult issues: How many lobsters will Indians be able to take in pursuit of a "moderate livelihood?" Who will regulate their catch? Will white fishermen have to reduce their take? Does the newly articulated Indian right extend to Metis and non-status Indians, or to status Indians only? Will American Indians, such as the Pasamaquoddy, who also claim to be involved in these treaties, be allowed to share in lucrative Canadian fisheries such as lobsters and scallops?

The implications of the *Donald Marshall* decision may extend far beyond Maritime fisheries. Some Indian leaders (with support from Bob Nault, minister of Indian and northern affairs) are claiming that the rights of gathering and exchange articulated in *Donald Marshall* extend also to natural resources such as timber and minerals. Micmac negotiator Bernd Christmas says: "We've never surrendered our land or our resources and that's the question that has to be answered. In our view, the treaty is just an offshoot of that notion of aboriginal title. And aboriginal title covers all aspects – whether it's hunting, fishing, mining, land, or return of our land."[19] A judicial extension of treaty rights thus tends to merge with an assertion of unextinguished aboriginal rights and title.

In 1979, just before the Liberals' defeat in that year's election, the federal cabinet took the position that aboriginal title in the Maritime provinces had already been extinguished or "superceded [sic] by law."[20] According to Allan MacEachen, then federal cabinet minister with political responsibility for Nova Scotia, "the Government informed the Union of Nova Scotia Indians that native title in Scotia has been superceded [sic] by law. This means that in Nova Scotia, the actions of successive pre-Confederation governments in opening up the lands of the Province to settlement ... has [sic] the effect of overriding and removing the existence of native title in all areas, other than Indian reserve lands. It is highly likely that the same would apply to New Brunswick and Prince Edward Island."[21] Because MacEachen's reasoning resembles the doctrine of implicit extinguishment rejected by the Supreme Court in *Delgamuukw*, one might guess that when a properly prepared case comes forward, the courts will hold that native title still exists in eastern Canada, as in British Columbia.

Indeed, a case that got under way in Nova Scotia Provincial Court in July 1999 may lead to that result. Thirty-one Micmac defendants have been charged with illegal logging. Their lawyer intends to argue that their title to land has never been extinguished: "The essence of our position is that the Micmac originally occupied all of Nova Scotia and Cape Breton, including the areas where the harvesting took place. At no time, through treaties or otherwise, did they cede their right to use and occupy that land. They were pushed aside by the British at various points in time, but the net result was not to extinguish the underlying title."[22]

In the meantime, aboriginal groups in eastern Canada are claiming extensive logging rights, whether treaty or aboriginal in character, leading to tense stand-offs in both New Brunswick and Quebec when insurgents block roads in pursuit of their claims to be able to cut timber at will.[23] Governments in both provinces responded by allocating Indians a share of the total allowable cut, but this solution has its own problems because of internal factionalism in aboriginal communities.[24] In both provinces there were serious internal disputes about who would get control over the increased allocation. Don Cayo, president of the Atlantic Institute of Market Studies, admits that "the talks taking place are neither comprehensive nor particularly well advanced," but writes, nonetheless, that "they ought to be welcomed as the first attempts in modern memory to bring Maritime native people into the broader economy."[25] Time will tell.

THE ONTARIO "TREATIES"

What are today known as the Ontario "treaties" are very different in character from the eighteenth-century agreements signed in eastern Canada. The latter were declarations of submission, made to cement peace after periods of fighting among the English and the French and Indian tribes. Those agreements had almost nothing to say about land or property rights. The Ontario agreements, in contrast, were real-estate conveyances, made to extinguish the Indian title to land so that settlement could proceed in Upper Canada.

The Ontario agreements were influenced by two factors: the Royal Proclamation of 1763, which recognized the existence of aboriginal property rights and stipulated that they be surrendered only to agents of the Crown and not to private purchasers; and the urgent need to settle Loyalist refugees from the American Revolution, including Indian allies of the British, who started to stream north in the late 1770s. In 1781 the British authorities began to negotiate the surrender of the Indian title on the north shore of the lower Great Lakes so that resettlement could proceed within a clear framework of property rights.[26]

The text of one of the earliest of these agreements, for the surrender of the island of Mackinac in the strait between Lakes Huron and Michigan, is illustrative. It simply says that, in return for "Five Thousand Pounds New York Currency," the undersigned chiefs "and all others of our Nation, the Chipwas, who have or can lay claim to the hereinmentioned Island ... do surrender and yield up [their rights to the island] ... and we do hereby make for ourselves and posterity a renunciation of all claims in future to said Island."[27] Ironically, the British lost their investment in this deal because the island ended up on the American side of the boundary when peace was concluded.

From 1781 to the War of 1812, the Crown entered into dozens of similar transactions in southern Ontario. According to the leading authority on the subject, all were "relatively simple arrangements. The Crown made a single, one-time payment in goods for a specific portion of territory."[28] There were no subsequent annual payments or any other continuing benefits. The agreements did not mention reserves because, at this stage, land was plentiful and Indians who sold a tract could move elsewhere. After a century and a half of exposure to Old World diseases and frontier warfare, the Indian population had declined so drastically that it was not hard to accommodate. Where reserves were required, they were set aside by executive proclamation, as in the case of the Six Nations reserve along the Grand River.[29]

There was a new wave of immigration to Upper Canada after the War of 1812, leading to another round of land-surrender agreements. From 1818 on, the Crown payed annuities instead of a one-time purchase price. This originated as an economy measure, because the money for the annuities could be derived from selling the surrendered lands, thus making the process self-financing.[30] After 1829 the annuities were changed from payments to individuals to appropriations for bands to spend collectively on housing or other needs.[31] But annuities in any form had the consequence of transforming the agreements from one-off real-estate deals into continuing relationships, because now the Crown had to make payments to the Indians every year. Nonetheless, the word "treaty" did not appear in the agreements of this period, which, like those prior to the War of 1812, were usually headed with contract-law terms such as "indenture" or "agreement." Hunting and fishing rights, while taken for granted in practice, were not explicitly mentioned in these early agreements, except for the fishing rights granted in the Mississauga surrenders of 1805–6, although all but one of these (the Etobicoke River) were extinguished in 1820.[32]

All these elements came together in the Robinson Treaties of 1850, which acquired the Indian title to large tracts of land north of Lakes Huron and Superior. These treaties provided for an initial purchase price of "two thousand pounds of good and lawful money of Upper Canada," plus a further "perpetual annuity" of five hundred pounds for the Superior Treaty and six hundred for the Huron. They also granted Indians the right to hunt and fish across the ceded territory, "excepting only such portions ... as may from time to time be sold or leased to individuals, or companies of individuals, and occupied by them with the consent of the Provincial Government." Finally, the Robinson Treaties established "reservations ... for the purposes of residence and cultivation," and included clauses giving the Indians the benefits of any minerals discovered on these reservations. Both texts were headed with the word "agreement," but the word "treaty" also appeared as a synonym within them.[33]

THE NUMBERED TREATIES

In 1871 Canada began a half-century of treaty-making to extinguish the Indian title in the newly acquired territories of Rupert's Land. British officials may or may not have intended to include the Hudson's Bay Company territories when they issued the Royal Proclamation of 1763, but the proclamation's policy of formal acquisition of Indian title had set a standard that, having been followed in Ontario, could not be ignored in the North-West. Thus, section 14 of the imperial order-in-council transferring Rupert's Land to Canada provided that "any claims of Indians to compensation for lands required for purposes of settlement shall be disposed of by the Canadian Government in communication with the Imperial Government; and the Company shall be relieved of all responsibility in respect of them."[34]

During its two-hundred-year tenure in Rupert's Land, the Hudson's Bay Company had used land for ports, docks, forts, trading posts, storehouses, gardens, and pastures; but it had been involved in only one formal surrender of Indian land rights. That was the so-called Selkirk Treaty, which Miles Macdonnell negotiated in 1817 in order to acquire land for Lord Selkirk's colonization project in the Red River Valley. In the Selkirk Treaty, an Ojibwa band and a Cree band surrendered two miles on either side of the Red and Assiniboine Rivers in return for an annual quit rent of a hundred pounds of tobacco to each band.[35] This land sale sufficed for the Red River Colony, but its validity was sometimes questioned because of suspicion that Macdonnell had dealt with the wrong Indians, the Ojibwa being relative newcomers on the scene.[36] Hence the Dominion decided to start afresh.

The eleven "Numbered Treaties" signed between 1871 and 1921 acquired for the Crown the Indian title to a truly enormous area that included all three Prairie provinces, the northeast part of British Columbia, the southeast corner of the Yukon, the Mackenzie Valley in the Northwest Territories, and that part of Ontario – most of the province – draining into Hudson Bay. Ironically, Canada embarked on this venture in the same year as the United States president lost his power to negotiate new Indian treaties.[37] The u.s. Congress had added these words to the Indian Appropriations Act: "Hereafter no Indian nation or tribe within the territory of the United States shall be acknowledged or recognized as an independent nation, tribe or power with whom the United States may contract by treaty."[38] After 1871 the United States dealt legislatively with Indians, even as Canada embarked on fifty years of treaty-making.

Treaties 1 and 2, negotiated in Manitoba in 1871, involved tracts of land more or less on the scale of the lands described in the Robinson Treaties. The procedure was also the same: the treaty commissioners held one meeting with an assembly of all the Indians inhabiting the territory and negotiated the surrender of land rights. In some of the subsequent Numbered Treaties, which covered much larger areas, the procedure had to be different because it was not practical to bring the whole population together. The commissioners would hold an initial meeting with as large a group as possible, negotiate terms, and then travel to other locations, inviting other groups to adhere on the same terms. It could take years or even decades to obtain the adhesion of all bands. Indeed, there are still bands – most famously, the Lubicon of northern Alberta – who claim to have been overlooked and never to have adhered to any treaty.[39]

There were some differences among the Numbered Treaties, depending upon the objective circumstances of the various Indian tribes as well as their relative bargaining position; but the differences were more than outweighed by the similarities. The following elements were typical:

- *A recognition of Canadian sovereignty.* Indians were styled as "subjects" in all the treaties.
- *An explicit surrender of Indian title to land.* Treaty 7, for example, contained these words: "the said Indians ... inhabiting the district hereinafter more fully described and defined, do hereby

cede, release, surrender, and yield up to the Government of Canada for Her Majesty the Queen and her successors forever, all their rights, titles and privileges whatsoever to the lands included within the following limits."[40] A similar statement was featured at the beginning of each of the Numbered Treaties. Extinguishing the Indian title and obtaining full rights over the land were clearly the federal government's chief objectives.

- *A statement of the Indians' right to continue hunting on surrendered land*, "subject to such regulations as may, from time to time, be made by the Government of the country, acting under the authority of Her Majesty; and saving and excepting such tracts as may be required or taken up from time to time for settlement, mining, trading or other purposes by her Government of Canada."[41] The right to hunt was not mentioned in Treaties 1 and 2 but was included in all subsequent treaties.

- *Land reserves to be held by the Crown for the use and benefit of the Indians*. The size of these reserves was set at 160 acres per family of five in Treaties 1, 2, and 5, and 640 acres per family of five in the others. In all cases, the reserves were to be held in trust for the Indians by the Crown.

- *A cash bonus to every man, woman, and child for signing, plus an annual payment thereafter*. Again, there was some variation in the size of the signing gratuities and the annuities and in the amount of extra money and goods provided for chiefs and headmen.

- *Educational assistance*. In the first six treaties, this benefit was phrased in terms of the government maintaining schools on the reserves; subsequently, it was described as the government paying teachers' salaries.

- *Assistance in earning a livelihood*. Depending on the location and circumstances of the signatories, this could include agricultural implements, seed grain, and livestock, as well as supplies for hunting, fishing, and trapping.

- *A promise by the Indians to obey the law and keep the peace with all other subjects of Her Majesty*.

These were first and foremost land-surrender agreements, but the many continuing elements in the Numbered Treaties – annuities, land reserves held in trust, hunting and fishing rights, educational assistance, and economic assistance – created an ongoing relationship more durable than a single real-estate transaction. This was partly due to necessity. The Indians of the plains had depended on the buffalo, and it was clear to everyone in the 1870s that the buffalo were on the edge of extinction. The plains Indians could not simply be left to shift for themselves.

The Numbered Treaties also rested upon a policy of civilizing aboriginal people and incorporating them into Canadian society. Alexander Morris expressed this eloquently in the final paragraph of his 1880 book *The Treaties of Canada with the Indians*:

And now I close. Let us have Christianity and civilization to leaven the mass of heathenism and paganism among the Indian tribes; let us have a wise and paternal Government faithfully carrying out the provisions of our treaties, and doing its utmost to help and elevate the Indian population, who have been cast upon our care, and we will have peace, progress, and concord among them in the North-West; and instead of the Indian melting away, as one of them in older Canada, tersely put it, "as snow before the sun," we will see our Indian population, loyal subjects of the Crown, happy, prosperous and self-sustaining, and Canada will be enabled to feel, that in a truly patriotic spirit, our country has done its duty by the red men of the North-West, and thereby to herself. So may it be.[42]

SHAKING THE MONEY TREE

On one side, the contemporary Indian approach to the treaties is a kind of literal fundamentalism, insisting on fulfilment of every jot and tittle and demanding compensation for every alleged instance of non-fulfilment, no matter how minor or remote in time. Since 1973, the Department of Indian Affairs has been dealing with such grievances under the heading of "specific claims." In 1991 the Mulroney government set up the Indian Claims Commission (ICC) to expedite the investigation of such claims. The ICC cannot make a legally binding determination, but it can mediate between the department and native claimants, conduct inquiries, and make recommendations. Bands also have the option of taking their claims to court, although that road is usually more expensive and less likely to succeed. Finally, they can seek redress directly from politicians, an option that has been particularly successful in Saskatchewan.

Although an infinity of specific claims can arise under treaty, the following are a few of the more common types.

Claims Relating to Size of Reserves.   Many bands in the Prairie
provinces allege that their reserves were too small from the beginning. Depending on the treaty, the reserves were supposed to be
160 or 640 acres per family of five; this seems straightforward
enough, but it was difficult to get an accurate count of native people
in the early years. Many spent extended periods hunting the last
buffalo in Montana; others initially presented themselves as Metis
but later switched to Indian status (some started as Indians, became
Metis, then went back again). There was also a lot of movement
from band to band. For these and other reasons, bands often argue
that they did not get their proper quantum of land at first survey,
reserves were not located precisely where the Indians wanted them,
certain desirable tracts of land were omitted, and so on.

Alone among the provinces, Saskatchewan has agreed to "top
up" reserve shortfalls using contemporary population data rather
than census returns from the time of first survey. Mel Smith has
estimated that, as of 1994, Saskatchewan's concession implied a
commitment of 97,112 acres (39,317 hectares) in land, plus
$454,368,157 in cash for cases where, as in most of the southern
part of the province, additional land could not be provided.[43]
Manitoba was involved in similar negotiations but, seeing the
expense of the Saskatchewan experiment, decided not to proceed.[44]

Claims Relating to Expropriation or Reduction of Reserve Land.
Many reserves across Canada (and not just those established under
treaties) have undergone reductions in size. Sometimes land was
expropriated (with compensation) for uses such as railways, highways, or military facilities; sometimes it was surrendered to the
Crown as surplus to need and then sold to private buyers, with the
proceeds placed in trust accounts for the use of the bands. With
the benefit of hindsight, bands often argue that undue pressure was
applied or that the compensation paid at the time of surrender was
inadequate, was not paid quickly enough, or was not accompanied
by sufficient interest in cases of delay.

Such claims have received an enormous boost from the doctrine
of "fiduciary obligation" proclaimed by the Supreme Court of
Canada in its 1985 *Guerin* decision. In *Guerin*, officials of the
Department of Indian Affairs had made a verbal promise to arrange
a lease of Musqueam Band reserve land upon certain terms. When
that deal fell through, they arranged a different and less favourable

lease without consulting the band. The court found this behaviour "unconscionable" and thus a violation of the fiduciary obligation owed by the Crown to the Indians whose land it held in trust.[45] However justified this particular decision may have been, it was soon seen as an open-ended invitation to Indian bands to re-examine every transaction in which they have ever engaged with the Crown. There is no objective standard inherent in "fiduciary obligation"; in the end, the doctrine will mean whatever judges say it means. It practice, it encourages judges to employ contemporary standards of justice to second-guess decisions made decades ago under assumptions of fairness and appropriate procedure commonplace at the time but that may now seem unacceptable. (It has also encouraged the Department of Indian Affairs to accelerate the trend to aboriginal self-government in order to reduce its chances of being sued for violation of fiduciary responsibility.)[46]

Another phrase now gaining currency that has the same effect is "the honour of the Crown." As expounded by David Arnot, the Saskatchewan treaty commissioner, it means acting "as if justice, honour, and the principles we so painstakingly negotiated in our national constitution come first, ahead of persons and parties."[47] But justice and honour are not self-evident concepts; they are always contested in debates over difficult practical issues. As demonstrated in the *Donald Marshall* decision, replacing the treaty text with a vague phrase like "the honour of the Crown" inevitably invites subjective and anachronistic reinterpretation of what was agreed upon at the time.

Claims Relating to Adequacy of Economic Assistance. Bands have sometimes challenged the adequacy of the economic assistance provided under the Numbered Treaties. Treaty 7 bands, for example, received $250,000 in 1974 for shortfalls in the delivery of the ammunition mentioned in the treaty: "the sum of two thousand dollars shall hereafter every year be expended in the purchase of ammunition for distribution among the said Indians; provided that if at any future time ammunition became comparatively unnecessary for said Indians, her Government, with the consent of said Indians, or any of the bands thereof, may expend the proportion due to such band otherwise for their benefit."[48] Likewise, the Siksika (Blackfoot) Nation, under Treaty 7, received $1,675,000 in 1984 for a deficiency in its treaty livestock entitlement: "the said

Indians shall be supplied as soon as convenient, after any band shall make due application therefor, with the following cattle for raising stock, that is to say: for every family of five persons, and under, two cows; for every family of more than five persons, and less than ten persons, three cows; for every family of over ten persons, four cows; and for every head and minor Chief, and every Stony chief, for the use of their bands, one bull."[49]

The investigation of specific claims has gone back more than two hundred years. The Indian Claims Commission recently announced that it had successfully mediated resolution of a claim based on the 1785 "Collins Treaty," which involved the acquisition of the right of passage along a footpath between Lake Simcoe and Georgian Bay. Indian Affairs agreed to accept this as a "fast-track claim," a special category for claims less than $500,000.[50] Such willingness to reopen the remote past is unique to Indian treaties. Neither international law nor ordinary contract law provides forums for parties to litigate breaches of agreement that allegedly occurred centuries ago.

Specific claims number in the hundreds and are increasing all the time. It is probably no exaggeration to assert that every band in Canada has made, is making, or is preparing to make at least one such claim. An impartial observer would no doubt find some of these to be justified – given the volume of dealings between Indians and the Crown over the centuries, government officials must have made some mistakes – but a thriving claims industry also has perverse consequences. It encourages First Nations to focus on the past rather than the future, to see themselves as victims, and to put their best efforts into proving victimization. It also reinforces the message that the way to advance is not to sell goods and services in the marketplace but to get money from the government through negotiation or litigation. Such strategies may succeed in their immediate objective of obtaining money, but they are unlikely to create the skills and attitudes associated with more permanent forms of prosperity.

Regrettably but not surprisingly, today's aboriginal orthodoxy encourages such compensation-seeking behaviour. The Indian Claims Commission, the Assembly of First Nations, and the Royal Commission on Aboriginal Peoples have all recommended replacement of the ICC with a new tribunal with the power to make legally enforceable decisions, not just to mediate, investigate, and recommend. The RCAP even recommended that the legislation creating such a tribunal include a privative clause barring appeals of the tribunal's decisions to the courts, which normally have jurisdiction over administrative and quasi-judicial tribunals.[51]

The Liberals promised in their 1993 election campaign to create such an independent tribunal for specific land claims, but Jean Chrétien's government has not yet finalized anything because of fears about cost: "In the past two decades, Ottawa has paid about $800 million [not adjusted for inflation] to resolve 185 specific claims."[52] Assembly of First Nations officials predict that a new tribunal could cost between $200 and $300 million a year. When practised on this scale and routinized over a long period of time, the pursuit of specific claims becomes, at bottom, a way of enlarging the Indian Affairs budget, using "justice" to override normal fiscal controls.

TRANSFORMING THE TREATIES

Although the language of the treaties is somewhat archaic, it is not hard to understand them as written texts. The eighteenth-century agreements in eastern Canada were expressions of submission to the Crown and promises to keep the peace, with mention of some specific issues, such as return of captives. The Ontario agreements were real-estate conveyances, though the later ones included a few elements that established an ongoing relationship. The Numbered Treaties also focused on the surrender of aboriginal land rights, and they imposed even more continuing obligations than the later Ontario agreements.

Contemporary jurisprudence, however, has broadened the understanding of treaties beyond the obvious meaning of the written text. A recent law-journal article summarizes some of the main developments, with concise quotations from leading decisions:

It is well accepted by the courts that treaties and statutes relating to Aboriginal peoples "should be given a fair, large and liberal construction in favour of the Indians." Ambiguities and doubtful expressions in the the text of treaties must be resolved in favour of Aboriginal interests, and "any limitations which restrict the rights of Indians under treaties must be narrowly construed." As the honour of the Crown is at stake in its dealings with Aboriginal peoples, the Crown is assumed to intend to uphold its promises, and no appearance of "sharp dealing" will be sanctioned by the courts. The treaties must therefore be interpreted in a manner consistent with the Crown's fiduciary duty. "... written terms alone often will not 'suffice to determine the legal nature of the document.'" In *R. v. Sioui*, the Supreme Court suggested that the analysis should never be confined to the written text of a treaty ... In ascertaining the obligations arising from a treaty, then, the courts place particular emphasis on the Aboriginal understanding of its terms. The written text is thus only one element of the terms of a treaty. It records "an agreement that had already been reached orally and ... [does] not always record the full extent of the oral agreement."[53]

In the 1988 *Horse* decision, the Supreme Court held that treaties should be interpreted in accordance with the normal rule for contracts, "that extrinsic evidence is not to be used in the absence of ambiguity."[54] Even though the Supreme Court reaffirmed this principle in its *Sioui* decision, advocates of the aboriginal orthodoxy continued to criticize the *Horse* decision and frequently invited the Supreme Court to overrule it.[55] Their goal was to promulgate a transformed understanding of treaties according to which the written words of the agreement would not be determinative because "the written text expresses only the government of Canada's view of the treaty relationship: it does not embody the negotiated agreement."[56] Their persistence paid off in the *Donald Marshall* decision when the Supreme Court effectively overturned the *Horse* doctrine, holding that "extrinsic evidence of the historical and cultural context of a treaty may be received even absent any ambiguity on the face of the treaty."[57]

The RCAP's discussion of treaties is a sophisticated version of the current aboriginal orthodoxy. For the RCAP, treaties are "nation-to-nation" agreements, "sacred and enduring."[58] They are neither international agreements nor ordinary contracts; they are *sui generis*, that is, unique, "because their central feature makes them irrevocable. The central feature of almost all the treaties is to provide for the orderly and peaceful sharing of a land ... Once this has been acted upon, it cannot be reversed."[59] They are "part of the Canadian constitution," and "fulfilment of the treaties is fundamental to Canada's honour."[60] Unlike other parts of the constitution, however, they cannot be interpreted by analysing the written terms:

"The commission believes that the unique nature of the historical treaties requires special rules to give effect to the treaty nations' understanding of the treaties. Such an approach to the content of the treaties would require, as a first step, the rejection of the idea that the written text is the exclusive record of the treaty."[61]

Above all, the proponents of the new orthodoxy object to the treaties' references to extinguishment, that is, to the surrender of aboriginal title:[62] "The treaty nations maintain with virtual unanimity that they did not agree to extinguish their rights to their traditional lands and territories but agreed instead to share them in some equitable fashion with the newcomers."[63] The term "sharing" has become the mantra of treaty revisionism: "Our ancestors did not sign a real estate deal as you cannot give away something you do not own. No, the treaties were signed as our symbol of good faith to share the land."[64]

The RCAP, conceding that "the text of the post-1850 treaties clearly provides for the extinguishment of Aboriginal title," argues that we cannot rely upon the text because "the people of the treaty nations reject that outcome."[65] Moreover, aboriginal people could not have surrendered their title because they did not understand the legal language of the treaties and their own cultures and languages did not contain concepts like rights, surrender, and extinguishment. "Thus, it is possible that Aboriginal title continues to coexist with the Crown's rights throughout the areas covered by treaties, despite the Crown's intention to include a cession of Aboriginal title."[66]

The RCAP concludes that Canada should henceforth act on the basis of this novel and untested legal theory and regard aboriginal peoples as co-owners of all land, even though they signed agreements extinguishing their land rights, have received substantial benefits for doing so, and continue to seek punctilious fulfilment of those treaty clauses from which they draw benefits. The commission's call for the "implementation and renewal of treaties"[67] comes down in the end to a one-sided reading of the treaties. Implementation means that any clause conferring benefits must be fulfilled to the letter, while renewal means that any clause by which the Indians gave up something must be ignored, reinterpreted, or replaced.

An early victory of this view of treaties was achieved in the campaign against Treaty 11. In 1973 sixteen chiefs in the Northwest Territories and northern Alberta attempted to register a caveat on about four hundred thousand square miles [a million square kilo-metres] of land ceded by Treaties 8 and 11. They succeeded in persuading Justice William Morrow of the Supreme Court of the Northwest Territories that "notwithstanding the language of the two Treaties there is sufficient doubt on the facts that aboriginal title was extinguished that such claim for title should be permitted to be put forward by the caveators."[68] At trial, the would-be cave-ators produced a series of elders who had been present (mostly as children) at the signing in 1921 and who testified, in the words of Chief François Paulette, that "no lands have ever been surrendered or ceded in the first treaty. It was sort of a peace treaty ... No land was mentioned. That peace treaty was with regard to whether the white people can come in without any conflict with the Indians and the Indians have no conflict with the white people."[69]

This view of the treaty was widely disseminated through the book *As Long as This Land Shall Last,* written by Father René Fumoleau, an Oblate missionary in the north. Morrow's decision in the *Pau-lette* case was overturned on appeal, but the political victory had been won. The federal government entered into negotiations with the Dene and Metis of the Northwest Territories (but not Alberta) for new land-claims agreements to replace Treaty 11. More recently, the minister of Indian affairs signed a memorandum of understand-ing with the "Treaty 8 First Nations of Alberta ... to establish a formal bilateral process to ... implement an inherent right of self-government consistent with the spirit and intent of the Treaty relationship."[70] Whether the renovation of Treaty 8 will amount to repudiation remains to be seen.

The repudiation of treaties has not yet spread beyond the Mac-kenzie Valley, perhaps because conditions there were unique. Because the land was still part of a federal territory, a provincial government did not have to agree to give up control of its Crown lands. Also, reserves had never been taken up, relatively little land had been alienated to private owners, and native people were still a demo-graphic majority outside of Yellowknife. But such differences mean nothing to the advocates of the aboriginal orthodoxy, who wish, in effect, to repudiate all treaties under the guise of renovation.

In the absence of wholesale renovation of the treaties, what we are likely to see is guerrilla warfare in the courts as partisans of the aboriginal worldview attempt to undo extinguishment by grad-ually undermining the Crown's control of public lands and natural resources. A recent example is a case tried by the Provincial Court of Saskatchewan on 26 August 1998, in which two Dene from Buffao Narrows were acquitted of the charge of hunting moose illegally on the Primrose Lake Air Weapons Range. Basing the relevant part of his judgment largely on Dene oral tradition, the judge held that Treaty 10, even though it contains the usual clause about surrender of title to the land, actually meant that "the land would thereafter be *shared* along principled lines."[71] This decision was overturned on appeal, but its implications remain troubling. Saskatchewan might have lost its control over resource development on Crown land and might have had to get permission from one or more Indian bands every time a project was contemplated. There could also have been major implications with respect to compensation for past development where the Crown acted as if it had a clear title.

Another example is the *RioAlto* case initiated by the Fort McKay First Nation in Alberta. RioAlto Exploration sought and obtained permission in the normal way from the Ministry of Environmental Protection to run some seismic lines in the Treaty 8 area. The band, alleging that the seismic exploration would interfere with its members' traplines, asked the Court of Queen's Bench for "an Order of Mandamus compelling the Minister of Environmental Protection to consult with the Applicants regarding the scope, nature and extent of the impact of all exploratory activities approved by that minister on the exercise of the Treaty and Aboriginal rights of the Applicants."[72] What the band is after is the right to approve, and receive compensation for, any economic development on Crown land in what it considers its traditional territory – in effect, a right of co-ownership with the province.

Inconveniently, Treaty 8 says that the Indians gave up all their rights and title to the land, but counsel for the band will base an argument on the treaty's guarantee of the continued right to hunt and fish on Crown land. Again, the language of the treaty is inconvenient, because it says that hunting and fishing can continue "saving and excepting such tracts as may be required or taken up from time to time for settlement, mining, lumbering, trading or other purposes."[73] In response, the Fort McKay First Nation will quote the oral promise of the treaty commissioners: "But over and above the provision, we had to solemnly assure them that only such laws as to hunting and fishing as were in the interest of the Indians and were found necessary in order to protect the fish and fur-bearing animals would be made, and that they would be as free to hunt and fish after the treaty as they would be if they never entered into it."[74] The Fort McKay First Nation will also bring forward various oral traditions purporting to show that its people never intended to give up their land rights. Indeed, because oral traditions are likely to be critical in all cases of this type, we will take a more careful look at them in the next section.

On 26 February 1999 the campaign against the treaties was taken to a new level when two statements of claim were filed in Alberta. The Samson Cree Nation now holds that in 1877, when it adhered to Treaty 6, it "agreed only to share the surface of the Traditional Lands with Her Majesty the Queen." They "did not surrender by *Treaty No. 6* their aboriginal title and aboriginal rights in and to the Natural Resources."[75] In a separate action, all Treaty 7 bands "deny they ceded, released, surrendered or yielded up their Aborig-inal title or right over the Treaty 7 Territory," claiming instead that "they were agreeing to share the Treaty 7 Territory with the Crown."[76] If actions of this type are successful, they will totally transform the treaties.

This is not just a problem for western Canada. More than two-thirds of Ontario is covered by Treaty 9, negotiated in 1905–6, and by the adhesions signed in 1929–30. University of Toronto law professor Patrick Macklem, a rising star in the field of aboriginal rights, recently published an article arguing that the extinguishment of aboriginal title in Treaty 9 is only "apparent."[77] According to Macklem's "expansive interpretation of the right to hunt, trap, and fish,"[78] the province cannot undertake or authorize any develop-ment that would cause aboriginal hunting, fishing, and trapping to become less successful than they have been, "measured by reference to the fruits of past practice."[79]

If extinguishment is undermined in the courts by an "expansive" interpretation of hunting rights, there will be an awkward dupli-cation of property rights. Indian bands will not receive ownership rights as such, but rather a veto, or perhaps the right to be consulted, on economic development projects that might affect hunting, fishing, and trapping in "traditional territories" whose boundaries are at present not defined. Provinces would lose the ability they now have to undertake or authorize projects on their own authority. It is, moreover, predictable that bands would have overlapping conceptions of their traditional territories, so that provincial authorities might have to deal with two or more bands, not just in major projects like dams, but in minor projects like seismic lines. If it comes to that, it would be better to grant Indian bands title in fee simple to larger tracts than to end up with an impossibly cumbersome system of dual or multiple property rights that can only stultify economic activity.

ORAL TRADITIONS

The Indian societies north of Meso-America were not literate, although they made some use of devices such as pictographs and wampum as mnemonic aides. They relied heavily on oral traditions to preserve the memory of their past, so they naturally conserved oral traditions about the treaties. More recently, researchers employed by Indian organizations have made systematic efforts to collect these traditions and commit them to writing, partly out of intrinsic interest but also to serve the organizations' struggles to seek compensation and transform the treaties. Two such books have been published about treaties in Alberta,[80] and parallel efforts are going on concerning treaties in other provinces.[81]

Prior to the 1990s, oral traditions played only a limited role in native-rights litigation. In the 1935 *Dreaver* case, the Exchequer Court heard testimony from Chief Dreaver, who had been present at the signing of Treaty 6 in 1876, and allowed him to state his understanding of the "medicine chest" clause in that treaty.[82] In 1971 Justice Morrow heard oral evidence from Indians who had witnessed the signing of Treaties 8 and 11. But neither of these cases had high legal (as compared to political) impact. Justice Morrow's decision was overturned on appeal, and *Dreaver* remained little known and was not even reported until the 1970s. Moreover, both cases exemplified not oral traditions in the true sense of stories passed down across generations, but non-literate witnesses recounting their own memories of events witnessed decades ago.

As noted earlier in this chapter, the Supreme Court of Canada said in its *Horse* decision (1988) that treaties should be interpreted in accordance with the normal rule for contracts, "that extrinsic evidence is not to be used in the absence of ambiguity."[83] In other words, the *Horse* rule was that oral traditions could be used as an aid to interpretation where courts found the wording of a treaty unclear. The Supreme Court's more recent *Badger* decision (1996) opened the door more widely to the use of oral traditions. Mr Justice Cory wrote:

The treaties, as written documents, recorded an agreement that had already been reached orally and they did not always record the full extent of the oral agreement ... The treaties were drafted in English by representatives of the Canadian government who, it should be assumed, were familiar with common law doctrines. Yet, the treaties were not translated in written form into the languages ... of the various Indian nations who were signatories. Even if they had been, it is unlikely that the Indians, who had a history of communicating only orally, would have understood them any differently. As a result, it is well settled that the words in the treaty must not be interpreted in their strict technical sense nor subjected to rigid modern rules of construction. Rather, they must be interpreted in the sense that they would naturally have been understood by the Indians at the time of the signing.[84]

The court's decision in *Badger* did not turn entirely, or even chiefly, on oral tradition, but it did make use of oral tradition, as recounted by a Cree elder, to help interpret the words of Treaty 8 as well as the accompanying promises made by government representatives during the negotiations.

The judicial standing of oral traditions received a further boost in 1997, when the Supreme Court of Canada handed down its *Delgamuukw* decision. The court ordered a new trial because in its view the trial judge, while he had admitted the oral histories of the Gitksan and Wet'suwet'en as evidence, had gone on "to give these oral histories no independent weight at all."[85] Chief Justice Lamer laid down the following principle: "Notwithstanding the challenges created by the use of oral histories as proof of historical facts, the laws of evidence must be adapted in order that this type of evidence can be accommodated and placed on an equal footing with the types of historical evidence that courts are familiar with, which largely consists of historical documents."[86]

Alexander von Gernet, an anthropologist making a special study of the use of oral traditions in aboriginal litigation, has offered a penetrating criticism of the *Delgamuukw* ruling. In von Gernet's view, the trial judge handled the oral evidence properly: "By admitting oral documents into evidence, recognizing that they are not *prima facie* proof of the truth of the facts stated in them, taking note of the context in which they were generated, evaluating them for internal consistency, comparing them with other available evidence, and carefully weighing them, the judge did precisely what his critics suggest he should have done with written documents."[87] Then, acording to von Gernet, the Supreme Court of Canada incoherently demanded that oral traditions be put "on an equal footing" with other types of evidence, even though that is what the trial judge had done when he subjected the oral evidence to the types of critical tests routinely used on written evidence. "The rejection of McEachern's critical analysis will almost certainly be regarded by some not merely as an effort to level the field or lower the standard, but as an outright abandonment of the rigorous scrutiny that is essential to any fact-finding process. When taken to its logical conclusion this would seem unworkable in conflict resolution and, as others have noted, it would open the way for a radical reinvention of the law itself."[88]

There are, to be sure, differences between *Delgamuukw* and treaty litigation. In *Delgamuukw,* there was no text to interpret because there was no treaty; the Indian plaintiffs were offering their oral traditions as evidence about their occupancy of land prior to the time when white settlers were present to write down their observations. In contrast, treaty cases focus on the interpretation of a text, and Indian oral traditions recount events that are also recorded in conventional documents. Nonetheless, the *Delgamuukw* decision is bound to raise the status of oral traditions in treaty litigation; and the *Donald Marshall* decision, which sanctioned the use of extrinsic evidence in all treaty cases, will strengthen that effect.

One can sympathize with the Supreme Court's desire to recognize aboriginal oral traditions. Although Lamer was wrong when he wrote that oral traditions "for many aboriginal nations, are the only record of their past"[89] (disciplines such as archaeology, linguistics, and palaeobotany have much to contribute), it is true that oral traditions are important to many aboriginal litigants. If they cannot introduce them as evidence, they may not be able to make much of a case. Nonetheless, to adapt the rules of evidence so that oral traditions "can be accommodated and placed on an equal footing"[90] with other forms of evidence will be difficult or even impossible. It all depends on what the phrase "equal footing" is taken to mean. Chief Justice Lamer's dictum that recognition of oral traditions as evidence "must be undertaken on a case-by-case basis" merely postpones confronting the difficulties.[91]

There is a profound similarity between the judicial process and modern historiography. Even though the judicial process contains some concepts, such as legislative intent, and rules of evidence, such as the prohibition of extrinsic evidence, that do not apply to the writing of history, they share certain assumptions, such as the following:

- The passage of time is a linear, irreversible process in which events can be dated precisely.
- Causation follows time's arrow. A later event cannot be the cause of an earlier event.
- There is an objective core of fact that in principle can be discovered by sifting the evidence (sometimes, of course, the necessary evidence is missing).
- Not all evidence is equally worthwhile. First-hand evidence is usually more reliable than hearsay. Contemporary statements are usually more reliable than those elicited long after the event. Human memory is fallible, and people sometimes do not tell the truth, so it is essential to seek corroboration from multiple sources.

The underlying similarity between historiography and the judicial process is not surprising, since both are products of post-Enlightenment Western civilization. Within that context, both aim at establishing the truth about what happened in the past. Oral traditions, in contrast, differ from both historiography and the judicial process in important ways. As the RCAP has emphasized, the oral traditions of aboriginal peoples are based on a cyclical rather than a linear view of time,[92] and a different understanding of time implies a different view of causation and agency. As in the Australian "Dreamtime," the stories that make up Indian traditions often involve the Creator and other suprahuman beings who move in and out of time. Oral traditions express the perceived meaning of existence in an ordered cosmos; they do not reflect the Western concept of objective fact tested by evidence. In particular, oral traditions do not discriminate among types of evidence according to criteria of reliability and closeness to the event. One authority (herself quite favourable to oral traditions) has written that "the contradictions in what constitutes history – oral and written – cannot be resolved. The narratives can be juxtaposed ... but not necessarily reconciled into a seamless whole."[93] Outlined below are three concrete examples of the difficulties of resolving such contradictions, all drawn from one of the oral history projects undertaken in Alberta.

First, aboriginal oral traditions often contradict Western conceptions of rationality and knowledge. When the Cree elder John Buffalo was asked in 1975 about the disappearance of the buffalo from the prairie, he replied, "Some old men said that the buffalo entered the earth somewhere, but I do not know. It must be true, as there are none left."[94] Saying that the buffalo entered the earth may be an emotionally moving, mythic, or poetic way of describing their disappearance, but it is not compatible with the rational explanations sought in the judicial process as well as in the writing of history.

Second, oral traditions often contradict facts that can be established by overwhelming documentary evidence. Another Cree elder, Fred Horse, was asked if the Indians who signed Treaty 6 had any knowledge of earlier treaties:

Interviewer: Before Treaty Six was signed, there were about four treaties signed in Eastern Canada. Did the Indians in this part of the country know anything of the treaties coming to them?

Horse: No, they were not aware of a treaty that was to be signed. It was only when it was here they realized what was happening.

Interviewer: Did the elders or ancestors know of the treaties in the United States?

Horse: No, they did not know of them. They only knew of what was taking place with them.

Interviewer: Did the Indians at the time want the treaty?

Horse: Well, it was brought to them and that is how they negotiated with the Queen's commissioners. That is how it was completed.[95]

But we know from many sources that the Treaty 6 Indians had discussed earlier treaties with their relatives in other bands and tribes, were well informed about these treaties, and used that knowledge to prepare the demands articulated during the negotiations at Fort Carlton.[96]

Third, aboriginal traditions often contradict each other. Consider the following statements about Treaty 8 made by various elders. Chief François Paulette, from Fort Smith, testified before Justice Morrow in 1973: "No lands have ever been surrendered or ceded in the first treaty. It was sort of a peace treaty ... No land was mentioned. That peace treaty was with regard to whether the white people can come in without any conflict with the Indians and the Indians have no conflict with the white people."[97] Compare Paulette's testimony with the words of Jean-Marie Mustus, in conversation with interviewer Richard Lightning in 1975:

Lightning: Do you know how much land was given up or sold to the white man?

Mustus: The amount of land they gave up was written down on paper. I am wondering whether it was one foot underground or more. It was written down, but I do not know where the paper could be found.

Lightning: And you do not know how much was to be used?

Mustus: No, I do not know, but whatever they selected for themselves they kept; the rest was taken. I do not recall my grandfather telling me about the depth underground.

Lightning: Did he ever tell you anything about underground minerals or oil?

Mustus: Yes, these things were mentioned, as was the timber within the reserve; the Indians had a right to anything underground.[98]

Paulette and Mustus are both contradicted by Felix Gibot of Fort Chipewyan, also interviewed by Richard Lightning:

Lightning: When the commissioner came here to make treaty, were his intentions to sign treaty on a friendly basis or was it to acquire the land?

Gibot: That is something that always puzzles me when I think of it. It appears as though he wanted to claim the land, to own the land for the government. That is why they took that action.

Lightning: Did the Indians of long ago ever imagine or think that anything valuable would be found underground?

Gibot: You mean the elders of long ago? No, they never mentioned anything about *money* [gold or minerals] to be found underground or even petroleum to be found below the surface. I never heard my grandfather, although he was intelligent, mention anything. Even after my grandfather died, I never heard anything mentioned.

Lightning: They never told stories of the commissioner discussing these things?

Gibot: No, the commissioner never mentioned them. The only thing he mentioned was how the people would be cared for by the government as promised in the treaty.[99]

The oral traditions proffered by these three aboriginal informants differ markedly with respect to the core meaning of Treaty 8. Paulette says that it was only a treaty of peace and friendship and had nothing to do with the land. Mustus says that the Indians surrendered the surface of the land but retained the mineral rights. Gibot says that the government acquired the land but that minerals were never discussed. These contradictory versions of history cannot all be factually true at the same time. Such contradictions do not matter when oral traditions are understood as expressions of people's beliefs; but their use in judicial proceedings demands that they be understood as evidence about what actually happened, not just what some people now think may have happened. At that level, the contradictions matter a great deal and must be resolved if courts are to deliver rational verdicts.

In 1996 the Department of Indian and Northern Affairs commissioned von Gernet to carry out an extensive review of the literature on oral traditions. He found that oral traditions, while sometimes demonstrably true, are not consistently so: "When independent evidence is available to permit validation, some oral traditions about events centuries old turn out to be surprisingly accurate ... [However,] there is ... overwhelming evidence that many oral traditions do not remain consistent over time and are either inadvertently or deliberately changed to meet new needs. Aside from the fallibility of human memory and inter-individual transmission, the factor that most contributes to the changing expression of any given oral tradition is the social and political context of the 'present' in which it is narrated."[100]

The three factors cited by von Gernet are all applicable to aboriginal oral traditions. First, oral traditions are held in the human memory, and everyone's memory is fallible. "Contrary to common belief," notes von Gernet, "there is no evidence that people who depend more on orality have inherently better memories."[101] Writing was a tremendous advance precisely because it transcended the limitations of individual memory.

Second, an oral tradition is a memory of a memory and depends on person-to-person telling and retelling, which offers more opportunities for omission, distortion, and error to creep in. The noted anthropologist Bruce Trigger has commented that oral traditions "frequently reflect contemporary social and political conditions as much as they do historical reality and even in cultures where there is a strong desire to preserve their integrity, such stories unconsciously may be reworked from generation to generation."[102]

Third, context can have a crucial effect. For example, the oral traditions published in the book *The Spirit of the Alberta Indian Treaties* were collected "by a team of staff and consultants of the Treaty and Aboriginal Rights Research (T.A.R.R.) group of the Indian Association of Alberta."[103] In other words, the work was sponsored by an aboriginal political organization under the highly evocative label of "treaty and aboriginal rights." Given the close-knit character of Indian communities, it is impossible that the partisan spirit of the enterprise would not communicate itself to those who were interviewed and exercise an influence upon their memories.

None of this means that oral traditions are always unreliable. In any particular instance, an oral tradition may have much to teach us. However, it does mean that we must be cautious about believing that oral traditions convey what the Treaty 7 Elders call "the true spririt and intent" of the treaties,[104] that is, that oral traditions reveal what is concealed in written documents. Oral traditions cannot be accepted as factual if they have not undergone the critical scrutiny that both historians and courts apply to all other kinds of evidence, including archaeological remains, written records, electronic data, and photographic images.[105] Critical scrutiny implies investigating the provenance of sources, asking questions such as who generated the sources, what were their motives, how knowledgeable were they about the events they witnessed, how were the sources transmitted, are we sure we have authentic versions, and so on. It also means comparing sources against each other to establish the most likely account of what happened – what in civil litigation might be called "the balances of probabilities." This, in my view, is the proper interpretation of Chief Justice Lamer's dictum that oral traditions must be placed "on an equal footing" with other forms of evidence. Equality means treating all forms of evidence in the same way.

The use of aboriginal oral traditions in treaty litigation will be constructive as long as these procedures are observed and as long as oral traditions are treated as one of many kinds of historical evidence. However, advocates of the aboriginal orthodoxy often speak as if oral traditions were intrinsically different from other forms of evidence, containing a superior truth not amenable to empirical testing. In that perspective, equality would mean "separate but equal" and would demand the suspension of normal historical methods. If the Supreme Court's *Delgamuukw* decision is interpreted in that spirit, the treaties will be transformed from intelligible, enforceable agreements to unpredictable relationships in which everything is up for renegotiation.

CHAPTER 9

Making a Living

Throughout the vast wilderness of northern Canada, traditional aboriginal life remained viable during the nineteenth century and, in some places, even into the second half of the twentieth. Aboriginal people continued to support themselves largely by hunting, fishing, and selling furs. Where conditions permitted, they also planted gardens and raised a few horses and cattle. In hard times – to give only two examples, a period of famine in northern Alberta in the 1880s[1] and a lethal epidemic of influenza in the Mackenzie Valley in the 1920s[2] – the Hudson's Bay Company, Northwest Mounted Police, missionaries, and Indian Affairs officials distributed relief in the form of food, clothing, and medicine; but aboriginal communities in the North generally remained independent and self-supporting.

As time went on, fish and game came under increasing pressure from large-scale commercial exploitation as well as from the side-effects of mining and lumbering, and the natives turned to these new industries for employment. Frank Tough's economic history of northern Manitoba shows how, in the 1880s and 1890s, some natives found jobs in the burgeoning commercial fisheries on Lake Winnipeg and Lake Manitoba, even as others continued to pursue their traditional fishing practices. In the same period, some Manitoba Indians became lumberjacks. A Manitoba lumber tycoon said, "I have employed Scots from Glengarry, French-Canadians from Quebec, Swedes from Sweden and all kinds of lumberjacks, but the Fisher River Indians are better than any others."[3] In British

Columbia, natives also worked extensively in both lumbering and commercial fishing.

One should not glorify or whitewash what happened. The work was hard, often dangerous, and subject to seasonal layoffs and the cyclical ups and downs besetting all natural-resource industries. The point is simply that, even as industrial civilization gradually spread into the Canadian north, native people continued to support themselves by combining their traditional pursuits with new opportunities for wage labour. Their material standard of living was low by modern standards, but they were not dependent on the government for their livelihood.

In the southern part of eastern Canada, farming played a much larger role. All Indians in eastern Canada derive from either the Algonquian or Iroquoian linguistic groups, both of which had horticultural traditions to build on. As they settled on reserves, they gradually expanded their cultivation until it resembled Canadian agriculture in its systematic use of animals and farm machinery and production for commercial sale. To take one example, agriculture on the Grand River Reserve reached its peak in the 1890s. The reserve was divided into family farms of about twenty to forty hectares in size, each worked by a father and his sons. Like their white neighbours, the Six Nations farmers planted wheat, oats, and hay, and raised cattle, horses, pigs, and poultry. There was even the weekly Six Nations *Indian Magazine,* subsidized by the Farmers' Institute.[4]

While they adopted agriculture, Indians in southern Ontario still devoted much energy to the traditional pursuits of hunting and gathering. They collected maple syrup in the early spring, then hunted ducks and geese returning from the south. In late spring and early summer, they fished for pickerel, whitefish, and sturgeon, and also planted their fields. In late summer and early fall, they harvested crops and picked wild berries. Later in the fall, they collected wild rice, hunted deer, and fished for lake trout when the cooler temperatures brought the fish back to the surface. In the winter, they cut firewood, repaired equipment, cared for livestock, and ran traplines.[5]

As in the north, Indians in the south also worked for wages. Harvesting for neighbouring farmers was common. Lumberjacks were needed in most parts of Canada in the winter, and many Indian men did that kind of work. Others filled more specialized occupational niches. The Mohawks of Kahnawake became famous first as river pilots, then as high-steel workers in the construction industry.[6]

There was also a small but important number of Indians who acquired formal education and entered professional careers. Holy orders was the most open pathway because both the Catholic and Protestant churches wanted native clergymen. The Mississauga Methodist minister Peter Jones is perhaps the most famous example, but there were many others. Although the numbers were not great, there were also native lawyers, doctors, engineers, civil servants, and military officers.

Native adaptation to civilized life was more difficult on the western prairies. When the plains Indians settled on the reserves allocated to them under Treaties 4, 6, and 7, signed between 1874 and 1877, their situation was desperate. The buffalo, on which they depended so heavily, had vanished as an economic resource. Except for the Ojibwa, who had migrated from the Great Lakes region around the turn of the century, they had no agricultural traditions. The Canadian government wanted them to take up farming, but the dry climate, tough prairie sod, and short growing season made agriculture difficult in the west. Under the treaties, the government was required to supply implements, seed, and livestock for the Indians to begin farming, but the infrastructure for delivering the assistance hardly existed. In practical terms, it was obviously going to take many years before the prairie Indians could raise enough food to feed themselves.

In this emergency, the federal government resorted to the large-scale, long-term provision of rations, unheard of elsewhere in Canada. Rations became an important, indeed the most costly, component of federal expenditures on Indians in the North-West. By 1882, the annual expense had climbed to over half a million dollars, a significant amount of money by the standards of the day. In a decade when the Indian Affairs budget hovered around a million dollars a year for the entire country, relief for western Indians took up more than 40 per cent of the entire departmental budget.[7] The government, moreover, continued to distribute rations long beyond the decade of the 1880s. In the fiscal year 1902–3, there were still 5,928 Indians on the rations list, receiving 991,050 pounds of flour, 1,206,715 pounds of beef, and 135,887 pounds of bacon.[8]

Maybe there was no practical alternative to providing rations, but the practice had many unfortunate effects. People – Indians or anyone else – who are fed for free are less likely to work to feed themselves. That is particularly true when the work is hard and unfamiliar, as in the case of prairie Indians taking up agriculture for the first time. Indian agents therefore pursued a work-for-rations policy, doling out bacon and flour to those who took their turn at the plow while withholding food from those who didn't. This perhaps necessary but degrading policy cannot have increased the Indians' love of agriculture, the reserves, or the Canadian government.

There were other reasons, too, why Indian agriculture was slow to develop on the prairies. As Sarah Carter has shown in detail, government policies in the late nineteenth century were often misconceived.[9] The first policy – setting up so-called Home Farms to teach agricultural techniques – did not work well and was phased out by 1884. It was followed around 1890 by the equally misconceived "peasant policy," whereby the Indians were encouraged to cultivate one-acre plots by hand and refrain from producing surplus for sale. Although this program too was dropped after a few years, it played a role in delaying progress. Scholars have also criticized the permit policy, which required farmers on reserves to obtain the Indian agent's permission for any economic transaction, such as selling surplus hay to a neighbouring rancher. These policies, combined with the department's practice of concentrating its limited investment capital on a few outstanding reserve farmers, meant that only a small number of Indians ever succeeded in large-scale farming with modern machinery. Others had to do the best they could with hand and animal power, and many planted little more than gardens and supported themselves chiefly as agricultural labourers, on or off the reserve.[10]

For all these reasons, progress was uneven and slow, but it did occur. By the 1920s at the latest, agriculture was relatively well established on many prairie reserves, and rather than supporting whole tribes, rations had been reduced to the relief of destitute individuals.[11] I have had occasion to study the history of the four Cree reserves near Hobbema, Alberta, in some detail.[12] By 1929, the residents of these reserves

- had increased in population to about 900, from a low of about 500 in 1894;
- were cultivating over 5,000 acres in various grains;
- owned about 1,200 horses and 500 cattle;

- owned about 400 plows and other planting machinery, plus over 250 mowers and other pieces of harvesting machinery;
- were cutting about 19,000 tons of hay; and
- had trust funds totalling almost $200,000, mainly derived from the sale of land they were not cultivating.

When the Hobbema Cree settled on their reserves around 1880, they had virtually nothing. Fifty years later, they had a viable agricultural community with houses, cultivated fields, livestock, roads, schools, churches, and money in the bank. Strikingly, the level of subsidy required had become very low by the 1920s. In 1925 only $1,120.27 was spent at Hobbema on "supplies for the destitute" – the equivalent of welfare or social assistance in modern terms. The Department of Indian Affairs' total expenditures for the Hobbema Agency averaged only $11,800 a year for the period 1916–27. This means that the government of Canada, through the agency, was spending about $13.90 per resident per year to support the Hobbema reserves. These data show that the Indians at Hobbema, both as individuals and as a community, had managed to come close to self-sufficiency by the end of the 1920s.

Naturally, prairie Indians, like those elsewhere, pursued as much of their traditional economy as they could. Those located near the Rocky Mountains or other wilderness areas hunted, fished, and trapped. They also cut timber, dug coal, and worked as ranch hands and harvesters for their neighbours. Stoney chief John Snow has described his childhood in the 1930s on the Morley Reserve in the foothills of the Rockies:

Like most band members my family earned some income through hunting and trapping and some by cutting timber for rails, posts, and firewood. My father's trapline was along the foothills just north of the Morley Reserve, and he would catch lynx, silver fox, red and cross fox, coyotes, marten, mink and squirrels.

Our family's worldly goods were about average for the reserve. Most of it was the vehicles and animals we needed for our livelihood. We had two wagons, a buggy, a big wagon for hauling logs, and a sleigh. We had three teams of horses, about fifteen saddle and pack horses, and about a dozen head of cattle.

No home had electricity, central heating, running water, or indoor plumbing. Quite typically our entire family lived in a one-room cabin, with a woodburning stove for heating and cooking ... even though there was little money, we had dried meat, pemmican, wild meat, rabbits, grouse, and bannock to eat. Somehow, we always managed to get by.[13]

Again, I don't want to glamorize Indian life in this period. Just how hard it was is suggested by the statistics on Indian population. There were 102,000 status Indians in 1871 and 129,000 in 1931, representing an increase of only 26 per cent in sixty years, in spite of high birth rates. Actually, the natural increase was probably greater than suggested by these official statistics, since some Indians in the west gave up their status to take Metis scrip and since Indian women everywhere lost their status when they married Metis or white men. Still, population growth was slow, reflecting low material standards of living as well as the effect of Old World diseases (resistance to these diseases takes generations to develop).[14] In the 1940s, infant mortality among Indians was still more than three and a half times higher than among the general population.[15]

But if the Indian standard of living was low, it was not much lower than that of the hundreds of thousands of other rural Canadians who survived by performing hard and often dangerous work. Homesteaders, cowboys, hunters, trappers, fishermen, prospectors, and lumberjacks also lived in small wooden cabins far from the amenities of urban life. What was different about Indians was not so much their low material standard of living as their segmentation from the rest of society. Prior to the Second World War, almost all Indians lived in small and remote rural communities located several days' or even weeks' travel by horseback from the nearest city. They could not vote in either federal or provincial elections. They received no benefits from provincial or municipal governments, such as education for their children or relief in time of distress, because they paid no taxes to those governments. They received education, relief, and any other benefits from the Department of Indian Affairs. In the small worlds in which they lived, there were only four public authorities – the chief, the Indian agent, the missionary, and the Mountie.

This extreme segmentation limited their horizons, but it also protected them from social pathologies. Church attendance was common, even if old beliefs sometimes survived alongside Christian orthodoxy. Marriage was a universal norm, even if occasionally polygamous. As in all human communities, there was plenty of infidelity and tangled relationships, but divorce was rare. Alcohol was illegal on most reserves and in practice required some effort to obtain. Hard drugs were unknown. Crime was deterred by the cohesiveness of small, stable communities. Welfare dependency was unattractive when the only handout was a bag of flour from the Indian agent, who would make you chop wood or clear brush if you could get out of bed. This rural and segmented way of life allowed Canadian Indians to arrest their demographic decline and adapt gradually to the demands of civilization. But it could not continue unchanged in the second half of the twentieth century. At least four factors combined to undermine it.

The first was the end of isolation. With the coming of automobiles and paved roads, reserves that used to be worlds unto themselves were suddenly only a short drive from the city. Sometimes cities expanded to border on reserves or even envelop them. How could you keep alcohol and drugs off the reserve when anyone could drive to town and return in a matter of minutes or hours? Television also meant that English was everywhere on the reserve, undermining the native language.

The second factor was the mechanization of agriculture. Mechanization had led to the need for larger farms, and this collided head-on with the size of reserves. The collision perhaps came earliest on reserves that had sold surplus acreage in the period of land surrenders, but it was destined to come to all. Even the largest reserves, based on 640 acres (260 hectares) per family of five, were not big enough for everyone to be supported by agriculture when neighbouring family farms were now measured in thousands of acres. The capital-intensive nature of mechanized agriculture was also a problem. Canadian farmers are always in debt, finding it impossible to function without borrowing money for equipment, seed, and livestock; but Indians were cut off from credit because the Indian Act made both real and personal property on reserves immune from seizure by off-reserve creditors.[16] Without more land, credit, and machinery, Indian farms became uncompetitive and the most rational thing Indians could do was to lease the land to outside operators. This brought in a little income but also produced unemployment on the reserve.

Another aspect of mechanization was the decline in demand for agricultural labourers. Many Indians had never farmed intensively on their own reserves but had eked out a living as farmhands for their neighbours. Helen Buckley writes of the "collapse" of the "precarious reserve economy" in the 1950s: "Farming had failed and wage work, the only alternative, was fast following suit. The people would have to find new ways to support themselves, but, already handicapped by poor education, they were rapidly becoming more so as education and skill levels in the mainstream labour force moved steadily upwards."[17]

The third factor undermining the Indians' way of life was the gradual but inexorable decline of hunting, trapping, and fishing. Every road into the wilderness, every mine, every clearcut, every dam meant loss of habitat. The new mines, dams, and forestry projects offered some employment to northern Indians, but much less than one might have hoped. These were large developments with bureaucratic management and a unionized workforce – not a promising environment for Indians with their low levels of formal education and little experience of structured employment.

The fourth was the demographic explosion in the native population that began in the 1920s and accelerated after the Second World War. Today there are more than six hundred thousand status Indians, compared to slightly over a hundred thousand in the early part of the twentieth century. Reserves that once seemed ample became crowded with residents unable to make a living there.

The combined impact of these four factors meant that the old pattern of life on reserves could not be sustained and large numbers of Indians would have to seek new opportunities in towns and cities. In one sense, this was part of the general movement from country to city that transformed society in the twentieth century. Millions of Canadians, finding that their labour was no longer needed on mechanized farms or in the small towns where farmers used to shop, moved to Montreal, Toronto, Vancouver, and other great cities. This transition, however, was bound to be especially difficult for Indians, who generally had low formal education, often spoke limited English, and had no traditions of urban life. It was a challenge comparable to that faced by the prairie Indians when they suddenly had to take up agriculture in order to survive. Just as the transition from buffalo-hunting to agriculture was slowed by the provision of rations necessary to avoid mass starvation, the transition from rural to urban life was slowed, in an even more damaging way, by the welfare state. The extension of the welfare state to Canadian Indians just as their rural economies were breaking down has proved to be one of the greatest policy disasters in Canadian history.

THE WELFARE TRAP

In the nineteenth century and first half of the twentieth, the dole was a local matter in Canada, administered by provincial and municipal authorities who regarded Indians as outside their jurisdiction. Moreover, Indians were not covered by the Old Age Pension Act of 1927, Canada's first public pension scheme.[18] The Department of Indian Affairs provided relief to the aged and other indigents on reserves, but in a minimal way. Relief consisted of rations, not cash; work was required when it was physically possible; assistance was withheld when family members could provide; and Indian agents required bands with trust funds to use their own money to pay for rations. A senior official told a parliamentary committee in 1947: "It is the policy of the Branch to assist Indians to be self-supporting rather than issue direct relief. Because of this, the scale of relief supplied to able-bodied Indians must err on the parsimonious rather than on the generous side. Our instructions to agents state that relief is not the right of any Indian but is given at the pleasure of the Branch to prevent suffering."[19]

Indians were included in the Family Allowance Act of 1944, but initially they received benefits in kind. The first time they started to get sizable amounts of cash from a federal program was in 1951, when they were included in the Old Age Security program, which paid forty dollars a month to everyone over seventy.[20] This was a large sum of money by the standards of most Indians, and it came directly to the individual rather than through the control of the Indian agent. Meanwhile, social workers and politicians started to criticize the relief system. In response, Indian Affairs made the ration scales more generous and lessened the demand for work, leading to a rapid increase in expense. In 1958 Treasury Board authorized the replacement of rations with cash.[21] The process had to be gradual because many Indians lived in remote areas where no cheque-cashing facilities were available; even seven years afterwards, more than 40 per cent of Indian relief was still in the form of rations.[22]

In 1964 the federal government adopted the system that still prevails. The provinces would be responsible for providing welfare to all aboriginal people off reserve, although some of the money would come from the federal government through the Canada Assistance Plan (replaced by the Canada Health and Social Transfer in 1995). The federal government would take complete financial responsibility for welfare payments on reserve but, rather than impose a national standard, would match the level of benefits and eligibility rules prevailing in the provinces where the reserves were located. The main change since 1964, other than the vastly increased expense of operating the program, is that on-reserve welfare has been brought under the rubric of aboriginal self-government, so that employees reporting to band councils distribute the money.

The result of these changes has been a staggering level of welfare dependency. By the time the Canada Assistance Plan was passed in 1966, about 36 per cent of reserve residents were receiving welfare assistance each year. That figure continued to grow, reaching 42 per cent by 1992, compared with a national utilization rate of less than 10 per cent for other Canadians in the same year.[23] The on-reserve rate of welfare dependence was reported to be 45 per cent in 1998, and Indian Affairs has estimated that it might rise to 57 per cent by 2010.[24] These figures are for recipients aged fifteen and older; if children were included, the percentage of reserve residents relying on welfare would be even greater, particularly given the high Indian birth rate.[25]

There is, to be sure, considerable regional variation. On-reserve welfare utilization is in the 20–30 per cent range in Ontario and Quebec, 40–50 per cent in British Columbia, and 60–80 per cent in the Prairie provinces and Atlantic Canada.[26] There are many western and northern reserves where the figure is over 80 per cent, which means that virtually everyone is on welfare except for the chief and council, a few band employees, and seniors living on Old Age Security. Even more disturbing, on-reserve welfare dependency is disconnected from the general economy. It has continued to rise for three decades whether the Canadian economy was in prosperity or recession. Moreover, "a 1991 DIAND [Department of Indian Affairs and Northern Development] analysis found no statistically significant relationship between economic development spending and Aboriginal social assistance expenditures."[27] Carleton University scholars Allan Moscovitch and Andrew Webster (who, incidentally, are proponents of the welfare state) conclude that on-reserve welfare has become a way of life, passed on from generation to generation, and often rationalized by recipients as a treaty right.[28]

None of this is any secret among aboriginal people themselves. The Manitoba Metis playwright Ian Ross won the Governor General's Award in 1997 for *fareWel*, a play about welfare dependency on Indian reserves. In one scene, two characters discuss the virtues of being an Indian. One says, "You won't go bald-headed ... And we're teachers ... We're going to teach the white people again how to live ... Lots more white people are gonna be poor. And they're gonna be on welfare. And because we already know how to live on welfare, we're gonna teach them how to live again."[29] Ross's play reportedly held native audiences spellbound when it toured northern Manitoba in 1998.

The welfare dependency of off-reserve aboriginals is not as bad. In 1991, when the figure for on-reserve Indians was 41.5 per cent, it was only 24.8 per cent for off-reserve Indians, in the same range as the 22.1 per cent reported for Metis and 23.5 per cent for Inuit.[30] But even if the situation is better for aboriginal people living off reserve, it is still shocking; their welfare-utilization figures are between two and half and three times higher than those for other Canadians.

I emphasize statistics on welfare utilization because they seem the most reliable means for measuring the overall engagement of aboriginal people with the productive economy. Unemployment rates are not very meaningful for aboriginal people because so many of them are not in the labour force at all. Average income is also a problematic indicator for two reasons: Indians receive a lot of in-kind income that does not get factored into reported averages; and income rises with age and the aboriginal population is much younger than the Canadian average. Welfare-utilization rates are far from perfect as data, having nothing to say about those aboriginal people who are doing well, but at least they identify the proportion of those who are outside the productive economy.

Why aboriginal people, and on-reserve Indians in particular, are so much more likely than other Canadians to turn welfare into a way of life is a complicated question. Racism, discrimination, cultural differences, and poor formal education may play a part; yet other ethnic groups with similar problems have not become so tightly ensnared in the welfare trap. We have to consider the cornucopia of benefits from the welfare state that flow only to Indians, and especially to Indians living on reserves.

All Canadians receive physicians' and hospital services through Medicare, but status Indians get a great deal more, including unlimited free prescriptions, eyeglasses, prosthetic appliances, physiotherapy, and ambulance trips. For those on reserves, band councils build homes. The housing may be of poor quality and in short supply, but it is virtually free to those who obtain it. All education through high school is paid for by the federal government rather than by property or other taxes, and many reserves offer financial assistance to band members who attend college and university. Government transfers create public-sector employment on every reserve, from the chief and council down through administrative, clerical, and maintenance staff. Income earned on the reserve is untaxed, so those with the better jobs may have a considerable cash flow to help support others in their extended families.

Welfare in the narrow sense is only part of a much larger stream of taxpayer-funded benefits directed to Indians, particularly those living on reserves. If the band offers a place to live, if the government pays for every bit of health care, if some government jobs are available and there is a tradition of sharing the benefits with family members, and if all of this is tax-free, is it surprising that so many people stay on the reserves even if no real jobs are available there? Those who take minimum-wage, entry-level jobs in town would lose their welfare cheque, would have to pay taxes and rent, and would be cut off from the informal distribution network on the reserve. They would almost certainly be worse off than if they had stayed at home.

The welfare trap, of course, works not just against Indians. Anyone who receives money without working faces the equivalent of a high marginal tax rate for giving up welfare and trying to earn a living in the labour market. Given all the expense of time and effort in holding a job, the material standard of living may be only slightly higher. But the situation is aggravated for on-reserve Indians, particularly if they have to go off the reserve to obtain employment. They face a set of perverse incentives unique in Canadian society (although those that destroyed the Atlantic cod fishery and trapped so many Newfoundlanders may be almost as bad). Unless they have high levels of education, special skills, or good connections, most Indians will be financially better off if they draw welfare on the reserve than if they enter the labour market at the bottom and try to work their way up the ladder.

THREE DECADES, TWO REPORTS

In October 1966, after two and a half years of research, the Hawthorn research team presented its report, *A Survey of the Contemporary Indians of Canada,* to the minister of Indian affairs and northern development. The director of the group was Harry Hawthorn, a prominent anthropologist at the University of British Columbia, known as an authority on Indians. He had put together a team of scholars from anthropology, sociology, economics, political science, law, and education. There were no native people among them. The research group took an academic approach in which Indians were the subjects of study. They carried out research and did not hold public consultations.

The Hawthorn report was very much a product of its time. The movement for the integration of Negroes, as they were then called, was reaching its peak in the United States, and President Lyndon Johnson had announced the "war on poverty" in 1964. Not surprisingly, the Hawthorn group framed its recommendations for Indian policy "essentially as one special part of the government's war on poverty."[31] It appeared, however, to reject the American notion of integration, or at least of assimilation, when it wrote that "the Indian should [not] be required to assimilate, neither in order to receive what he now needs nor at any future time."[32] But those words were effectively contradicted by recommendations to the effect that as many Indians as possible should be encouraged to leave their reserves and find jobs in the wider economy.

Specifically, Hawthorn recommended spending money on housing and welfare on reserves to obtain a minimum standard of living, but only that. The major expenditures should come in areas like education, job training and counselling, and off-reserve housing: "What is suggested is that, in so far as the economic development of Indians lies primarily in wage and salaried employment, and that for most Indians such employment lies beyond commuting distance of their reserves, a large and increasing part of an expanded Indian Affairs Branch budget should be used to support Indians who wish to leave their reserves."[33]

Northern reserves still dependent on hunting, fishing, and trapping might have to be subsidized for the sake of residents who could never adjust to a different life,[34] but not much money should be poured into the promotion of farming on southern reserves because "in most cases the same amount of investment and expenditure in money, time and effort for special training by expert personnel, could better be used for equipping Indians to engage in urban-industrial types of employment rather than farming."[35] In the same vein, Hawthorn urged that Indians should receive health, education, and welfare services from provincial authorities. Not only would the quality of the services be better than those previously provided by federal authorities, but a provincial system of benefit delivery would promote the integration of Indians into Canadian society.

This approach may have been integrationism, but it was not based on a classical liberal philosophy of small government. Hawthorn called for an expensive assortment of coordinated policy initiatives: "All told, therefore, any program that is seriously designed to raise the Indian population to a level of competitive equality with Whites will have to be a truly massive undertaking by comparison with the limited bits-and-pieces program that has been followed hitherto ... We must expect that it will cost thousands of dollars per capita, and hundred of millions per annum in the aggregate, to provide Indians with the facilities and services needed to bring them up to White standards."[36] In an anticipation of affirmative action, Hawthorn coined the slogan "citizens plus,"[37] emphasizing special expenditures on Indians to overcome decades of neglect.

The spending of massive amounts of money was the only part of Hawthorn's vision that was ever really implemented. The budget of the Indian Affairs Branch at the time of the report was about $60 million, with another $20 million being spent by Indian Health Services, the two together amounting to a little over 1 per cent of the federal programs budget.[38] Other departments spent little or nothing on Indians in that era. Three decades later, at the end of the twentieth century, expenditures on Indians – mostly, but by no means entirely through Indian Affairs – amounted to $6.3 billion, about 6 per cent of the federal programs budget.[39] Over those years, the population of status Indians slightly more than doubled. Thus, in a period of time in which the welfare state came to maturity and federal spending increased more rapidly than at any time in history, Indians not only shared in the overall growth but almost tripled their relative share on a per capita basis.

In other respects, things did not go according to the Hawthorn plan. Only a few years after his report was submitted, reaction to the federal government's 1969 White Paper touched off a new era in native politics, the master themes of which were aboriginal rights, land claims, and self-government rather than the war on poverty and "citizens plus." Indian leaders continued to demand an improved standard of living but rejected any transfer to provincial jurisdiction and emphasized their separateness from, rather than their integration into, the larger society. Money for housing, education, welfare, and economic development poured onto reserves, making it more attractive for the residents to stay. In spite of such enormous expenditures, the proportion of status Indians living off reserve has now reached 42 per cent; one can only speculate what it might have been if the relative parsimony of the pre-Hawthorn era had continued.

Thirty years after the Hawthorn report came the RCAP *Report,* which differed from the former in many ways. The royal commission was appointed by the prime minister, whereas Hawthorn simply executed a contract from the minister of citizenship and immigration. The RCAP study took much longer, engaged far more people, and cost much more money. More importantly, native people had a predominant role within it. They were a majority on the seven-member commission and made up a large portion of the staff and researchers. There were also elaborate consultations in which native organizations and individuals could make presentations. Academic researchers were also involved, but they did not dominate as they had in the Hawthorn study.

These differences in structure and process no doubt influenced the RCAP recommendations, but one must also take the *Zeitgeist* into account. In the mid-1960s, integration and the war on poverty were major enthusiasms, whereas the mid-1990s were characterized by debates over collective identity and group rights. The Hawthorn and RCAP reports were similar in that each distilled the conventional wisdom of its era into a remedy for the ills afflicting aboriginal people. They also shared a central irony, of which neither seemed aware. While both passionately indicted the Canadian government for decades of policy failure in dealing with aboriginal people, both called upon that same government to undertake a new, wide-ranging, expensive program of policy initiatives to undo the damage. Neither seemed to consider the possibility that government was the problem, not the solution.

Hawthorn spoke rather vaguely of spending "hundreds of millions [of dollars] per annum in the aggregate." In contrast, the RCAP appeared to be more precise in calling for "an investment of up to $2 billion per year for 20 years [above present expenditures]."[40] In the earlier years, this money would mainly fund improvements to human services designed to make aboriginal people more capable of being productive and self-supporting. In the later years, it would be more a matter of transferring land, natural resources, and investment capital so that aboriginal people could develop their own economies.

Building "aboriginal economies" is the RCAP's leading idea, in sharp contrast to Hawthorn's emphasis upon encouraging Indian participation in the general economy. In that respect, the RCAP's economic proposals are of one piece with its definition of aboriginal peoples as nations and its promotion of the inherent right of aboriginal self-government: "The desire of Aboriginal peoples to be self-governing political entities can be fully realized only with a transformation in their capacity to provide for themselves. A nation does not have to be wealthy to be self-determining. But it needs to be able to provide for most of its needs, however these are defined, from its own sources of income and wealth."[41]

At the extreme, this economic nationalism leads the RCAP to the discredited idea of "import substitution" – that is, producing goods rather than importing them. It is presumed that people in aboriginal communities who practise import substitution should reduce the "economic leakage" that occurs when they deal with external vendors.[42] This profoundly regressive notion, which repudiates the economic principles of division of labour and comparative advantage, has caused incalculable damage to Third World countries, such as India, that have tried to implement it. Fortunately, however, most of the RCAP's economic development strategy is not so obviously flawed. Its report summarizes the key components as "measures to restore control, secure resources, master professional and technical skills, develop enterprises, broker employment, and relate income supplements to productive activity."[43] We should look at these components in some detail:

- *Restoring control and securing resources* means transferring property to aboriginal people. "The single most important factor in the medium term will be the restoration to Aboriginal people of fair shares in the lands and resources in this country."[44] This implies (1) negotiation of land claims in areas of Canada where treaties were never signed; (2) "renovation" of existing treaties; (3) settlement of specific claims involving land surrenders and alleged non-fulfilment of treaty provisions; and (4) creation of a Metis land base. The net result would be that aboriginal people would own a considerable portion of the Canadian land mass with its natural resources, and would also have accumulated billions of dollars of investment capital through the monetary side of settling claims.

- *Developing enterprises* means that aboriginal people would enter the business world as collective owners and managers of their treasure trove of natural resources. They would sign partnership agreements with corporations to explore for oil and gas, exploit mineral deposits, harvest forests, and open hotels, golf courses, and shopping malls. Much of this would take place through "community-owned enterprises," although there would also be room for individual entrepreneurship.[45]

- *Mastering professional and technical skills* and *brokering employment* are closer to Hawthorn's approach of encouraging aboriginal participation in the labour market, but there is still a difference. The aboriginally owned and managed sector envisioned by the RCAP would create employment opportunities within itself. Aboriginal people might seek training and experience in the outside world, but they would have a reasonable hope of eventually working in the native-owned sector. In this way, the RCAP avoids the integrationism that pervaded the Hawthorn report.

- *Relating income supplements to productive activity* means welfare reform. The basic idea is to take the money now spent on welfare and give it to aboriginal communities free of legal restrictions. Aboriginal governments could decide to tie payments to work effort or training programs rather than simply dole out support payments as entitlements. The intent is to provide new resources for aboriginal development projects while breaking the cycle of welfare dependency.[46]

The RCAP's economic vision has two particularly attractive features. First, it is unapologetically pro-capitalist. It does not call for a socialist revolution, or for expropriation without compensation, or for the creation of state monopolies. It praises ownership and entrepreneurship and accepts that making profits has social utility. Also, except for its brief flirtation with import substitution, it avoids interventions that most economists condemn, such as production quotas, price controls, protectionism, and regulated markets. The underlying premise is that aboriginal people can compete effectively in the market, both individually and collectively, if they own and control capital and resources. There are problems with this assumption, which I discuss below; but at least it is compatible with a market economy and is thus capable of being improved.

The second attractive feature is that the RCAP is clear about the harmful effects of welfare dependency: "While welfare provides a basic income, it does not even provide a partial solution to the economic problems facing communities."[47] Perhaps once band administrations feel they are distributing their own money, they might revert to the tough-minded attitude displayed by some chiefs when cash welfare first came to reserves in the 1960s. The Hawthorn study team reported one incident in southern Ontario: "The first winter when _____ was chief, they also started a work program under the welfare scheme. They paid able-bodied welfare recipients only if the latter went out and cut four cords of pulp wood ... On the winter's operation the band came out two or three hundred dollars to the good! This is, of course, highly illegal, and the council and welfare administrator got themselves bawled out for doing this."[48]

There would be major difficulties implementing tough-minded welfare policies on the reserves unless Canada simultaneously reformed its own welfare policies. Stringent aboriginal workfare schemes would drive residents off reserve and onto welfare rolls in nearby towns, and there would no doubt be some truly pitiable cases among them. Also, given the factionalism of reserve politics, welfare payments might often be withheld for political purposes, again promoting a flow of refugees from reserves. Nonetheless, it is an intriguing thought that aboriginal communities might pick up the torch of welfare reform from the Conservative premiers of Alberta and Ontario, Ralph Klein and Mike Harris.

In spite of these attractive features, however, the RCAP's economic vision is unlikely to succeed in practice. One reason for this, though not the most fundamental, is that the extra two billion dollars a year of aboriginal spending will not be forthcoming. Existing expenditures for native programs will probably continue to escape cuts, as they have in the past, but there are not likely to be major enhancements. But even if much more money were available, the RCAP's stated goal of making aboriginal people self-supporting would remain elusive for other reasons.

One problem is the RCAP's focus on land and natural resources. Given the remote location of Indian and Metis communities, most RCAP-style "aboriginal economies" would depend on some combination of mining, forestry, fishing, agriculture, and perhaps tourism. Natural-resource industries are notoriously cyclical; there is, moreover, a long-term tendency of commodity prices to fall in world markets, which is one reason why the currencies of commodity-exporting countries such as Canada, Australia, and New Zealand have been declining in value. Of course, these industries remain essential to human welfare, and producers continue to make profits over the course of the business cycle; but they do so only by the application of ever more sophisticated technological and organizational techniques. Ownership of resources, in and of itself, is of diminishing importance.

The RCAP's emphasis on ownership of land and resources reflects deeper fallacies in the new aboriginal orthodoxy – its twin beliefs that the land produces wealth and that aboriginal people were deprived of wealth because colonial settlers took their land. In fact, only human ingenuity and effort produce wealth. The European newcomers could generate greater wealth from the land because, through their participation in world civilization, they possessed more advanced techniques of production and organization. Ownership of resources may produce some royalty flow, which allows the recipients to purchase consumer goods as long as the flow lasts; but unless the rentiers acquire the skills and attitudes – the human capital – needed in a modern economy, the royalties will quickly be dissipated.

The hydrocarbon-rich Morley and Hobbema reserves of Alberta furnish outstanding examples of this truth. These reserves have earned huge royalties, and some residents have become well off; but large majorities on the reserves are still dependent on welfare and suffer from all the attendant social pathologies. Cash flow is not the same as prosperity. Royalties bought new houses and pick-up trucks for the residents, but few ever became self-supporting wage-earners.

Another problem is the very uneven distribution of land and resources among aboriginal communities. Remember that there are 625 different First Nations plus Metis villages. Under the RCAP land-and-resources scenario, some of these communities would control rich mines, valuable forests, or productive fisheries, but most would own nothing of exceptional value. Even if the lucky communities were to manage their resources well, involve their people in steady work, and become self-supporting, what about the others? The RCAP wants the hundreds of aboriginal communities to consolidate themselves into sixty to eighty aboriginal nations, but there is no evidence that this is happening. Wealthy bands in the past have not often shared their wealth with others, and it is hard to believe they will in the future.

Still another problem stems from the small size of aboriginal communities. Assume that a Chipewyan band of two thousand members in northern Saskatchewan gets a large amount of land through settling a specific claim, plus monetary compensation of $50 million. Lucrative deposits of diamonds are discovered on the new land, which the band is willing to exploit in conjunction with a mining company. Because the band has its own money, it can be an active investor and partner. Development of the mine will create well-paid jobs – managers, geologists, engineers, computer specialists, accountants, airplane pilots, heavy-equipment operators, and so on. How many of those jobs will go to band members? Probably not very many, because two thousand people is a small pool from which to draw all these specialists. As owners of the resource, the band's leaders will want to develop it profitably in the interest of the band; but to do so, they will have to rely on employees recruited elsewhere. It would be the same situation if the mine were developed near a town of two thousand white people.

Then there is the problem of property rights. Aboriginal lands and resources would be collectively owned by communities acting through their institutions of self-government. Direct involvement of elected politicians in aboriginal business enterprises would likely be corrupt and inefficient, just as it is in the outside world. A better solution would be to set up development corporations at some distance from aboriginal politicians. These could certainly work up to a point – there are many moderately successful examples already in existence – but they would be hampered by the collective nature of aboriginal property rights. Indians cannot sell or mortgage inalienable aboriginal land, and they could not sell a development corporation to outside interests, even if that would be the rational course of action (ordinary corporations do such things all the time in the interests of their shareholders).

The inflexibility of aboriginal property rights means that aboriginal development corporations would be handicapped in the long run as competitors in the market. Many would probably require continuing subsidies from their band governments, land-claim revenues, or federal programs, just as non-aboriginal corporations would if they were not free to sell, mortgage, and reorganize their assets. Can self-sufficiency be built upon subsidized business entities?

In the last analysis, the RCAP's economic vision is a new version of regional economic development, with the depressed "region" consisting of the widely dispersed aboriginal archipelago rather than a specific region of the country. There are, to be sure, some factors in the aboriginal situation that differentiate it from Canada's other experiments in regional development – the claim to nationhood, the emphasis on self-government, the transfer of resources not only in money but also in land – but in an economic sense the picture is largely the same. The RCAP proposes to bring about prosperity by transferring wealth, buttressed by a wide range of government programs and services, to areas where this wealth would not flow under conventional economic incentives. Sadly, it will not work any better for aboriginal communities than it has for Atlantic Canada.

I will not rehearse the familiar litany of failures – bankrupt corporations, unpaid debts, rusting factories. Let me point only to the most perverse result: regional economic development tends to increase unemployment in the receiving areas. The reasoning behind this far from obvious conclusion is elegantly explained by economist Fred McMahon in his prize-winning book *Looking the Gift Horse in the Mouth:*

In an independent nation, an inflow of foreign funds leads to a currency appreciation which raises domestic wages and prices relative to foreign wages and prices. The implications for Atlantic Canada are that an increase in regional subsidies would result in an increase in regional wages relative to the Canadian average. This in turn would lead either to an increase in regional prices relative to the rest of Canada or – if Atlantic Canada's integration into the national economy blocked local suppliers from raising prices faster than elsewhere in the nation – to an increasing unemployment gap with the rest of the nation ... In fact, regional wages rise at exactly the predicted rate. Regional prices continue to rise at about the average Canadian rate, and thus, as expected, the unemployment gap between the region and the rest of Canada increased.[49]

My prediction, then, is that implementation of the RCAP's economic vision would actually increase unemployment, welfare dependency, and human misery in aboriginal communities. Of course, with that much money sloshing around, some people would do very well. Fortunes would be made by an aboriginal entrepreneurial elite, just as fortunes were made in Russia when well-placed people took over management of resources previously controlled by the Soviet state. At a lower level, the new aboriginal professional class of lawyers, administrators, consultants, teachers, and social workers would find employment managing the government programs that would supposedly facilitate economic development, and some skilled workers would find steady, well-paid jobs in aboriginal enterprises. But more and more ordinary aboriginal people would be spending less and less time at work.

There is already substantial evidence that this scenario is in the process of coming true:

- While spending on aboriginal people grew almost a hundredfold in nominal terms from the 1950s to the 1990s, welfare dependency grew with it, is now higher than ever, and still appears to be increasing.
- Many land claims, both comprehensive and specific, have been settled, so that native people now own more land and resources.
- Beginning around 1980, there was a progressive transfer of power to band governments, so that today over 80 per cent of spending decisions are taken at that level.
- The "inherent right of aboriginal self-government" may not have been entrenched in the constitution, but it is close to a working reality on the ground.

Yet even though Indians are controlling more land, spending more money, and implementing aboriginal self-government, the situation has gotten worse rather than better, as the RCAP itself noted: "In fact, disparities between Aboriginal and other Canadians are increasing, and they will likely continue to do so unless policies are radically altered. Between 1981 and 1991, the unemployment and income gaps widened."[50]

Similar trends are visible in Australia. Since the mid-1970s, spending on Aboriginal programs has multiplied manyfold, while huge amounts of land have been transferred. Aborginals, 2 per cent of the population, now own half of the Northern Territory and 14 per cent of the whole continent.[51] Much of this land is desert or arid plain, but that does not mean it is without value, for Australia is one of the world's great storehouses of minerals. Yet in this period of time the average material standard of living for Aboriginals seems to have improved hardly at all. One study found that between 1979 and 1991 life expectancy for Aboriginal men in the Northern Territory rose a little, but not as much as for other Australian men, while the life expectancy of Aboriginal women actually fell.[52] In 1999 a review of Aboriginal land rights in the Northern Territory found "that the dilemma with the Land Rights Act is that it has delivered land to Aboriginal People but land is an economic *cul de sac*. The Land Rights Act has been extraordinarily successsful in delivering huge tracts of land to Aboriginals, but in terms of economic advancement that has taken them off in the wrong direction."[53]

New Zealand has also embarked in recent decades upon a broadly similar course of enhanced government spending on Maori programs combined with settlement of land claims. Yet in 1993 the acclaimed Maori writer Alan Duff, probably known to many Canadians through the film version of his novel *Once Were Warriors,* published a best-selling indictment of his own people.[54] The details sound familiar – loss of the work ethic, widespread welfare dependency, half of Maori children living in single-parent families, crime rate six times higher than the New Zealand average, rampant alcoholism and drug addiction. Duff's view is that the Maori need to cultivate more broadly those virtues that have given many of their race outstanding careers in New Zealand's national game of rugby: hard work, perseverance, and self-discipline. The book is not a quantitative analysis, but its qualitative portrait suggests that the average Maori condition is getting worse in spite of, or perhaps because of, all the land-claims settlements and remedial programs.

But things have not gotten worse for everyone. This is also the time in world history when the aboriginal entrepreneurial elite and professional class have started to come into their own. There is an evident explosion of aboriginal entrepreneurship in Canada, with an estimated six thousand aboriginal-owned businesses in 1989 and more than twenty thousand in 1998.[55] Most are small, but some are quite large, including a trust company, an airline, lumber mills, shopping malls, hotels, golf courses, and casinos. This rapid expansion of aboriginal entrepreneurship should receive closer scrutiny than it has thus far from business journalists. As a political scientist, I lack the knowledge of accounting, economics, and business practices to do this kind of research properly, but I can certainly see signs that further investigation is warranted.

Take one example, the St Eugene Mission Resort now being built on the St Mary's Reserve near Cranbrook, British Columbia. The plan is to convert an old residential school into an international resort by remodelling the building, adding some new accommodations, and building a golf course, tennis courts, and other recreational facilities. Is this an ambitious, imaginative, profit-making private-sector venture, as described in the promotional literature, or is it a regional-economic-development project that will lose bundles of money and eventually have to be shut down? Would it ever have been launched except to create the platform from which the promoters have applied for a casino licence from the provincial government?

The project's financial structure is not reassuring.[56] According to projections in early 1998, the total cost will be $24 million, of which $9.1 million will consist of grants or soft loans from federal and provincial agencies:

Aboriginal Business Canada	$1.0 M	grant
Indian and Northern Affairs	.5	grant
Human Resources Development	.4	grant
Columbia Basin Trust	3.5	grant
Western Economic Diversification	3.7	loan

Although they are apparently putting in no cash, the Indians are receiving equity credit of $2.2 million for land and buildings and $1.3 million for "work completed to date," whatever that means. Coast Hotels and Resorts has contributed $1.5 million and has also guaranteed $2 million of a $9.5 million loan from the Royal Bank of Canada (RBC). This firm also has a twenty-year management contract for the completed project that will, no doubt, allow it to recoup its investment. The government of British Columbia has guaranteed another $6 million of the RBC loan, leaving Canada's largest bank, which has been trumpeting its commitment to aboriginal enterprise, with an exposure of only $1.5 million in this project. Does the Royal Bank know something that taxpayers should also know?

To put it another way, in this $24 million project, only $1.5 million of private money has been directly invested, plus $3.5 million in unguaranteed or privately guaranteed loans. The rest of the investment – $19 million – consists of grants, soft loans, publicly guaranteed loans, and values assigned to land, buildings, and improvements – items that have no true market value because, being located on an Indian reserve, they cannot be sold. If this were a truly profitable project, would so much public money be required to get it off the ground?

Aboriginal enterprises, at least the larger ones, are generally started with some combination of federal and provincial grants, guaranteed loans, proceeds of land-claims settlements, and resource revenues. Money from such sources is often used to subsidize losses that may go on for years. As an example, "Bill Namagoose, executive director of the Grand Council of the Crees, estimates [James Bay] Cree ventures over the years have lost about $32 million."[57] Ownership is held by the band government, which usually does not require the enterprise to return a profit. Since there are no shares to be publicly traded, the stock market cannot evaluate the worth of the enterprise and send signals to the public about how well it is managed. Aboriginal enterprises seldom compete directly in the broader marketplace; much of their business comes from untendered contracts with governments or corporations operating in a highly regulated environment. For example, the Tsuu T'ina Nation's Wolf's Flat Ordinance Disposal Corporation has had contracts in several countries, but it is sustained by a $35-million contract with the Department of National Defence to clear a firing range on land leased from the Tsuu T'ina Reserve.[58]

In some ways, aboriginal enterprise bears a striking resemblance to the "crony capitalism" that flourishes in countries where politicians control resources and allocate business opportunities to their relatives, friends, and supporters. Crony capitalism can certainly make an entrepreneurial elite very well off. And, as aboriginal participation rates in higher education approach those of other Canadians, the aboriginal professional class will grow and flourish. Taken together, these trends point to an internal polarization of the aboriginal population, in which the emergence of well-to-do entrepreneurial and professional minorities has been accompanied by increasing unemployment and welfare dependency of the majority.

Thomas Sowell found the same pattern of polarization in his worldwide study of preferential policies: "Because preferential benefits tend to be concentrated on more lucrative or prestigious things, they are often within striking distance only for the fortunate few who have already advanced well beyond most other members of the preferred group ... The less fortunate members of designated beneficiary groups have often not only failed to share proportionately in benefits but have actually retrogressed during the era of preferential policies."[59] In this instance, as in many others, the law of unintended consequences produces a paradoxical outcome. While trying to help an entire group, we end up helping only a fraction – the least needy members of the group – while actually harming the life chances of the majority.

CHAPTER 10

This Octagon Is a Stop Sign

Figure 10-1 shows the themes of the preceding chapters arrayed as the corners of an octagon – a geometrical representation of the aboriginal orthodoxy.

Each line between two points represents the connection between two leading ideas of the prevailing orthodoxy. I have numbered the eight lines making up the perimeter of the octagon as well as six interior lines connecting opposed points on the perimeter. One could draw fourteen more of these interior lines, but that would make an already complicated figure impossible to decipher. There is enough in the figure as it stands to illustrate how the ideas of the aboriginal orthodoxy are interconnected and how, through mutual reinforcement, they make up a logically consistent system of thought.

Let me identify the connections represented by the fourteen lines shown in Figure 10-1:

1. *Aboriginality–Civilization.* Because all cultures are functionally equivalent ways of meeting human needs, and because there is no hierarchical scale of civilization, being first does not mean being primitive.

2. *Civilization–Sovereignty.* Because aboriginal cultures were on the same level as European civilization, aboriginal peoples possessed sovereignty in the full sense of a governmental organization exercising jurisdiction over a fixed territory.

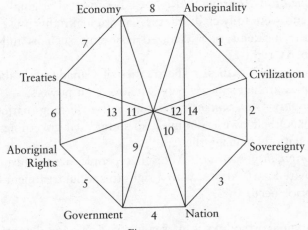

Figure 10-1
The Aboriginal Octagon

3. *Sovereignty–Nation.* Just as nations are sovereign in the context of modern European civilization, so the sovereign entities of aboriginal cultures are nations.

4. *Nation–Government.* Because nations by definition have a right to govern themselves, aboriginal nations must control their own destiny under their "inherent right of self-government."

5. *Government–Aboriginal Rights.* The inherent right of self-government is one of many aboriginal rights, along with aboriginal title to the land.

6. *Aboriginal Rights–Treaties.* Treaties are the means by which aboriginal rights, including self-government and aboriginal title, are recognized and entrenched in the constitution.

7. *Treaties–Economy.* Treaties are the means by which aboriginal peoples secure the resources necessary to create and direct their own economies.

8. *Economy–Aboriginality.* Being first in the Americas entitles aboriginal peoples to receive from later arrivals the same standard of living that the newcomers are able to provide for themselves.

9. *Aboriginality–Government.* The inherent right of self-government exists in virtue of first arrival.

10. *Economy–Nation.* Nations have their own economies. Just as there is a Canadian economy, so there is a Tsuu T'ina or Stoney economy.

11. *Civilization–Aboriginal Rights*. Because aboriginal peoples are and were fully civilized, their aboriginal rights must contain all the incidents of a civilized economy, such as full-fledged property rights.
12. *Sovereignty–Treaties*. The treaties of Canada with aboriginal peoples are agreements between sovereign powers.
13. *Economy–Government*. Just as self-governing nation-states manage their own economies, so should self-governing aboriginal nations manage theirs.
14. *Aboriginality–Nation*. Aboriginal peoples are not just nations, they are First Nations, with a right to special treatment because of prior occupancy.

The aboriginal orthodoxy is internally consistent, but the logical consistency of an ideology is not the same as its utility in the real world of politics and economics. Three grave problems associated with the aboriginal octagon make it a stop sign for human progress, just as the octagons on our highways are stop signs for vehicular traffic.

First, the aboriginal orthodoxy is at variance with liberal democracy because it makes race the constitutive factor of the political order. It would establish aboriginal nations as privileged political communities with membership defined by race and passed on through descent. It would redefine Canada as an association of racial communities rather than a polity whose members are individual human beings. The "third order" of aboriginal government would not mesh with the existing federal and provincial levels because aboriginal government would be based on a closed racial principle, whereas Canada's other governments are based on open individual and territorial principles. Because the aboriginal element is small relative to Canada's population, the third order of aboriginal self-government might not destroy the country, but it would be a continuous irritant. Its very existence would also be a standing invitation to other racial or ethnic communities to demand similar corporate status.

The Canadian philosopher James Tully has celebrated this prospect in his book *Strange Multiplicity*, but I find it troubling.[1] Through painful trial and error, the Western world has developed a form of polity – liberal democracy – which, though patently imperfect, confers upon ordinary people a degree of freedom, respect, and security of expectations unmatched in any other political system.

Do we really want to jeopardize this accomplishment by embarking upon the troubled waters of racial and ethnic politics?

The second problem is that the aboriginal orthodoxy wrongly encourages aboriginal people to see others – so-called Eurocanadians – as having caused their misfortune and, therefore, as holding the key to their improvement. Most aboriginal advocates define "doing better" as succeeding not by their own efforts, but by getting something from the oppressors. They rationalize the attainment of land and natural resources, bigger budgetary appropriations, and financial compensation for residential schools as entitlements – things that Canada owes aboriginal people because they were here first. But obsession with political campaigns to repair injustice, even if the injustices are real, does not produce independence and prosperity.

What Thomas Sowell has written about the United States is equally true of Canada, that "emphasis on promoting economic advancement has produced far more progress than attempts to redress past wrongs, even when those historic wrongs have been obvious, massive, and indisputable."[2] Japanese-Canadians, who experienced relocation and confiscation of property during the Second World War, are today one of the most prosperous ethnic groups in Canada. So are Jewish Canadians, who had to overcome a long history of racial discrimination and exclusion.[3] In a functioning liberal democracy, prosperity, independence, and respect are like an arch built one brick at a time. The bricks are the decisions people make as they pursue their goals of work, family, and community service. Individual effort mortars them into place.

The third problem is that the aboriginal orthodoxy encourages aboriginal people to withdraw into themselves, into their own "First Nations," under their own "self-governments," on their own "traditional lands," within their own "aboriginal economies." Yet this is the wrong direction if the goal is widespread individual independence and prosperity for aboriginal people. Under the policy of withdrawal, the political and professional elites will do well for themselves as they manage the aboriginal enclaves, but the majority will be worse off than ever. In order to become self-supporting and get beyond the social pathologies that are ruining their communities, aboriginal people need to acquire the skills and attitudes that bring success in a liberal society, political democracy, and market economy. Call it assimilation, call it integration, call it adaptation, call it whatever you want: it has to happen.

What, then, can be done? Let me be clear that I do not propose a magic-wand solution of abolishing the Department of Indian Affairs, dissolving all the reserves, and declaring Indians to be Canadian citizens pure and simple. There are far too many legal and political obstacles for this to happen. Rather, we must acknowledge where history has brought us and think about making small steps in the right direction.

A crucial fact is that a substantial majority of aboriginal people are already on their way towards integration into Canadian society. Forty-two per cent of the 610,000 status Indians counted in the 1996 census lived off reserve, as did almost all of the 210,000 Metis and non-status Indians. The most important consideration that we can give those already outside the reserve system is to avoid setting up obstacles to their gradual integration into the larger society, which is of necessity a slow process. Two policies would be particularly damaging – the first, to create non-territorial forms of self-government for Metis and off-reserve Indians, and the second, to establish a land base for the Metis and in other ways to begin treating them like Indians, as was implied in the fortunately defeated Charlottetown Accord. *Primum non nocere* –·"first do no harm." Let social processes proceed without creating new political entities and administrative systems to reinforce the separateness of those who are already well on the way to integration.

Also, we must be aware that dedicating additional money to reserves tends to keep people there, or even bring them back. With such a large population now off the reserves but having the right to return if they wish, much of the benefit of additional investments on reserves will be quickly diluted by increasing population. Large transfers to reserves can create jobs in the local public sector – classroom aides, welfare counsellors, and so on – but these are unlikely to start most families on the road to economic self-improvement. The best analogy is provided by the decades of public-sector investments and social programs that have kept the population in the Atlantic provinces artificially high while depressing the general standard of living.

However, no matter how smoothly and quickly integration proceeds, aboriginal territorial enclaves – Indian reserves, Metis colonies, and other "traditional lands" that may be allocated through land-claims settlements – will remain a fixture of the Canadian polity for decades and perhaps centuries to come. It is, therefore, vital that they be governed as well as possible. Good government will have to be self-government, for the age of administration through Indian agents is past. Here are three of the many things that need to happen.

First, aboriginal self-governments need to become more accountable to the people over whom they preside, because accountability to the Department of Indian Affairs is getting weaker all the time. Better auditing would help, as would the creation of a professional, politically neutral corps of aboriginal public servants. But the introduction of "self-funding" through taxation far outweighs any other initiative. Aboriginal self-governments will never be held accountable by their own people as long as the money they spend comes from outside. Under those circumstances, people and government collude to get as much from the public treasury as they can. The residents of aboriginal communities must feel that they are reaching into their own pockets to support the activities of their own governments.

Just for a moment imagine that the $6.3 billion now spent every year by the federal government on aboriginal programs was simply divided up as cash grants among the 610,000 status Indians. Each man, woman, and child would receive a little over $10,000 a year – more than enough for an ordinary Canadian family to live, if not lavishly, at least respectably. Once they had the money, the recipients would be allowed to tax themselves to support whatever collective activities they wished their aboriginal governments to undertake. Would they vote to pay heavy taxes so that their governments could own all the housing and let people live in it for free, or would they prefer to buy houses for themselves, as most Canadians do? Would they vote to fly their chiefs business class to Ottawa, or would they rather use the money to pay for a family visit to the West Edmonton Mall? Would they vote to give large portions of their money to be invested in band enterprises that were managed by government officials, or would they prefer to buy Canada Savings Bonds? Would they vote for schools that spent a lot of time and money trying to revive extinct languages, or would they vote for better English-language instruction in the basic subjects – reading, writing, and arithmetic?

At the present time, aboriginal people do not face these choices. They have little sense of real-world trade-offs because everything their governments do for them is paid for by other people. They never have to give up anything in order to get additional government programs. If they had to make the same choices that other Canadians routinely make, they would, I predict, take the axe to many of the governmental programs proliferating luxuriantly in their communities.

A second reform, less sweeping but still useful, would be to break up the concentrated power of elected band councils. No small group of elected politicians should have control simultaneously of people's land, housing, schools, jobs, and social assistance. There should be school boards to manage the schools, housing commissions to allocate housing, boards of directors to manage band businesses, and so on. All of these bodies should be made independent of the band council, through popular election or appointment for fixed terms of office, as appropriate. Dispersion of power would help to dampen the familial factionalism that curses aboriginal politics.

Finally, it will be essential to introduce a regime of individual property rights. As I argued in an earlier chapter, housing would be a good place to start, but there is much more that needs to be done. As long as the land and natural resources on reserves are collectively owned, they will be the *de facto* property of the band council. The same is true of the other economic assets that bands are beginning to acquire – everything from airlines and trust companies to shopping centres and resort hotels. Since most of these are new creations, operating where nothing existed before, they may appear for a time to be competitive and even profitable. But in the long run, private ownership is necessary if there is also to be the incentive to hire efficient management and the option to reorganize or sell companies when management fails. Aboriginal businesses will need to devise some system of tradeable shares to solve their long-term ownership problems.

Aboriginal self-government will be a failure if it means nothing more than transferring the powers of the Department of Indian Affairs to band councils. Civil society cannot thrive without containment of political power and wide dispersal of private ownership. The challenge for self-government is to "civilize" aboriginal communities in the sense of creating the conditions for civil society to emerge. Above all, that means getting government out of the way – especially the kind of "self-government" that exercises total control over community affairs.

CHAPTER 11

Update 2008

HOW EARLY WAS EARLY?

When I wrote the first edition of this book, the "Clovis model" of the settlement of the Americas – i.e., that people from northeastern Asia first came to the Americas about 13,000 or 14,000 years ago, moving south through the gap between retreating glaciers in Alberta – was under some pressure but was still espoused by many authorities. Since then, however, support for the Clovis model has receded, although there is no consensus on what should replace it.

One challenge to Clovis comes from the genetic evidence. Analysis of mitochondrial DNA confirms Asia as the source of America's population, but the diversity of Amerindian haplotypes seems to require a longer time than the 13–14,000 years of the Clovis model.[1] Another challenge comes from archaeology's increasing validation of pre-Clovis sites such as Monte Verde in Chile and Meadowcroft in Pennsylvania.[2] However these sites have not yielded human skeletal remains, only artifacts that can be difficult to date and may arise from causes other than human manufacture. Some authorities, such as the widely published archaeologist Brian Fagan, still believe that all, or at least most, Palaeo-Indians came to the Americas across the Beringia land bridge and through the gap between melting glaciers in Alberta,[3] while others have concluded that humans were in America before, perhaps long before, the Clovis model would allow.

If so, how did they get there? Perhaps the earliest settlers came from Asia by boat during the last Ice Age, exploiting marine resources as they island-hopped along the southern edge of the Arctic glaciers from Siberia to Alaska and then further south. This maritime model is plausible, but it is difficult to prove archaeologically because the oceans have risen over 100 meters with the end of the Ice Age and the melting of the glaciers, covering the sites on which these putative pioneers would have camped.[4]

All this is fascinating to anyone interested in human pre-history but does nothing to change the fact that human presence in Canada is relatively recent, having become possible only as the glaciers gradually receded after 13,000 BP. Despite the creationist theories of some aboriginal writers, the scientific evidence continues to show that Indian and Inuit habitation preceded European settlement of Canada by thousands, not tens of thousands, of years.

FIRST AND OTHER NATIONS

The practice of referring to Indian bands as First Nations has continued to grow in the last ten years. Today politicians, civil servants, and aboriginal leaders would not use any other terminology when speaking in public. Terms such as "Indian," "status Indian," and "non-status Indian" are heard only in court proceedings or other legal situations where clarity and precision are important in speaking about the constitution and legislation.

Ordinary people, however, seem to find terms such as "First Nations," "First Nations person," and "First Nations people" to be too much of a mouthful. Thus the word "native," common in the 1960s, has come back as a portmanteau label for Indians, Metis, and Inuit. It is now common to read, for example, about "native reserves," even though Inuit and Metis don't have and have never had land reserves in the same sense as Indians, and non-status Indians have no right to live on reserves, which are reserved for status Indians. The loss of precision is regrettable because it leads to confusion about the different situations in which the various subcategories of Canada's aboriginal people find themselves and makes news reports about aboriginal affairs less informative and more difficult to interpret than they were twenty years ago.

At the time of the first edition, the government of Canada had begun using First Nations terminology for status Indians but was still refusing to use the vocabulary of nationhood to describe Quebec. That changed somewhat in early December 2006 when the House of Commons passed a resolution moved by Prime Minister Stephen Harper declaring that "the Québécois form a nation within a united Canada."[5] Although no one was thinking about the implications for aboriginal nationalism at the time, this phrase opens the path for a sensible understanding of First Nations rhetoric. Just as the Québécois were declared to be not a nation *tout court* but a nation "within a united Canada," it makes little sense to call Indians "First Nations" unless they are part of some grouping involving other nations. If First Nations were to become sovereign states, as some of the Mohawk leaders desire, I doubt that they would still call themselves First Nations: they would just be nations in the eyes of the Poles, Ethiopians, and other members of the world community. At the end of the day, then, First Nations rhetoric has been domesticated. It remains an awkward, politically correct way to refer to status Indians, but it has lost the potential separatist connotations that it originally possessed.

Unlike First Nations, the Metis Nation has no land base, except for the seven Metis settlements in northern Alberta established as a result of provincial initiative in the 1940s. Metis leaders have been trying for decades to acquire a land base, both through negotiations with government and by litigation. Negotiation hasn't yielded much, but litigation has had some returns.

In its 2003 *Powley* decision, the Supreme Court of Canada upheld the right of two Metis men living near Sault Ste Marie, Ontario, to hunt for food without a license. In a ruling strongly conditioned by the facts of the case, the Court found that the Powleys (father and son) belonged to a Metis community that had lived around Sault Ste Marie since the days of the fur trade and whose members had always supported themselves by hunting and fishing. Under these circumstances – the existence of an "identifiable Metis community" characterized by "continuity and stability" – the Court held that section 35 of the Constitution Act, 1982, guaranteed the members of that community a "site-specific aboriginal right" to hunt and fish for subsistence.[6] The phrase "site-specific" means that the Metis of Sault Ste Marie could hunt without a license in the area around that city where their ancestors had been accustomed to hunt but could not claim that right elsewhere in Canada.

Strictly speaking, the *Powley* decision applied only to one group of Metis in Ontario, but it put other provinces on notice that they might have to recognize Metis hunting and fishing rights in some way, just as they have long recognized Indian hunting and fishing rights. Alberta moved quickly in the wake of *Powley* to establish a regime for Metis "harvesting," including hunting, fishing, and trapping. The result was the Interim Metis Harvesting Agreement (IMHA), approved 28 September 2004.[7] Driven by Premier Ralph Klein's widely publicized sympathy for native people, the IMHA went far beyond the site-specific and continuous community aspects of *Powley*, treating all of Alberta as a single territory and all Metis as a single group. It allowed anyone accepted as a member of the Metis Nation of Alberta to hunt, fish, and trap for subsistence on all unoccupied Crown lands in Alberta, in provincial parks and protected natural areas if wildlife harvesting was allowed there, and on privately owned lands with permission of the owner. The IMHA was controversial from the start and was soon overtaken by politics when the new government of Ed Stelmach, who became premier in December 2006, cancelled it. When a new agreement is eventually reached, it will probably be more in line with the "site-specific" wording of *Powley*.

However defined, hunting and fishing rights are a far cry from a full-fledged land base. The Manitoba Metis Federation (MMF) is attempting to obtain a true land base by suing the Crown over the implementation of the Manitoba Act of 1870. "Towards the extinguishment of the Indian Title to the lands in the Province," section 31 of the Manitoba Act set aside 1.4 million acres of Manitoba land "for the children of the half-breed heads of families," and subsequent legislation awarded Metis adults $160 scrip redeemable in Dominion lands for the same purpose.[8] In a thirty-year-old claim, which was finally heard in spring 2006, the MMF argued that the implementation of both pieces of legislation was so faulty that the Metis share of aboriginal title had not been extinguished, with the implication that government would now have to negotiate with them as if they were an Indian tribe that had never taken treaty. Such negotiations would presumably lead to creation of a Metis land base on unoccupied Crown land in Manitoba, together with a financial endowment. However, the MMF suffered a jarring setback in this case at the end of 2007, when the decision of the Manitoba Court of Queen's Bench rejected all of their key arguments (disclosure: I was an expert witness for the federal Crown). Indeed, the MMF not only failed to advance, it actually lost ground because the court rejected the notion, which the MMF had taken for granted, that the Metis had ever enjoyed aboriginal title to Manitoba.[9]

Despite this setback, numerous Metis land, scrip, and hunting and fishing lawsuits are percolating through the courts in various provinces and territories.[10] It is possible that this strategic litigation campaign will extend Metis hunting and fishing rights, and perhaps even lead to creation of a land base in one or more provinces. Progress, however, has been slow and is likely to remain that way, so the Metis will continue to be a landless nation for the foreseeable future.

PROBLEMS OF SELF-GOVERNMENT

First Nations? Second Thoughts dwelt at length on the problems of "familistic factionalism" in the government of Indian reserves, as manifested in frequent disputes over election results, widespread patronage, misuse of public funds, and lack of financial transparency and accountability. Jean Chrétien's government resolved to tackle these problems, leading Indian Affairs Minister Robert Nault to introduce Bill C-7, the First Nations Governance Act, on 14 June 2002.[11] The bill proposed three major reforms:

- Bands in which chief and council were elected would have to adopt a clear code of electoral procedure. "Custom" bands, which choose their leaders by some mode other than election, would also have to adopt a transparent code of procedure.
- All bands would have to adopt a financial code providing for annual budgets and reports, audits, and other modern financial tools aimed at promoting transparency and accountability in the use of public money.
- Section 67 of the Canadian Human Rights Act would be repealed, allowing complaints about discriminatory conduct by First Nations governments to be brought before the Canadian Human Rights Commission. This might have allowed Indian women, for example, to complain that they were not being treated equally with Indian men in the allocation of housing by the band council.

As soon as C-7 was introduced, the Assembly of First Nations, which is composed of the chiefs of Canada's approximately 600 Indian bands, opposed it vociferously while parliamentary committee hearings were held around the country. Although the bill appeared to be on track for passage, everything depended on Jean Chrétien's support as prime minister, and Chrétien was pushed out of that office by Paul Martin during 2003. Martin, when he became prime minister, announced that he would not proceed with C-7.

The Conservative government of Stephen Harper did not attempt to revive C-7 except for the provision that would have made First Nations governments subject to the Canadian Human Rights Act. Legislation to that effect was introduced by Indian Affairs Minister Jim Prentice (Bill C-44) but was opposed by the Assembly of First Nations and died when Harper prorogued Parliament. It was reintroduced in fall 2007.[12] The new bill, now known as Bill C-21, was substantially amended in committee, where the three opposition parties combined to water it down by inserting a reference to native traditions as grounds for overriding the Canadian Human Rights Act. At the time of writing (May 2008), C-21 had been approved in the House of Commons and was under consideration in the Senate. It will not take effect until three years after final passage.

Until we see the final version of such legislation, it is difficult to say what its impact might be. It will almost certainly enable status Indian women to go to the Canadian Human Rights Commission and bring complaints of sexual discrimination in the allocation of housing and jobs on reserves. Depending on the wording, it may also enable non-Indian employees and contractors, who are sometimes treated high-handedly by band councils, to complain about discrimination based on race. The Congress of Aboriginal Peoples hopes it will allow non-status Indians to complain about the fact that they are denied band membership and benefits under the Indian Act on the basis of their ancestry.[13] Winning such cases could have advantages for individuals but lead to new challenges for some reserves, if, for example, they were required to provide housing to previously excluded non-status Indians. At the extreme, extending the jurisdiction of the Canadian Human Rights Commission to status Indians might allow them to challenge a wide range of federal policies as being discriminatory toward Indians in general.

Whatever may happen over decades if this new decision-making process is established, it will do little or nothing to deal with the current problems of self-government on Indian reserves. Familistic factionalism arises from a combination of small size, remote location, legislation that does not require transparency and accountability, and almost total reliance on transfer payments without revenue from self-taxation. Bringing in the Canadian Human Rights Commission will not change any of that.

Overall, reform of reserve self-government does not seem very likely in the foreseeable future. The Assembly of First Nations showed that it had the political weight to obstruct and outwait even the cunning and experienced Jean Chrétien, a prime minister backed by majorities in both the House of Commons and the Senate. The minority government of Stephen Harper would have little chance of success if it were to embark upon a project of fundamental reform in this field. Given what happened to Chrétien and Nault's attempts at modest reform, it may be a long time before any federal government seizes the nettle again.

When the first edition was written, there was still a lot of momentum towards recognizing an inherent right of aboriginal self-government and "nation to nation" relations between Canada and aboriginal peoples. The RCAP (Royal Commission on Aboriginal Peoples) had proposed a set of institutional changes that moved in the direction of creation of a third level of aboriginal government within the Canadian federal system, with aboriginal seats in the House of Commons, Senate, and Supreme Court. Such changes were never implemented, and one hears less self-government rhetoric today. Now, when Phil Fontaine speaks as National Chief of the Assembly of First Nations (AFN), it is usually not to demand greater jurisdictional autonomy but to ask for more money – to compensate residential school survivors, to implement the Kelowna Accord, or to address native poverty. The AFN puts a tagline on its press releases maintaining its view that Indians are in but not of Canada ("The Assembly of First Nations is the national organization representing First Nations citizens in Canada"[14]), but the supplicant posture belies the profession of independence.

The main area where aboriginal self-government still has momentum is British Columbia, where the attempt to negotiate modern-day treaties is ongoing. The first such treaty was the Nisga'a agreement, which came into effect in 2000.[15] Although negotiated outside the main process, it will inevitably serve as the benchmark for subsequent agreements, such as the Tsawwassen Final Agreement, which was going through its approval process at the time of writing.

The Nisga'a Agreement provides for native government legislation in certain areas to prevail over federal or provincial legislation in case of inconsistency. The stipulated areas include the administration of Nisga'a lands plus health, education, and family matters; such legislation would not apply to Nisga'a people who choose to live outside Nisga'a lands. Probably the most controversial area of jurisdiction is citizenship, which gives the Nisga'a government the right to determine who can vote in tribal elections.

Several other features of the agreement limit Nisga'a jurisdiction. The final agreement does not alter the Constitution of Canada, and it specifies that the Charter of Rights and Freedoms will apply to the Nisga'a government. It also states explicitly that federal and provincial laws will apply on Nisga'a territory in all areas where the Nisga'a are not explicitly given paramount jurisdiction. Thus, the agreement does not turn the Nisga'a community into an *imperium in imperio,* able to disregard the laws of Canada and British Columbia as it chooses.

Beyond this, there are several features of the agreement that are consistent with the arguments made in *First Nations? Second Thoughts.* It puts the Nisga'a outside the Indian Act, and it gives them ownership of their lands in fee simple rather than as a Crown reserve. The Nisga'a will have the ability to subdivide their lands and create private property among their members, if they wish, as well as to sell some of their lands to outsiders. There is negotiated immunity from some taxes for a period of time, but not perpetual immunity from all taxes on reserve as there is under the Indian Act.

The Nisga'a, therefore, are outside the Indian Act but inside the Canadian constitution, both of which I support. They do, however, have a status far superior to that of other Canadian cities or rural municipalities, which cannot pass enactments to override provincial or federal laws, even in limited areas of jurisdiction. Critics argue that this feature of the treaty is unconstitutional because it ignores the division of powers between Parliament and the provincial legislatures laid down in sections 91 and 92 of the Constitution Act, 1867.

This aspect of the Nisga'a agreement was highly controversial before passage and has already given rise to considerable litigation. The provincial Liberals challenged it in the Supreme Court of

British Columbia but chose not to appeal further after they lost.[16] Since then, a new challenge has arisen among the Nisga'a themselves. A faction led by James Robinson (also known as Chief Mountain) and supported financially by the Canadian Constitution Foundation claims:

... that the Nisga'a Final Agreement violates Canada's constitution by creating a semi-independent Nisga'a state whose laws prevail over Canadian law ...

The Nisga'a Agreement came into force in 2000. It created a Nisga'a government in north-western B.C. with the power to grant or withhold Nisga'a citizenship – even from individuals of Nisga'a descent. Only Nisga'a citizens are allowed to vote in elections, so that the Nisga'a government can effectively select the voting population. The Nisga'a Agreement expressly states that Nisga'a law prevails over Canadian federal and provincial law in fourteen areas of jurisdiction.

Chief Mountain opposes this "third order" of government created by the Nisga'a Treaty, stating, "It hurts our people by taking away our ancestral lands and human rights. It hurts all Canadians by undermining the Canadian constitution. I vow to fight for my people's rights to be Canadian citizens and to be protected by the Charter of Rights. Those rights have been taken away illegally, by the Nisga'a treaty."[17]

A decision in this case is still years away because the dissident Nisga'a group did not win their procedural battle to allow them to bring this suit until October 2007.

Finally on the self-government front, it is encouraging to report that, after years of pushing by Manny Jules, chief of the First Nations Tax Commission, there is at least a modest trend towards taxation on Indian reserves. There are now 113 First Nations that levy property taxes on reserve land, 29 that have some form of sales tax, and 12 (mostly in the Yukon) that are experimenting with personal income tax.[18] At present most of these taxes fall on outsiders who lease land, do business, or shop on the reserve, but a few First Nations, including Westbank in British Columbia, Whitecap Dakota in Saskatchewan, and several in Yukon, are taxing their own people. When the Institute on Governance interviewed administrators from these bands, they received positive reports about the effect self-taxation had in enabling bands to pay for services, increasing members' interest in band government, and promoting transparency and accountability: "In a self-government context, one interviewee spoke of a 'complete transformation' of a First Nation that had been mired in debt and partisan politics twenty years earlier. Taxation had contributed its part to different attitudes of citizens, better governing institutions, better services, and better relations with other governments and non-Aboriginal parties within a reasonably short period."[19] Taxation is not a magic wand that will make everything right, but it is encouraging to see that the results of early experiments seem consistent with the argument made in the first edition of this book.

WHO OWNS WHAT?

Almost as soon as *First Nations? Second Thoughts* was published, I realized that its sketchy treatment of individual property rights on Canadian Indian reserves was inadequate. Fortunately, a talented graduate student, Chris Alcantara, helped me correct the deficiency.[20] Alcantara and I found that while all land on Canadian Indian reserves is owned by the Crown, and most of it is controlled by band councils subject to approval by the minister of Indian Affairs, a substantial amount of it is subject to three different forms of private rights:

- *Customary rights*, based on lengthy family possession. Depending on the reserve, the basis of these rights ranges from pure oral tradition to a high degree of formalization, including land surveys, approval by band council, and recording in a land registry. These rights enable many Indians to own their own homes, as well as to engage in farming, ranching, and other businesses, but they are not enforceable in Canadian courts and may be lost through adverse claims by neighbours or confiscation by the band council.[21]
- *Certificates of possession (CPs)*, as authorized in the Indian Act. Once granted, after approval by the band council and the minister of Indian Affairs, CPs are much like ownership in fee simple, except that they cannot be sold or otherwise transferred to anyone who is not a member of the band. This restriction lowers their cash value because there is no real market for CPs. Nonetheless, they are useful to their owners because Canadian courts will enforce the rights that attach to them, thus offering protection against seizure by band councils or depredations by neighbours,

two types of conflict that often occur on reserves. CPs are prevalent in southern Ontario and southern British Columbia, but much less common elsewhere. Where they have been granted, they are used not only for owner-occupied housing on reserve but can also be leased to outsiders for commercial or residential development.

• Subject to various approval processes, it is possible to lease band land, customary land, and land held under certificates of possession. Depending on how the leases are drawn, they may become a form of private property right that can be sold to anyone, thus transcending the limitations of CPs, at least for the duration of the lease.

This panoply of private property rights is far from perfect but still useful to those who live on reserves. Starting in the 1960s on the Six Nations reserve in Ontario, various communities have devised ways to use customary rights and certificates of possession to facilitate individual ownership of housing. The difficulty of obtaining a mortgage has always been a barrier to on-reserve home ownership. Banks and trust companies will not loan if they cannot attach the property in case of default, and the Indian Act prevents Indian property from being subject to "charge, pledge, mortgage, attachment, levy, seizure, distress or execution in favour or at the instance of any person other than an Indian or a band."[22] But this limitation can be overcome if the band council, or some entity set up by the council, guarantees the mortgage. The lender thus receives the security necessary to make the loan, while the band council has authority under the act to seize a certificate of possession or withdraw permission to use customarily held property.

Building on four decades of Indian experience, on 20 April 2007 the minister of Indian Affairs, Jim Prentice, announced the establishment of a $300 million First Nations Market Housing Fund to promote individual home ownership on reserves.[23] This welcome initiative is intended to help finance 25,000 owner-occupied homes over a period of years, but it is far from a complete solution to Indian housing problems. Many reserve residents, particularly on poor reserves in remote locations, are simply too poor to qualify for a mortgage, even with the most favourable terms and generous subsidies.

Beyond home ownership by members of First Nations, leases have become the basis of real estate development on many reserves, sometimes on quite a large and sophisticated scale... A developer, for example, can get a head or first lease from the band and then sell subleases to non-Indians who can use the land to build houses, which in turn can be resold. It is rather like owning a home in Banff, where all homes are built on land leased from the National Parks. The main problems associated with such leases, as compared to ownership in fee simple, are that they last only for a fixed period, may not always be renewed, and do not carry the right to participate in the reserve's decision-making processes, such as in setting property tax rates. Because of such limitations, the Supreme Court of Canada held in the *Glass* case that lease land on the Musqueam reserve was worth only half as much as similar fee simple land in the surrounding city of Vancouver.[24]

The complexities surrounding Crown ownership, customary rights, certificates of possession, and leases do not forestall economic development on reserves, but they certainly slow it down and make it more difficult. Entrepreneurs seeking to protect their investments have to invest time and money in extra legal work to create complex third-party arrangements because they cannot purchase the land on which their shopping centres, industrial parks, or housing developments will be located. Aboriginal leaders pursuing economic development are, therefore, beginning to show some interest in the type of fee simple ownership that other Canadians enjoy in their property. Fee simple ownership is provided for in some recent treaties, such as the Nisga'a Agreement, and the First Nations Tax Commission headed by former Kamloops Chief Manny Jules has commissioned quite sophisticated research showing the potential advantages of fee simple ownership on Indian reserves.

There is, indeed, little doubt about the economic advantages. The Canadian commercial economy is based on ownership in fee simple, and it will obviously be easier for First Nations to participate in that economy if their land is held in the same way. Fee simple ownership, however, carries with it the possibility that land could be sold to people who are not members of the band. Instead of signing long-term leases, homeowners might want to buy their residential lots or investors might want to buy the sites for casinos or shopping centres. In the present climate of opinion, most band members would regard that as a loss of control over their reserve and a threat to their land base. To assuage these fears, First Nations governments will probably have to retain the underlying title to fee-simple lands, as well as exercise a higher degree of control, perhaps under the heading of zoning and land-use bylaws, than other local governments. Such restrictions may lower the value of fee-simple land on reserve as compared to fee-simple land off reserve, but that may be the unavoidable cost of surviving as separate ethnic entities.

SPECIFIC CLAIMS

In June 2007, Prime Minister Harper announced a "Specific Claims Action Plan," containing four key initiatives:

- Create a new tribunal staffed with impartial judges who will make final decisions on claims when negotiations fail;
- Make arrangements for financial compensation more transparent through dedicated funding for settlements in the amount of $250 million a year for ten years;
- Speed up processing of small claims and improve flexibility in the handling of large claims; and
- Refocus the existing Indian Claims Commission to concentrate on dispute resolution.[25]

The Speech from the Throne in October 2007 reaffirmed the government's commitment, and Bill C-30, the Specific Claims Tribunal Act, received first reading on 27 November 2007. At the time of writing, it had been approved in the House of Commons.

The existing Indian Claims Commissions can investigate, mediate, and recommend settlements for specific claims that arise out of the implementation of treaties or of the Indian Act, but it does not have the quasi-judicial power to impose a settlement. An independent tribunal for specific claims will resemble administrative tribunals in fields such as human rights and labour relations, which have the power to make binding awards within legislated limits but with their decisions subject to judicial review in the Federal Court of Appeal.

The demand for an independent tribunal is not new: it goes back to the creation of the Indian Claims Commission in 1991. In fact, Canada almost got an independent tribunal when Jean Chrétien was prime minister. Comprising part of Robert Nault's reform package, the Specific Claims Resolution Act was passed and received royal assent in November 2003, but Paul Martin, who had a different view of aboriginal issues than Chrétien, decided not to proclaim it. The Assembly of First Nations favoured establishing an independent tribunal able to make binding decisions, but it had many criticisms of the Specific Claims Resolution Act's details. In particular, it objected to the $10 million limit that the tribunal would be allowed to award for any single claim and to the fact that the government could set a limit on what it would pay for claims each year.

We are not talking small change here. At the end of 2006, there were 861 unsatisfied claims filed by 445 First Nations, and the historical pattern is for about 60 new claims to be lodged every year. One expert told a Senate committee that it would cost $4 to 5 billion over a five-year period to "stabilize the situation," whatever that means.[26] Based on the size of past awards, it could cost $10 billion to deal with existing claims, to say nothing of those not yet filed. Harper's commitment of $2.5 billion over ten years is a substantial amount of money, but it is almost certainly far from enough to settle all the claims that may be brought.

In at least one important respect, however, Bill C-30 represents an improvement over the never-proclaimed Specific Claims Resolution Act. That legislation would have established a tribunal composed of six lawyers appointed by order in council, whereas in the new bill the tribunal members must be superior court judges.[27] The requirement of judicial status should help forestall the extravagant decisions that sometimes emanate from human rights and labour tribunals, whose members are lawyers, not judges.

A weakness in the bill, however, is that it contains no cutoff date for the filing of claims. In this respect, it ignores the precedent of the United States Indian Claims Commission, which sat from 1946 to 1978 and was then wound up, with all unsettled claims transferred to the United States Court of Claims. Not only that, but the bill specifically forbids the tribunal to "consider any rule or doctrine that would have the effect of limiting claims or prescribing rights against the Crown because of the passage of time or delay."[28] Specific claims generally arise out of Indian treaties, which were negotiated from the late eighteenth century up to 1923. First Nations have had twenty-five years to look for specific claims since the policy was announced in 1982; it is not as if this is a new concept that needs more time to be explored.

The typical claim deals with a set of facts more than a hundred years old. Were all band members counted when the reserve was allocated? Did Indian Affairs send seed grain, livestock, and farm implements in the quantity and quality implied by the treaty? If a piece of the reserve was surrendered, did the Indian agent notify all male band members to meet to discuss the sale, and did he properly explain the deal? Did Indian Affairs obtain a fair price for whatever land and resources were sold? One can imagine the difficulty of answering such questions more than a century afterwards when everybody involved is long dead. In normal civil litigation, statutes of limitation and doctrines such as laches prevent ancient grievances from being turned into litigation; why should there not be similar constraints in the field of aboriginal specific claims?

Without a filing deadline, specific claims may never end, because teams of lawyers, historians, and anthropologists can discover an infinite number of new ones. The specific-claims process may become not a one-time way of dealing with past grievances but an ongoing method of shaking the money tree. If that happens, the main beneficiaries will be the lawyers and consultants who research the claims and argue them before the Tribunal. The main losers will be First Nations themselves, who will be led to spend their time searching for ever more tenuous past injustices rather than focusing on improving their future prospects. In the words of Calvin Helin: "It is time for indigenous people to stop dwelling on the rancorous injustices of the past.... no matter how unfairly or badly indigenous people were treated in the past, we cannot do anything about history. Our actions now, however, can impact the future."[29]

The mother of all specific claims, though it may never get into the actual process, is the Six Nations' demand for control over the entire Haldimand Grant, which was conferred upon the Mohawks in 1784 when they took refuge in Canada after supporting the losing side in the American Revolution. The Haldimand Grant consists of six miles on both sides of the Grand River, from its source to the point where it enters Lake Erie, totaling about 951,000 acres (385,000 hectares). Only about 5% of the original grant remains in the Six Nations Reserve, the rest having been lost over the years through administrative actions, land surrenders to the Crown, and sales.[30]

In early 2006, Six Nations activists occupied Douglas Creek Estates, a housing project under construction near Caledonia, Ontario. The occupation continues at the time of writing, although the government of Ontario has purchased Douglas Creek Estates from the developer and is holding it in trust pending a resolution of the dispute.[31] In late 2007, the Six Nations also set up the Haudenosaunee Development Institute in an attempt to levy development charges elsewhere in the area of the Haldimand Grant.[32] The value of the lands at stake goes far beyond the fiscal capacity of the government's proposed specific-claims process. Because the Haldimand Grant contains many urban areas, including the city of Kitchener and some of the outer suburbs of Hamilton, its contemporary value would be many billions of dollars. In any case, this is not so much a conventional specific claim as an assertion of political jurisdiction. It will ultimately have to be settled by force if Six Nations activists continue to violate Canadian law, claiming it does not apply to them because they are part of a sovereign Iroquois nation.

LEGAL CONFUSION

First Nations? Second Thoughts pointed out the uncertainty created by Chief Justice Antonio Lamer's jurisprudence, culminating in his 1997 decision in *Delgamuukw*. "In spite of its attempt at conceptual sophistication, the Lamer doctrine left most of the pressing practical issues unsettled. As one critic [Mel Smith] has said, '*Delgamuukw* undermined everything but settled nothing.'"[33] The Supreme Court of Canada is now led by Chief Justice Beverley McLachlin, who sometimes writes the majority decision in important aboriginal cases. The Court has been trying, with mixed success, to clarify the confusion that resulted from *Delgamuukw*.

In *Mitchell* (2001), the Court ruled that the Mohawks did not have an aboriginal right to bring goods across the international border between the United States and Canada for the purpose of trade – a right that would have exempted them from Canadian customs regulations. Overturning the Federal Court of Appeal, the Supreme Court found no persuasive evidence that the Mohawks had ever engaged in more than negligible acts of trade across the St Lawrence. The Court's dictum in *Mitchell* about standards of evidence was important in clarifying *Delgamuukw's* vagueness about what it means to put oral evidence "on an equal footing" with other forms of evidence:

a consciousness of the special nature of aboriginal claims does not negate the operation of general evidentiary principles. While evidence adduced in support of aboriginal claims must not be undervalued, neither should it be interpreted or weighed in a manner that fundamentally contravenes the principles of evidence law.[34]

In the *Bernard* and *Marshall* cases (2005), the Supreme Court overturned both the Nova Scotia and New Brunswick Courts of Appeal to hold that the Mi'kmaq possessed neither a treaty right nor an aboriginal right to engage in commercial lumbering without regard to provincial regulations. On the treaty side, the Court differentiated this case from *Donald Marshall* (1999), in which it found that the "truck house" clauses of treaties signed in 1760–61 gave Donald Marshall a right to earn a "moderate livelihood" by catching and selling eels outside of provincial regulations. Without overturning the earlier *Marshall* decision, the Court held that the Mi'kmaq, though they had cut trees and made use of timber at the time of the treaties, had not engaged in anything comparable to commercial logging. "Logging was not a traditional Mi'kmaq activity. Rather, it was a European activity, in which the Mi'kmaq began to participate only decades after the treaties of 1760–61."[35] With respect to aboriginal rights, the Court found that the Mi'kmaq had not established aboriginal title to the areas on which they were logging, so they could not claim they were simply making use of their own property. Though they may have occasionally visited or passed through these areas, they had not produced evidence that they had had exclusive occupation of the land before the establishment of European sovereignty.[36]

That the Supreme Court of Canada had to overturn the Federal Court of Appeal as well as the Courts of Appeal of New Brunswick and Nova Scotia to arrive at its decisions in *Mitchell, Marshall,* and *Bernard* illustrates the state of judicial confusion after *Delgamuukw.* But at least in the these decisions the Supreme Court did its job of laying down rules for interpreting aboriginal rights and treaty claims that lower courts should be able to follow. Unfortunately, while the Supreme Court was producing more clarity, it was also creating new confusion about the right of consultation.

In the 2004 cases of *Taku River* and *Haida Nation,* the Supreme Court found that the "honour of the Crown" required the government of British Columbia to consult First Nations about the use of lands that might be part of an as yet unproved claim of aboriginal rights and title. The Court's fundamental position is hard to fault. *Delgamuukw* held that aboriginal title has never been extinguished in most of British Columbia, so claims for aboriginal title might be proved valid almost everywhere. It hardly seems fair to aboriginal claimants to have lands over which they hope to assert title stripped of their minerals, timber, or fish and game while the claim is being negotiated. Hence the requirement on the provincial government to consult claimants before issuing mining permits or timber licenses.

But even if the basic idea is sound, the way in which the Court phrased the duty of consultation seems extraordinarily difficult to put into practice:

The government's duty to consult with Aboriginal peoples and accommodate their interests is grounded in the principle of the honour of the Crown, which must be understood generously. While the asserted but unproven Aboriginal rights and title are insufficiently specific for the honour of the Crown to mandate that the Crown act as a fiduciary, the Crown, acting honourably, cannot cavalierly run roughshod over Aboriginal interests where claims affecting these interests are being seriously pursued in the process of treaty negotiation and proof. The duty to consult and accommodate is part of a process of fair dealing and reconciliation that begins with the assertion of sovereignty and continues beyond formal claims resolution. The foundation of the duty in the Crown's honour and the goal of reconciliation suggest that the duty arises when the Crown has knowledge, real or constructive, of the potential existence of the Aboriginal right or title and contemplates conduct that might adversely affect it. Consultation and accommodation before final claims resolution preserve the Aboriginal interest and are an essential corollary to the honourable process of reconciliation that s. 35 of the *Constitution Act, 1982,* demands.

The scope of the duty is proportionate to a preliminary assessment of the strength of the case supporting the existence of the right or title, and to the seriousness of the potentially adverse effect upon the right or title claimed. The Crown is not under a duty to reach an agreement; rather, the commitment is to a meaningful process of consultation in good faith. The content of the duty varies with the circumstances and each case must be approached individually and flexibly. The controlling question in all situations is what is required to maintain the honour of the Crown and to effect reconciliation between the Crown and the Aboriginal people with respect to the interests at stake. The effect of good faith consultation may be to reveal a duty to accommodate. Where accommodation is required in making decisions that may adversely affect as yet unproven Aboriginal rights and title claims, the Crown must balance Aboriginal concerns reasonably with the potential impact of the decision on the asserted right or title and with other societal interests.[37]

This decision imposes impossibly high standards of knowledge upon the civil servants who must carry out consultations. They must make a preliminary assessment of the strength of the claim, even though the claim has not been approved or perhaps even heard yet. They don't have a duty to reach agreement with the First Nation, but they have to negotiate in good faith, whatever that means ("The content of the duty varies with the circumstances and each case must be approached individually and flexibly"). Government must uphold "the honour of the Crown" while balancing aboriginal claims against "other societal interests." Such open-ended language is an invitation to second-guessing by the various layers of the judiciary as decisions are made and appealed. Instead of clearly delineating property rights, it gives ownership to no one and the right to be consulted to everyone, as represented through provincial, local, and First Nations governments.

Taku River and *Haida Nation* applied only to the special situation of British Columbia, but they have ramifications in other provinces where groups of (sometimes non-status) Indians maintain they were left out of treaty negotiations and are pressing comprehensive claims to aboriginal title. One such case flared up in the fall of 2007, when two groups of non-status Algonquin set up barricades to block uranium exploration near Sharbot Lake, Ontario. In simple terms, their argument was that, since they had lodged a comprehensive claim including this area, resource extraction could not go ahead without their approval.[38]

In 2005 the Court extended the uncertainty beyond British Columbia in the *Mikisew* decision, which found that the Mikisew had a right to be consulted in northern Alberta, even though the area has been subject to Treaty 8 since 1899. The dispute began when the federal Department of the Environment proposed to build a winter snow road through a portion of Wood Buffalo National

Park that is also a reserve for the Mikisew Cree First Nation. After protests, the department agreed to reroute the road so that it would go around the reserve rather than cross it, but the Mikisew still demanded to be consulted, on the grounds that the road would affect their hunting and fishing off the reserve. Treaty 8 gives signatories the right to hunt, trap, and fish on Crown land off reserve, "saving and excepting such tracts as may be required or taken up from time to time for settlement, mining, lumbering, trading or other purposes."[39]

In reasoning rather similar to *Taku River* and *Haida Nation*, the Supreme Court overruled the Federal Court of Appeal, finding that the federal government had a duty to consult with the Mikisew Cree even though the proposed road was on land that had been surrendered in 1899 as part of Treaty 8:

The Crown, while it has a treaty right to "take up" surrendered lands, is nevertheless under the obligation to inform itself on the impact its project will have on the exercise by the Mikisew of their treaty hunting, fishing and trapping rights and to communicate its findings to the Mikisew. The Crown must then attempt to deal with the Mikisew in good faith and with the intention of substantially addressing their concerns. The duty to consult is triggered at a low threshold, but adverse impact is a matter of degree, as is the extent of the content of the Crown's duty. Under Treaty 8, the First Nation treaty rights to hunt, fish and trap are therefore limited not only by geographical limits and specific forms of government regulation, but also by the Crown's right to take up lands under the treaty, subject to its duty to consult and, if appropriate, to accommodate the concerns of the First Nation affected ...

Here, the duty to consult is triggered. The impacts of the proposed road were clear, established, and demonstrably adverse to the continued exercise of the Mikisew hunting and trapping rights over the lands in question. Contrary to the Crown's argument, the duty to consult was not discharged in 1899 by the pre–treaty negotiations.[40]

If these sorts of decisions continue, all Indian bands, including those who long ago surrendered their aboriginal title in return for clearly defined land reserves and other benefits, will soon be able to claim a right to be consulted on development proposals across vaguely defined "traditional territories" that extend far beyond their own reserves. Federal, provincial, and local governments, as well as private owners, will find that their property rights no longer entitle them to make decisions about their own land, at least not without protracted and expensive consultation and legal appeals. Let's hope the Supreme Court starts to limit the fallout from these decisions, just as it has taken steps to reduce other types of damage from *Delgamuukw*.

THE ENTREPRENEURSHIP EXPLOSION

The first edition correctly assessed the St Eugene Mission Resort in British Columbia as a financially shaky project whose real objective was to serve as a platform for getting a casino license.[41] In the event, the enterprise went bankrupt soon after the casino license was obtained.[42] It has, however, been reorganized under outside aboriginal investors and is functioning under new management. Situated in a stunningly beautiful location, it can perhaps thrive over the long term now that the original defects of capitalization have been washed out.

The St Eugene story may be ambiguous, but fortunately there has been tremendous progress in aboriginal entrepreneurship over the last ten years. Without any pretence of offering a complete list, here are some examples of success stories, both big and small:

- The Fort McKay First Nation, located about an hour's drive north of Fort McMurray, owns the Fort McKay Group of Companies, composed of seven corporations. With a mainly aboriginal work force, they offer corporate clients in the oil sands of northeastern Alberta various kinds of construction, transportation, and labour services, ranging from simple janitorial services to the sophisticated operation of heavy machinery.[43] More recently, the Fort McKay Group has entered a joint venture with Shell for development of oil sands leases on its treaty lands.[44]
- In partnership with ATCO, the Tlicho Government of the Northwest Territories owns a logistics company that sells services to the Diavik diamond mine and the Colomac gold mine.[45] As of 2006, 50 tribal members were among the 130 people who worked for Tli Cho Logistics.
- The Membertou First Nation, located near Sydney, Nova Scotia, has built a business empire with revenues of $75 million in 2007. Enterprises include a fishing company, a gas station, an industrial

park, and a casino. Under the leadership of Bernd Christmas, the band pulled itself out of debt, balanced its annual budget, and became a significant employer in the Sydney area.[46]

• The Enoch Cree Nation and the Tsuu T'ina Nation, located on the western edges of Edmonton and Calgary respectively, have opened Alberta's first native casinos. Several other native casinos are in the works for Alberta, while others already exist or are being built in British Columbia, Saskatchewan, Manitoba, Ontario, and Nova Scotia.[47] Native gaming in Canada will probably not produce anything like the huge concentration of wealth produced by the Pequots' Foxwoods Casino in Connecticut,[48] because the provincial authorities who regulate the industry have imposed arrangements to distribute profits among all First Nations as well as the government of the province.

• The Westbank First Nation near Kelowna, BC, has seen a great deal of real estate development on the west side of Lake Okanagan. Most of the reserve had been previously divided into certificates of possession, and many holders of these have leased their land for commercial or residential real-estate projects, so that now fewer than 5 per cent of the people who live on the reserve are band members.[49] Meanwhile the Kamloops Indian Band has taken a different approach, granting a head lease on band land to a developer, who in turn is selling the leases in the local residential real-estate market.

• The Osoyoos Indian Band, under the leadership of Chief Clarence Louie, has become the biggest producer of grapes in the Okanagan valley. In addition to operating its own Nk'Mip winery, the band sells grapes to many other wineries up and down the valley. It also operates recreational and tourism enterprises.[50]

• As detailed in the first edition, the Samson Cree Nation, located near Hobbema, Alberta, has had difficulties in using its oil revenues for the benefit of all its people. But some of the royalties went into establishing the Peace Hills Trust Company, which now has 20,000 customers, eight regional offices, and an Internet operation.

This list could be multiplied many times over. All across Canada, aboriginal organizations own casinos, hotels, and resorts; shopping centres and industrial parks; sawmills, mines, and oil wells; banks and trust companies; airlines and trucking companies; and many other kinds of enterprises. All Canadians should welcome this explosion of entrepreneurship, which will create a class of well-to-do aboriginal owners and managers as well as providing manual and white-collar jobs for many ordinary aboriginal people.

Nevertheless, it is necessary to keep the limitations of aboriginal entrepreneurship in mind. Most of the success stories come from capitalizing on specific advantages, such as having fertile land or natural resources on the reserve, or being located near an urban centre or in an attractive holiday area. But most reserves in Canada do not have such assets and will find it more difficult to go down the entrepreneurial path. Moreover, in any society, only a relatively small number of people will become entrepreneurs, while most people will work in enterprises owned and managed by others. This is just as true of aboriginal people as of all other Canadians. And working in a business that happens to thrive on a particular reserve may not be a good fit for many individual Indians. If you have the skill set of a carpenter, there may not be a rewarding job for you at the local casino after it has been built. No matter how much aboriginal entrepreneurship there is – and I hope there is a lot – most aboriginal people, like most Canadians, will have to look for work in the wider economy.

Notwithstanding the limits to aboriginal entrepreneurship, it will, over time, have a major impact on relationships between aboriginal communities and Canadian society. Initially, aboriginal entrepreneurship may seem like a form of autonomy. "Finally," one might think, "we will control our own future by setting up our own businesses, creating our own jobs on the reserve, and giving up dependence on government handouts." But in practice indigenous entrepreneurship will create an ever denser network of ties with the surrounding society. All but the smallest projects will require partnerships with outside investors and financial institutions. Moreover, any aboriginal business will have dealings with agents, suppliers, and maintenance and service companies. To maintain such ties will require band councils to play by ordinary commercial rules, resisting the temptation to use their governmental authority arbitrarily. The American authors David Haddock and Robert Miller call this the "sovereign's paradox": "the greater a sovereign's power to insist on an outcome that is favorable to itself during potential future disputes, the less its present power to conclude agreements that require time to reach fruition."[51] In the context of American tribal sovereignty, this often means tribal governments agreeing to be bound by the commercial law and courts of the state in which they are located, thus affording more predictability to investors and suppliers.

Also, even if aboriginal enterprises try to promote the employment of their own people, they will often need to hire managers and skilled workers from outside the reserve. If they are selling retail goods and services to the public in casinos, resorts, and shopping centres, they will need to make the reserve a welcoming place for non-resident customers and clients. And there will inevitably be an ever-growing web of affiliations with nearby cities, rural municipalities, and provincial authorities because on-reserve business enterprises require electric power, water and sewerage, highway connections, and police and fire protection that only outside governments can provide.

All of these factors will work together to make indigenous entrepreneurs ever more involved in the Canadian economy and civil society. What began as the dream of autonomy will end in the reality of interdependence.

PROGRESS FOR PEOPLE?

There are many difficulties in measuring whether aboriginal people in general, or subgroups within that larger community, are making economic and social progress. The first layer of problems has to do with the collection and reporting of data. Statistics Canada has several ways of classifying aboriginal people:

- By origin (respondents who claim some degree of aboriginal ancestry);
- By identity (respondents who identify themselves as aboriginal, subdivided into Indian, Metis, Inuit, and mixed);
- Registered (status) vs. unregistered (non-status) Indians.

This looks like a wealth of information, but it creates multiple difficulties:

- All categories except registered Indian are subjective and self-defined, so reported membership fluctuates with political and social trends. For example, the number of self-reported Metis

rose by a third from 292,305 in 2001 to 389,785 in 2006.[52] Only
a small part of such a large increase can be explained by natural
growth: the rest must be due to changing self-perceptions on the
part of those who have some degree of aboriginal ancestry. But
such great changes introduce a correspondingly large element of
uncertainty into any attempt to track health, income, or educational attainments across time, because those calling themselves
Metis in 2006 include many who did not label themselves that
way in 2001.

- The count of Indians on reserve is imprecise because some band
councils will not allow Statistics Canada to gather information
on their reserves. According to Statistics Canada, there were
seventy-seven incompletely enumerated reserves in 1996, thirty
in 2001, and twenty-two in 2006.[53] Thus Statistics Canada estimated a total of 698,025 North American Indians in 2006,
whereas the Indian Affairs register had 763,555 at the end of the
same year.[54] The latter figure is likely more accurate than the
former, but no one knows for sure because information submitted
to Indian Affairs is also subject to manipulation (band councils
have incentives to underreport deaths and departures in order to
keep grants high).
- Many status Indians frequently move off and on reserve, so the
actual people reported as living on reserve and off reserve in any
two census years may be quite different. Again, this makes
compilation and interpretation of time series difficult.
- Legal definitions are subject to change. The mother of all changes
was Bill C-31, passed in 1985, which restored Indian status to
women (and their children) who had lost it by marrying outside
the band. By the year 2000 there were about 107,000 C-31 persons on the Indian Register, representing about one-sixth of the
whole status Indian population.[55] This large infusion of people
has changed the composition of the Registered Indian population
in substantial ways because non-status Indians, though they lost
their Indian Act benefits, benefited from intermarriage with members of the non-Indian population and generally enjoy higher
levels of income and education than status Indians. Their return
to Indian status tends to increase economic and social indicators
for the whole group of Registered Indians, even though there were
no changes in the situations of particular individuals.

Table 11.1
Human Development Index, Registered Indians and Other Canadians, 1981–2001

Year	Registered Indians	Increase over previous census	Other Canadians	Increase over previous census	Gap
1981	626	–	806	–	180
1986	644	18	823	17	183
1991	706	62	852	29	146
1996	739	33	863	11	124
2001	765	26	880	17	115

Around the time that *First Nations? Second Thoughts* was published, Indian Affairs launched an ambitious and sophisticated research program in an attempt to track the well-being of the Registered Indian and Inuit populations for which it is responsible. The program involves extensive cooperation between the staff of the INAC Research and Analysis Directorate and sociologists and demographers at several universities, particularly the University of Western Ontario. One result of this collaboration is the Registered Indian Human Development Index (HDI), modeled upon the more famous United Nations Human Development index. Without going into all the technical details, the HDI combines data on life expectancy, formal education, and income. As with all such indices, the construction and weighting of the components is controversial (critics say it gives too little weight to income), but it does provide a standardized yardstick for measuring social trends over time.

Table 11.1 presents the HDI results for 1981–2001.[56] (Unfortunately, it was not possible to process the results of the 2006 census of Canada in time to update HDI to that year.) The HDI is normally presented as a decimal between 0 and 1.0, but for ease of reading a complicated table I have multiplied all values by 1000 to get rid of the decimals. The adjustment does not affect the interpretation of the results.

At first reading, Table 11.1 seems to demonstrate substantial progress for First Nations. Over a twenty-year period, their HDI increased from 626 to 765, and the gap between their score and that of all other Canadians declined from 180 to 115. At that rate of progress, First Nations might hope to catch up with other Canadians in a couple more generations. The news, however, is not as good as it seems. Note that the increase in the Registered Indian HDI was above average in the period 1986–1996, particularly in the five-year period 1986–1991. These were the years when most non-status Indians became Registered Indians under Bill C-31. Thus much of the progress in those years was a statistical artifact caused by counting as Registered Indians people who had not previously been considered Indians. No one has tried to estimate the precise magnitude of the C-31 effect, but it was obviously important while it lasted, so we can expect the future rate of increase in the Registered Indian HDI to slow down. It will be a long time, not just a generation or two, before Registered Indians catch up to other Canadians.

As expected, the HDI score for Indians living off reserve is higher than for those on reserve – 802 vs. 725 in the census year 2001.[57] This gap has been painfully slow in closing: it was 77 points in 2001 and 80 in 1991. It seems safe to assume that the well-being of the on-reserve population will lag well behind that of other Canadians and off-reserve Indians for the foreseeable future.

Researchers have also devised a Community Well-being (CWB) index to measure how communities, as distinguished from individuals, are doing. Its components are income, housing quality, labour force participation, and level of formal education. In 2001, the CWB for 541 aboriginal communities – mainly Indian reserves – was 66, compared to 81 for 4,144 other Canadian communities.[58] That 15-point gap had been 21 points in the 1981 census data,[59] so again there seems to be some evidence that First Nations are catching up. However more refined analysis leads to a less optimistic conclusion. Communities, both Indian and other, which had lower CWBs in 1981 tended to have larger increases over time. Because there were far more Indian communities in the lower ranges of the distribution, their aggregate improvement from 1981 to 2001 was greater than for other Canadian communities. *But at every level of the distribution, other Canadian communities made more progress than First Nations in improving their CWB scores.*[60] Indian reserves appeared to make progress relative to other communities only because they were concentrated near the bottom of the distribution. In fact, when compared to other communities at the same starting point, Indian reserves made less progress.

The CWB has great potential for future research because it can be used to see whether First Nations that adopt different forms of government, property regimes, or treaty agreements produce better or worse results for their people. One interesting study of this type has already been carried out – an inquiry into the effect of specific claims settlements – with negative results. In the anodyne words of the researchers, "it is not possible to identify a significant linkage between the claims process and the outcome measure used."[61] Of course, there could be many explanations of this finding. Perhaps the settlements have been too small to matter, or there has not been enough time for them to have an impact. Or perhaps band councils invested them unwisely, or distributed them to band members, who spent them on consumer goods that do not show up in the CWB.

Unfortunately, the 2006 census returns are not yet sufficiently processed to extend the HDI and CWB analyses closer to the present day. In the absence of those systematic data, let me pull together some scattered sources of information that give an idea of how things are going.

Life expectancy for registered Indians increased throughout the twentieth century, both in absolute terms and relative to the rest of the population. Based on the 2001 census, there was a gap of 5.8 years between life expectancy for registered Indians and for other Canadians. To put this into perspective, this is similar to the gap between Canadian life expectancy and that in countries such as China, Serbia, Oman, and the Dominican Republic. It is much smaller than the gap of thirty or even forty years between Canada and countries such as Haiti and Zimbabwe.[62] Infant mortality rates of Indians living on reserve have also fallen, from 27.6 per 1,000 live births in 1979 to 7.2 in 2001. Over the same period of time, the comparable Canadian figure fell from 10.9 to 5.2.[63] As with Indian life expectancy, there has been considerable improvement in Indian infant mortality in recent decades, but there is still room for further progress.

The relative rate of improvement is slowing down because the easiest gains have already been made. When we look behind the aggregate statistics, there is evidence of widespread health problems among the Indian population. Incidence rates for suicide, alcoholism, smoking, obesity, diabetes, and tuberculosis are all higher for Indians, particularly those living on reserve, than among the general population.[64] Tuberculosis can be treated with antibiotics, but other health-related conditions are tied to lifestyle issues that are not amenable to easy change.

Housing is also an indicator of well-being. According to Statistics Canada, 33 per cent of people living on Indian reserves were in "crowded housing" (defined as more than one person per room) in 1996, whereas that number had fallen to 26 per cent by 2006. That appears to be progress, though the total is still far above the figure of 3 per cent that prevailed for the non-aboriginal population in both census years. On another indicator of housing, however, things seem to be moving backward. In 1996, 36 per cent of on-reserve housing needed "major repairs," but that percentage had grown to 44 per cent by 2006. The comparable figures for the non-aboriginal population were 8 per cent in 1996 and 7 per cent in 2006.[65] If we can take these figures at face value, on-reserve housing seems to be less crowded but in poorer condition than it was ten years ago.

Another perspective on how well First Nations are doing comes from data on social assistance on Indian reserves in comparison to utilization of welfare among the general population. The peak year for welfare utilization in recent Canadian history was 1994, when almost 11 per cent of the population relied on social assistance at some point during the year. By 2003, that figure had dropped by half, to about 5.5 per cent, partly because of better economic conditions and partly because of provincial reforms to benefits and eligibility, particularly in Ontario and Alberta.[66] First Nations' dependence on welfare also hit a peak in 1994, when about 46 per cent of the on-reserve population benefited from social assistance during the course of the year.[67] By 2003, that figure had dropped to 36 per cent.[68] (Percentage calculations for First Nations must be taken as approximate because of considerable uncertainty as to how many people actually live on reserves.)[69]

It was surely good news that on-reserve welfare utilization dropped by 10 percentage points, or 22 per cent, from the mid-1990s to the mid-2000s. But over the same period the general Canadian rate of welfare utilization fell by nearly 50 per cent. Data supplied to me privately by Indian Affairs suggest that nothing much has changed since 2003 and that in fact the situation may be worsening. The number of on-reserve welfare beneficiaries increased from about 146,000 in 2003 to about 159,000 in 2007 – an all-time high.[70] That may well represent a percentage increase as well an absolute increase in receipt of social assistance on reserves, although estimates of the on-reserve population are so variable that it is hard to know. In any case, reduction in welfare dependency on reserves since the 1990s, though real, has been modest and certainly slower than in the larger society. Advocates of the aboriginal orthodoxy might explain that result by saying that First Nations were starved of resources and deprived of jurisdiction, while a critic would say it shows that opportunities for self-improvement are greater off reserve than on.

Formal education is a critical factor for self-improvement in a modern society. Many observers predicted that Indian education would get better as the residential schools were shut down and responsibility for running schools on reserves was transferred to First Nations governments. In 1997, sociologist Rick Ponting wrote optimistically that with "the policy of 'Indian control of Indian education' ... [and] the hiring of qualified Indian teachers and teachers aides, and with the incorporation of elders in the teaching of traditional languages and ways, the dropout/pushout rates have fallen." He could point for confirmation to increases in aboriginal school retention rates and in post-secondary attendance.[71]

Since then, however, doubts about on-reserve education have multiplied. In a 2000 review of Indian Affairs Elementary and Secondary Education, the Office of the Auditor General concluded that the department "cannot demonstrate that it meets its stated objective to assist First Nations students living on reserves in achieving their educational needs and aspirations."[72] The report pointed to the lack of supervision for most on-reserve schools as well as an absence of data for evaluating cost effectiveness and student performance. The auditor general made another review in 2004 and found only "limited progress" in responding to the 2000 critique: "The Department does not know whether funding to First Nations is sufficient to meet the education standards it has set and whether results achieved are in line with resources provided."[73]

There has been some progress, as shown in Table 11.2. Unfortunately, Statistics Canada has changed its definitions and protocols for collecting information about educational attainments, so Table 11.2 cannot be extended through 2006. However, the 2006 census does allow some comparison with the past in terms of university degrees held by the 25–64 age group (Table 11.3).

The good news is that the percentage of university degree holders increased in all categories of aboriginal people between 2001 and 2006. The not-so-good news is that the rate of increase is about the same as that of the general population. At this rate, it will take

Table 11.2
Percentage Over the Age of 15 with at Least a High School Education

	All Canadians	Indians on reserve
1991	61.8	31.4
1996	65.2	36.6
2001	68.7	41.4

Table 11.3
Percentage of 25–64 Age Group with University Degrees[74]

	2001	2006
Indians on reserve	3	4
Indians off reserve	7	9
Métis	7	9
Inuit	2	4
All aboriginal identity	6	8
All Canadians	20	23

generations to close the education gap between aboriginal and non-aboriginal people.

Self-government, then, has not been a cure-all for aboriginal education. Michael Mendelson remarks that in practice aboriginal self-government has led to "a stand-alone village school model of education – a model that was outdated in the rest of Canada before the Second World War."[75] He proposes federal legislation to create First Nations consolidated school boards, which could provide supervision and support to isolated reserve schools. Indeed, a step in that direction was taken in 2006 with the creation of the British Columbia First Nations Education Authority.[76] John Richards also supports the idea of First Nations school boards but emphasizes that most aboriginal children, including a large minority of those on reserve, are actually educated in provincially run public schools. He proposes a number of strategies, including systematic evaluation of individual student performance, to improve aboriginal performance. Again, British Columbia has been a leader in this respect.[77] Looking at a specific experience of success rather than broad statistical trends, Calvin Helin points to the Grandview Elementary School in Vancouver, which elevated the performance of its aboriginal students through a combination of corporate fundraising, high expectations, a traditional curriculum using tools such as phonics, and rejection of "a culturally centred curriculum for the Aboriginal kids."[78]

Overall, the partial and sometimes conflicting data available on First Nations health, life expectancy, housing, welfare dependency, and education make it difficult to give a clear answer to the question, how much progress are aboriginal people making at the start of this new century? Clearly, there was a lot of progress in the second half of the twentieth century. Fifty years ago, Indian life expectancy and infant mortality were close to Third World levels and virtually no aboriginal people went to college or university. But the earliest stages of progress came most easily and fastest. In the last ten years, improvements in longevity and infant mortality have been modest, housing on reserves has become less crowded but more in need of repair, welfare dependency on reserves has decreased, but less rapidly than among the general population, and First Nations high- school and university completion rates are increasing, but painfully slowly, and remain alarmingly behind general Canadian rates.

Clearly, the policy emphasis on self-government for First Nations has not correlated with any acceleration of improvement on measurable social and economic indicators of well-being. Senior Indian Affairs researchers have concluded that "there is no direct evidence to suggest that the disproportionate attention [paid to the] *rights-based agenda* (e.g., specific and comprehensive claims, self-determination, self-government, Indian status, membership, citizenship) ... has improved the quality of life of Aboriginal people and their communities."[79] In fact, improvement seems to have leveled off in the era of self-government. It may go too far to argue that self-government is interfering with social and economic progress: so many factors are involved that it is pointless to offer monocausal explanations. But, at the very least, it is apparent that self-government is no panacea for the social and economic ills that burden aboriginal people.

A CONFLICT OF VISIONS

The American economist and analyst of race relations Thomas Sowell wrote that "conflicts of interests dominate the short run, but conflicts of visions dominate history."[80] *First Nations? Second*

Thoughts analyzed the vision of the report of the Royal Commission on Aboriginal Peoples, which continues to animate the aboriginal political leadership in Canada. Appropriate names for this vision would be separation or autonomy. Beginning with the belief that natives and other Canadians constitute two different peoples, the separatist vision emphasizes and tries to perpetuate the difference. Native peoples are nations, indeed First Nations, and should have "nation-to-nation" dealings with other Canadians. As nations, they have an inherent right of sovereign self-government. They should also develop their own economies, based on management and control of their own land and resources. The two-row wampum belt of the Iroquois, symbolizing a treaty made with the Netherlands in 1613, is an icon of the separatist vision: "It is said that each nation shall stay in their own vessels, and travel the River of Life side by side. It is further said that neither nation will try to steer the vessel of the other, or interfere or impede the travel of the other."[81]

The other vision bearing on native issues is held widely but inarticulately by most Canadians. It could be called integration or assimilation. It holds that aboriginal people are not separate nations but Canadian citizens and should have all the obligations, rights, and opportunities that citizenship brings to Canadians. They should be able to vote in Canadian elections and serve in Canadian public office. They should have the same opportunities as others to make a decent life for themselves by working and investing in the economy. To that end, aboriginal people should receive an education similar to that of other Canadians in our schools and universities.

Indian reserves and the Indian Act were originally part of the vision of assimilation: they were supposed to protect aboriginal people while they learned the arts of civilization on the way to becoming full citizens. But reserves and separate legal status have been taken over by the autonomist vision, which now sees them as permanent elements of separate nationhood, not transitional institutions on the path to integration. The current situation of aboriginal people thus involves a mix of two incompatible visions. Aboriginal people are supposed to be simultaneously Canadians and First Nations, subject to Canadian law while exercising sovereignty and self-government, creating their own economies while depending on transfer payments from Canadian taxpayers. The aboriginal status quo is intellectually incoherent, but of course the same can be said of most aspects of life. Only utopian fantasts believe that reality is rational.

Proponents of each vision have their own agendas of reform. Advocates of autonomy would like to create a third order of government, control a much larger share of Canada's land and natural resources, continue forever to receive large financial transfers without being taxed, revive dying languages, and keep their own people segmented inside separate social institutions. At the extreme, like the Iroquois, they would like to declare sovereign statehood, join the United Nations, and take their place on the world stage. In contrast, advocates of assimilation would like to repeal the Indian Act, make a once-for-all settlement of treaty obligations,[82] shut down the reserves, and encourage education, participation in the workforce, home ownership, and other attributes of modern Canadian citizenship.

Both visions, and the reform agendas that flow from them, have powerful support in today's society. The vision of autonomy dominates the thinking of the aboriginal political leadership, with its network of tribal, provincial, and national organizations supported by sympathizers in the academy and social-justice organizations. Critics call it the "aboriginal industry."[83] Regardless of what you call it, it is politically powerful and deeply entrenched within Canadian government and politics. The assimilationist vision is not organized in the same way, but it represents the inarticulate beliefs of most voters, who are sympathetic to native people and see them as victims of oppression and neglect but envision them entering Canadian society rather than withdrawing from it.

With each having powerful support, the two visions tend to counterbalance each other, making coherent reform in either direction almost impossible. Evidence of immobility is easy to find. The Royal Commission on Aboriginal Peoples offered a sweeping plan for reform founded on the vision of autonomy, but the government of Jean Chrétien balked at the hard parts, such as vast new expenditures and a third order of government. Instead it offered token recognition through First Nations terminology and acceptance of victim claims from residential schools. Then, when the Chrétien government proposed a modest reform of First Nations government based on the vision of assimilation (making band councils function more like other governments in Canada), the Assembly of First Nations mobilized to defeat it. Even though Chrétien had secure

majorities in both Houses of Parliament, the AFN was able to delay
the legislation until a new Liberal leader, Paul Martin, withdrew it.
But when Martin in turn tried to tack modestly in the direction of
autonomy by negotiating the Kelowna Accord with the provinces,
which would have put another billion dollars a year into aboriginal
programming, that project was killed by a new prime minister,
Stephen Harper, who decried the lack of accountability in aboriginal
expenditures. At the provincial level, a sympathetic Alberta government gave the Metis the right to hunt almost without restriction,
but that was quickly rescinded when a new premier came into office.

My conclusion is that for the time being, and perhaps for a very
long time, sweeping reform of the aboriginal situation is politically
impossible. There are simply too many constitutional difficulties
and too many veto groups inspired by conflicting visions. No one
would choose the status quo if we could start from the beginning,
but we can't do that – we have to start from where we are.
Advocates of change like to say that the status quo is unacceptable,
but even an unacceptable status quo is inevitable unless there is
fairly wide consensus on how to move away from it – and the
conflict of visions prevents such agreement from developing.

Inertia is the dominant fact of the aboriginal situation, and no
grand scheme capable of changing it has much chance of being
legislated. Public policy, then, should be occupied with trying to
make improvements at the margin. On reserve, that ought to mean
more flexible property rights, more accountable and transparent
local government, and better education for new generations. Off
reserve, the dynamism of Canada's market economy and open
society offers enormous opportunities to those willing and able to
participate in it.

Some aboriginal people will move to the cities and do well for
themselves and some reserves, blessed with favourable location and
energetic leadership, will raise their standard of living through
entrepreneurship. Success, when it comes, will result less from
changes in public policy than from such exercise of individual
initiative. Sadly, the pattern of success will be uneven: no tide will
lift all boats. Some – too many – individuals and bands will remain
mired in poverty and social pathology. An aboriginal underclass
will continue to exist, just as a Black underclass still exists in the
United States, fifty years after the beginning of the Civil Rights
movement. But aboriginal success stories, though uneven and limited,

will also be real, and they will become cumulative as the children of successful native parents grow up in more favourable circumstances. Aboriginal success, then, is not a public-policy challenge to governments but a moral and spiritual challenge to the people themselves. Calvin Helin was right when he wrote, "Wai Wah – make it happen."[84]

Notes

PREFACE TO THE SECOND EDITION

1 Alan C. Cairns, *Citizens Plus: Aboriginal Peoples and the Canadian State*: Vancouver: UBC Press, 2000).

2 "An Exchange" (with Alan Cairns), *Inroads* 10 (2001), 101–22. Reprinted as "Flanagan and Cairns on Aboriginal Policy," *Policy Options* 22, no. 7 (September 2001), 43–53, and in *Inroads: The Best of Our First 20 Issues* 21(summer/fall 2007), 150–9.

3 Tom Flanagan, *Harper's Team: Behind the Scenes in the Conservative Rise to Power* (Montreal: McGill-Queen's University Press, 2007).

4 "National Aboriginal Leaders Call on Stephen Harper to Explain Position on Offensive Writings of Tom Flanagan, Conservative Party Of Canada's National Campaign Chair," joint release by Metis National Council, Assembly of First Nations, and Inuit Tapiriit Kanatami, 7 June 2004; see also "Notice to Aboriginal Voters: Globe and Mail confirms Thomas Flanagan still a part of Stephen Harper's Inner Circle," Liberal release, 10 January 2006.

5 Jean Allard, *Big Bear's Treaty*, http://www.bigbearstreaty.ca

6 http://www.fcpp.org/main/project_jump.php?ProjectTypeID=6& GraphicID=48.

7 John Richards, *Creating Choices: Rethinking Aboriginal Policy* (Toronto: C.D. Howe Institute, Policy Study 43, 2006), 127.

8 Calvin Helin, *Dances with Dependency: Indigenous Success through Self-Reliance* (Vancouver: Orca Spirit, 2006).

9 McGill-Queen's University Press, forthcoming.

CHAPTER ONE

1 Royal Commission on Aboriginal Peoples (RCAP), *Report.*
2 31 January–2 February 1997.
3 Flanagan, "Unworkable Vision of Self-Government."
4 Stanley et al., *Collected Writings of Louis Riel;* and Flanagan, *Riel and the Rebellion, Metis Lands in Manitoba,* "Adhesion to Canadian Indian Treaties and the Lubicon Lake Dispute," and *Louis 'David' Riel.*
5 In addition to the RCAP *Report,* see, for example, Tully, *Strange Multiplicity;* Manuel and Posluns, *Fourth World;* Watkins, *Dene Nation;* Asch, *Aboriginal and Treaty Rights;* Boldt, *Surviving as Indians;* and Ponting, *First Nations in Canada.*
6 Anderssen and Greenspon, "Federal Apology Fails to Mollify Native Leaders"; and Department of Indian Affairs, *Gathering Strength.*
7 Mill, *On Liberty,* 45.
8 Ibid., 46.

CHAPTER TWO

1 Fontaine, "No Lessons Needed in Democracy."
2 Miller, *Skyscrapers Hide the Heavens,* 4.
3 Ray, *I Have Lived Here Since the World Began.*
4 Wilson and Urion, "First Nations Prehistory and Canadian History," 34; and Gamble, *Timewalkers,* 204.
5 Gamble, *Timewalkers,* 211; Diamond, *Guns, Germs, and Steel,* 37; Cavalli-Sforza and Cavalli-Sforza, *Great Human Diasporas,* 123; and Stringer and McKie, *African Exodus,* 169.
6 Huck and Whiteway, *In Search of Ancient Alberta,* 60–4.
7 Ibid., 69.
8 Crosby, *Ecological Imperialism,* 276–7; and Stringer and McKie, *African Exodus,* 165–7.
9 Gruhn, "Language Classification," 102.
10 Dawson, *Ice Age Earth,* 45, 61.
11 Jackson et al., "Cosmogenic 36_{Cl} Dating," 195–9.
12 Dawson, *Ice Age Earth,* figure 5.7.
13 Wilson and Urion, "First Nations Prehistory and Canadian History," 37.
14 Ibid., 39.

15 Dawson, *Ice Age Earth*, figure 5.8.

16 Gruhn, "Linguistic Evidence," 33–61.

17 I refer to the Assiniboine people. The Dakota Sioux in Manitoba and Saskatchewan came north after the Minnesota Indian war of 1862.

18 Jones, *History of the Ojebway Indians*, 178–9.

19 Ibid., 180.

20 Ruhlen, *Origin of Language*, 207–13.

21 One estimate for the time depth of Iroquoian is four thousand years. See Campbell, *American Indian Languages*, 150.

22 Greenberg, *Language in the Americas*.

23 Ibid., 333.

24 "Word Study Bolsters Theory of Several Native Migrations from Asia," reporting on the research of Merritt Ruhlen.

25 This hypothesis goes back to the anthropologist Edward Sapir.

26 Ruhlen, *Origin of Language*, 166; and Gibbons, "Geneticists Trace the DNA Trail of the First Americans," 27–31.

27 Huck and Whiteway, *In Search of Ancient Alberta*, 65.

28 The skeleton of the so-called Kennewick Man (9300 BP), unearthed along the Columbia River in 1996, has caused some controversy because it allegedly does not have the typical characteristics of North American Indians. Hume, "9,300 Years after His Death, This Man Sparks a Lively Fight." But this finding has not yet been properly authenticated and studied, so the implications remain unclear.

29 Ruhlen, *Origin of Language*, 72, 78–9, 135.

30 Wilson and Urion, "First Nations Prehistory and Canadian History," 44–8.

31 Campbell, *American Indian Languages*, 206–59.

32 Nichols, "Linguistic Diversity and the First Settlement of the New World," 512.

33 Trigger, *Natives and Newcomers*, 62, 174–5.

34 "Iroquois Wars."

35 Desbarats, "The 150-Year Gap," commenting on the research of William D. Finlayson, professor of archaeology at the University of Western Ontario.

36 J.B. Tyrell, *David Thompson's Narrative of His Expeditions in Western America, 1784–1812*, cited in Howard, *Plains-Ojibwa or Bungi*, 11.

37 Milloy, *Plains Cree*, 5–20.

38 Ibid., 116–17.

39 Cumming and Mickenberg, *Native Rights in Canada,* 13.
40 From the opinion of Justice Lambert of the British Columbia Court of Appeal in the *Delgamuukw* case, cited in Bell and Asch, "Challenging Assumptions," 53.
41 *R. v. Van der Peet* [1996], 137 D.L.R. (4th), 303.
42 Mitchell, "Population Bomb Ticking on Reserves."
43 *Report of the Auditor General,* October 1997, 13–21.
44 Foot, "Ottawa Aims to Limit Supply of Free Drugs on Native Reserves."
45 Miller, *Skyscrapers Hide the Heavens,* 223.
46 Mitchell, "Population Bomb Ticking on Reserves."
47 The term "Siberian-Canadian" was inspired by Henry, *In Defense of Elitism,* 16.
48 Sowell, *Preferential Policies.*
49 Macklem, "Distributing Sovereignty," 1327–35.
50 Milloy, *Plains Cree,* 111–13.
51 Erasmus and Sanders, "Canadian History," 4.
52 Ground, "Legal Basis for Aboriginal Self-Government," 114.
53 Commissioners for Treaty No. 8 to Clifford Sifton, 22 September 1899, in Madill, *Treaty Eight,* 122.
54 Bell and Asch, "Challenging Assumptions," 72. Two of the many books tending to deconstruct the idea of civilization are Pearce, *Savagism and Civilization,* and Chamberlin, *Harrowing of Eden.*

CHAPTER THREE

1 John Snow, *These Mountains Are Our Sacred Places,* 5.
2 Plain, "Rights of the Aboriginal Peoples of North America," 33.
3 Arcand, "Clobbering the First Nations with a New 'Frontier Thesis.'"
4 RCAP, *Report,* vol. 1, 44–5.
5 Hobbes, *Leviathan,* 104. I have modernized the spelling.
6 DeWiel, "Conceptual History of Civil Society."
7 Williams, *Keywords,* 48–50.
8 Mill, "Civilization."
9 Sanderson, *Social Evolutionism,* 13.
10 Quoted in Williams, *Keywords,* 79.
11 Cited in D'Souza, *End of Racism,* 147.
12 Sanderson, *Social Evolutionism,* 16.

13 On the influence of Boas and his students, see D'Souza, *End of Racism*, 142–61; Degler, *In Search of Human Nature*, 61–104; and Freeman, *Margaret Mead and Samoa*.
14 Boas, introduction in Benedict, *Patterns of Culture*, 3–4.
15 Benedict, *Patterns of Culture*, 17–18.
16 Murphy, *Cultural and Social Anthropology*, 9.
17 Peoples and Bailey, *Humanity*, 166.
18 Gowlett, *Ascent to Civilization*.
19 Ibid., 172.
20 Fagan, *People of the Earth*, 343.
21 RCAP, *Report*, vol. 1, 37.
22 Ibid., 101–2.
23 Ibid., 103.
24 Ibid., 141.
25 Ceci, "Squanto and the Pilgrims," 77.
26 On levels of political organization, see Diamond, *Guns, Germs, and Steel*, 268–9.
27 Donald, *Aboriginal Slavery*, 17–32.
28 Jenness, *Indians of Canada*, 33.
29 Ibid., 28–9.
30 Miller, *Skyscrapers Hide the Heavens*, 10, 35.
31 Jenness, *Indians of Canada*, 28–39; and Diamond, *Guns, Germs, and Steel*.
32 In addition to Diamond, *Guns, Germs, and Steel*, see Crosby, *Columbian Exchange*, and McNeill, *Plagues and Peoples*.
33 Cavalli-Sforza and Cavalli-Sforza, *Great Human Diasporas*, 126.
34 Ibid., 149.
35 Renfrew, *Archaeology and Language*, 148–51.
36 Cavalli-Sforza and Cavalli-Sforza, *Great Human Diasporas*, 161.
37 Much of this section is condensed from Flanagan, "Agricultural Argument."
38 More, *Utopia*, 79–80.
39 Arneil, *John Locke and America*.
40 Locke, *Second Treatise of Government*, 17.
41 Ibid., 4.
42 Ibid., 22–3.
43 Ibid., 25.
44 Vattel, *Law of Nations*.
45 Ibid., 37.
46 Ibid., 38.

47 Ibid.
48 Ibid., 85–6.
49 Ibid., 38, 85.
50 Gauthier, review, 435.
51 Arneil, *John Locke and America.*
52 Louis Riel, address to the court, 1 August 1885, in Stanley et al., *Collected Writings of Louis Riel,* vol. 3, 548.
53 Vattel, *Law of Nations,* 85–6.
54 Alpheus Henry Snow, *Question of Aborigines,* 3.
55 Ibid., 7.
56 RCAP, *Report,* vol. 1, 263.
57 Ibid., 271.
58 Ibid., 14.
59 Schouls, Olthuis, and Engelstad, "The Basic Dilemma," 19.
60 Diamond, *Guns, Germs, and Steel,* 407.

CHAPTER FOUR

1 My translation from the extracts of the French original in Maritain, "Concept of Sovereignty," 44–6.
2 Hobbes, *Leviathan,* 143–4. I have modernized the capitalization.
3 Dickerson and Flanagan, *Introduction to Government and Politics,* 41.
4 Joint Council of the National Indian Brotherhood, "Treaty and Aboriginal Rights Principles," 338.
5 Schouls, Olthuis, and Engelstad, "The Basic Dilemma," 12.
6 RCAP, *Report,* vol. 1, 608.
7 Alfred, *Heeding the Voices,* 103–4.
8 Sheremata, "Flag of Inconvenience."
9 Melvin H. Smith, *Our Home or Native Land?* 163.
10 "Dene Declaration," 4.
11 Flanagan, "Lubicon Lake Dispute," 284–5.
12 RCAP, *Report,* vol. 2, 202–12.
13 Quoted in Melvin H. Smith, *Our Home or Native Land?* 160.
14 Ground, "Legal Basis for Aboriginal Self-Government," 123–5.
15 Wilkins, "Take Your Time and Do It Right," 4.
16 Ibid., 10.
17 Quoted in Green, *Claims to Territory,* 5.
18 Ibid., 7–17.

19 Keller, Lissitzyn, and Mann, *Creation of Rights of Sovereignty,* 6–22.
20 Flanagan, "Francisco de Vitoria and the Meaning of Aboriginal Rights," 422–3.
21 Cited in ibid., 424.
22 Cited in ibid., 428.
23 Cited in Green, *Claims to Territory,* 71.
24 For different views on Wolff, compare Green, *Claims to Territory,* 71, with Reynolds, *Aboriginal Sovereignty,* 49–52.
25 Cited in Green, *Claims to Territory,* 76.
26 Quoted in Reynolds, *Aboriginal Sovereignty,* 56.
27 RCAP, *Report,* vol. 1, 695.
28 Paenson, *Manual of the Terminology,* 294–6.
29 Gamboa, *Dictionary of International Law and Diplomacy,* 254.
30 Slomanson, *Fundamental Perspectives on International Law,* 134–5.
31 Reynolds, *Aboriginal Sovereignty* and *Law of the Land.*
32 Scott, "*Terra Nullius* and the *Mabo* Judgement."
33 *Mabo v. Queensland* [1992], 66 A.L.J.R., 422.
34 Island of Palmas decision, in R.Y. Jennings, *Acquisition of Territory,* 100.
35 Simsarian, "Acquisition of Legal Title to Terra Nullius," 128.
36 Slomanson, *Fundamental Perspectives on International Law,* 135.
37 Ibid.
38 Western Sahara Advisory Opinion, in Lauterpacht, *International Law Reports,* vol. 59, 56.
39 Berger, *Village Journey,* 179.
40 RCAP, *Report,* vol. 1, 609.
41 Quoted in Green, *Claims to Territory,* 76.
42 R.Y. Jennings, *Acquisition of Territory,* 23.
43 Quoted in Cumming and Mickenberg, *Native Rights in Canada,* 139. I have modernized the orthography.
44 In ibid., 291.
45 *Johnson v. M'Intosh* [1823], 21 U.S. (8 Wheat.), 259–60.
46 See the lengthy excerpts in Green, *Claims to Territory,* 105–13.
47 Barsh and Henderson, *The Road.*
48 Cited in Green, *Claims to Territory,* 122–3.
49 *Delgamuukw v. British Columbia* [1997], 153 D.L.R. (4th), 203.
50 Ibid., 273.

51 Anderson, *Sovereign Nations or Reservations?* 176.
52 *Johnson v. M'Intosh* [1823], 21 U.S. (8 Wheat.), 543.
53 *Cherokee Nation v. Georgia* [1831], 30 U.S. (5 Pet.), 16–17.
54 *U.S. v. Wheeler*, quoted in Pevar, *Rights of Indians and Tribes*, 48.
55 Skari, "Tribal Judiciary," 94.
56 Pevar, *Rights of Indians and Tribes*, 79.
57 Kickingbird, "Indian Sovereignty," 46.
58 RCAP, *Report*, vol. 5, 158.
59 Ibid., 159.
60 Ibid., 157.

CHAPTER FIVE

1 White, "What Is a Nationality?" 6–7.
2 *Oxford English Dictionary*, entry "nation."
3 Schapiro, *Liberalism*, 122.
4 Ibid., 180–1.
5 Quoted in Shafer, *Faces of Nationalism*, 64.
6 Schapiro, *Liberalism*, 129.
7 White, "What Is a Nationality?" 2.
8 Ibid., 3.
9 Waite, *Confederation Debates*, 50.
10 *Oxford English Dictionary*, entry "tribe."
11 Treaty of 1717, in Cumming and Mickenberg, *Native Rights in Canada*, 299.
12 Ibid., 307.
13 Ibid., 291.
14 Articles of Confederation, Article 5, in Hamilton, Jay, and Madison, *Federalist*, 579; and Constitution of the United States, Article 1, section 8, in ibid., 590.
15 Alexander Morris, *Treaties of Canada with the Indians*, 299.
16 *Cherokee Nation v. Georgia* [1831], 30 U.S., 16–17.
17 *Worcester v. the State of Georgia* [1832], 6 Peters, 558.
18 *Cherokee Nation v. Georgia* [1831], 30 U.S. (5 Pet.), 16.
19 See the decision of the U.S. Supreme Court in *Alaska, Petitioner v. Native Village of Venetie Tribal Government et al.*, 1998 U.S. Lexis 1449, 25 February 1998.
20 Barsh and Henderson, *The Road*.
21 Pevar, *Rights of Indians and Tribes*, 15.
22 Egan, "New Prosperity Brings New Conflict to Indian Country."

23 Derek G. Smith, *Canadian Indians and the Law,* 32–57.
24 More specifically, the word "tribe" was used in Treaties 1, 2, 3, 5, and 6. The word "nation" was never used in any of Treaties 1 through 7. See Alexander Morris, *Treaties of Canada with the Indians,* 313–75.
25 *St Catherine's Milling and Lumber Co. v. R.,* in Isaac, *Aboriginal Law,* 14.
26 Alexander Morris, *Treaties of Canada with the Indians,* 11.
27 An example is cited in LaViolette, *Struggle for Survival,* 117: a recommendation of the attorney-general in 1874 "that each nation of Indians be dealt with separately on their respective claims."
28 *Indian Act, 1876,* s. 3(1), in Derek G. Smith, *Canadian Indians and the Law,* 87.
29 Cited in LaViolette, *Struggle for Survival,* 129.
30 McFarlane, *Brotherhood to Nationhood,* 18. In his brief to the committee, Manuel also referred to "the various nations or tribes" that still possessed aboriginal title in British Columbia. Tennant, *Aboriginal Peoples and Politics,* 131.
31 *Calder et al. v. Attorney-General of British Columbia,* reprinted in Isaac, *Aboriginal Law,* 20–1.
32 Manuel and Posluns, *Fourth World,* 268 n. 12.
33 "Dene Declaration," 3–4.
34 Sanders, "Indian Lobby," 308–9.
35 *Native People,* 9 May 1980.
36 *Indian News,* August 1980.
37 Ibid., May 1982.
38 Canada's nationhood still survives in the title "National Chief" applied to the head of the AFN.
39 For example, "Indian nations are not recognized as founding peoples." Union of British Columbia Indian Chiefs communiqué, 16 October 1980, cited in McFarlane, *Brotherhood to Nationhood,* 266.
40 Another example of usage around this time was Opekokew, *First Nations,* iv. The author's acknowledgments are dated November 1980.
41 Declaration of the First Nations, 2 December 1980, in Sanders, "Indian Lobby," 313.
42 *Indian News,* December 1980.
43 *Report of the Special Parliamentary Committee on Indian Self-Government,* abridged in Ponting, *Arduous Journey,* 340–1 n. 1.

44 Tennant, *Aboriginal Peoples and Politics*, 211–12.
45 Bill C-49, which went through Parliament in 1999, uses "first nation" (lower-cased) instead of "band."
46 Ponting, *Arduous Journey*, 330.
47 Tennant, "Delgamuukw and Diplomacy," 6.
48 Indian and Northern Affairs Canada website, www.inac.gc.ca, "First Nations Profiles."
49 Ponting, *First Nations in Canada*, 72–3.
50 RCAP, *Report*, vol. 2, 179.
51 Ibid., 181.
52 Russell, "Dene Nation and Confederation," 165.
53 Ibid., 169.
54 Cardinal, *Rebirth of Canada's Indians*, 15.
55 Ibid., 141–2.
56 Boldt and Long, "Tribal Traditions and European-Western Political Ideologies," 537–44.
57 I predicted as much in 1985 in a critique of Boldt and Long. See Flanagan, "Sovereignty and Nationhood of Canadian Indians."
58 Morton, "New Nation," 140. See also Giraud, *Métis in the Canadian West*, vol. 1, 408.
59 Louis Riel to C.-J. Coursol, 24 June 1874, in Stanley, *Collected Writings of Louis Riel*, vol. 1, 368.
60 See Flanagan, *Louis 'David' Riel*.
61 Louis Riel to Paul Proulx, 10 May 1877, in Stanley, *Collected Writings of Louis Riel*, vol. 2, 119–20.
62 "Le peuple Métis-Canadien-français," August 1883, in ibid., vol. 4, 324.
63 Ponting and Gibbins, *Out of Irrelevance*, 197–8.
64 See Daniels, *Native People and the Constitution of Canada*.
65 Purich, *Metis*, 178.
66 The text is in RCAP, *Report*, vol. 4, 376–82.
67 Ibid., 220, 255.
68 White, "What Is a Nationality?" 16.
69 Ibid.
70 Ibid., 17.
71 Ibid.
72 Ibid., 17–18.
73 Adams, *Understanding the Nisga'a Agreement*, 8.

74 Matthews and Wakefield, "Resource Development on Traditional Aboriginal Lands," 203.
75 White, "What Is a Nationality?" 19.

CHAPTER SIX

1 Harrington, "Cree Comic Pokes Fun at Own People."
2 Lunman, Lowey, and Beaty, "Stoney Saga."
3 Dempster, "Reserve in Battle over Timber Profits."
4 Lowey, "Stoney Audit Will Last until Spring."
5 Lunman, "Stoney Probe Reveals Serious Problems."
6 Alberts, "Stoney Cleanup Costs $1.8 Million."
7 Lowey, "New Stoney Politicians Say Voters Want Change."
8 Beaty and Lunman, "Stoney Chiefs Received $450,000."
9 Lunman and Beaty, "Chief Used Public Funds for Nanny."
10 Beaty, "Province Takes Over Stoney Child Welfare."
11 Lowey, "Stoneys Turn Around Child Care Crisis"; and Lowey, "Province May Revoke Child Care Authority."
12 Lunman and Beaty, "Chief Used Public Funds for Nanny."
13 Lowey, "Stoneys Turn Around Child Care Crisis."
14 Beaty, "Once-Rich Stoneys Open First Food Bank."
15 Beaty, "Stoney Chief in Cardiology Ward."
16 Lunman and Beaty, "Arson Suspected in Stoney Reserve Fires."
17 Tibbets, "Feds Say 150 Bands Need Financial Aid."
18 Lowey, "Alexis Band Mired in Deepening Deficit."
19 Quoted in Alberts, "Indian Affairs Fails to Monitor $3.6B in Native Funding."
20 Bell, "Elders Outraged after Native Leaders Used Health Grant to Play Stock Market."
21 Truscott, "Native Bands."
22 Flanagan, "Indian Bands Unwise to Give Public Money to Political Parties."
23 Alberts, "Reserve Corrupt, Cree Charge."
24 Cheney, "Money Pit."
25 Cheney, "How Money Has Cursed Alberta's Samson Cree."
26 Zdeb, "Alberta Car Insurer."
27 See Cassidy, "Aboriginal Governments in Canada." Important subsequent works include Engelstad and Bird, *Nation to Nation;* Boldt, *Surviving as* Indians; Ponting, *First Nations in Canada;* and

the five-volume RCAP *Report* plus the other RCAP publications listed in *Report*, vol. 5, 330–2.

28 For example, Gibbins, "Citizenship, Political and Intergovernmental Problems with Indian Self-Government"; Boldt, *Surviving as Indians*; Melvin H. Smith, *Our Home or Native Land?*; Crowley, "Property, Culture, and Aboriginal Self-Government"; and Flanagan, "Unworkable Vision of Self-Government."

29 Buckley, *From Wooden Ploughs to Welfare*, 168.

30 Martin, *Antagonist*, 294.

31 Boldt, *Surviving as* Indians, 140

32 Franks, *Public Administration Questions*, 45.

33 Cassidy and Bish, *Indian Government*, 95–114.

34 Dust, "Impact of Aboriginal Land Claims and Self-Government on Canadian Municipalities," 481–94.

35 Ponting, *First Nations in Canada*, 98.

36 Gibbins, "Citizenship, Political and Intergovernmental Problems with Indian Self-Government," 375.

37 Hamilton, Jay, and Madison, *Federalist*, 61.

38 Hawthorn, *Survey of the Contemporary Indians of Canada*, vol. 2, 218–24.

39 Lithman, *Community Apart*, 142–61.

40 Carstens, *Queen's People*, 232.

41 Pocklington, *Government and Politics of the Alberta Metis Settlements*, 115, 118–19.

42 Long, "Political Revitalization in Canadian Native Indian Societies," 761.

43 Crowfoot, "Leadership in First Nation Communities," 313–15.

44 Driben and Trudeau, *When Freedom Is Lost*, 97.

45 See the data in RCAP, *Report*, vol. 4, 210–17.

46 Hamilton, Jay, and Madison, *Federalist*, 55.

47 Gibbins, "Citizenship, Political and Intergovernmental Problems with Indian Self-Government," 374.

48 Franks, *Public Administration Questions Relating to Aboriginal Self-Government*, 35–6.

49 Mill, *Principles of Political Economy*, 605.

50 Comeau and Santin, *First Canadians*, 149.

51 Adams, *Understanding the Nisga'a Agreement*, 22.

52 Melvin H. Smith, *Our Home or Native Land?* 228.

53 Cheney, "Money Pit"; and Adams, *Understanding the Nisga'a Agreement*, 12.

54 For an overview of the Indian tax exemption, see Isaac, *Aboriginal Law*, 275–303. The most recent decision at the time of writing was *Shilling v. Canada*, 9 June 1999, Federal Court of Canada Trial Division, www.fja.qc.ca

55 Isaac, *Aboriginal Law*, 366–8.

56 Melvin H. Smith, *Our Home or Native Land?* 243–5; Jules, "First Nations and Taxation," 163–4; Kesselman, "Living as Leaseholders."

57 Adams, *Understanding the Nisga'a Agreement*, 11.

58 Varcoe, "Stoney Nation, Velvet Exploration Sign Gas Deal."

59 Belabwi and Luciani, *Rentier State*; Brynen, "Economic Crisis and Post-Rentier Democratization" and "Neopatrimonial Dimension of Palestinian Politics."

60 Pipes, *Property and Freedom*, 160.

61 Brynen, "Economic Crisis and Post-Rentier Democratization," 86.

62 Belabwi and Luciani, *Rentier State*, 53.

63 Ibid., 52.

64 Pratt, "Federalism in the Era of Aboriginal Self-Government," 49.

65 Quoted in Alfred, *Heeding the Voices*, 95.

66 Maslove and Dittburner, "Financing of Aboriginal Self-Government," 152.

67 RCAP, *Report*, vol. 2, 292–3.

68 Maslove and Dittburner, "Financing of Aboriginal Self-Government," 146.

69 Pocklington, *Government and Politics*, 133.

70 Maslove and Dittburner, "Financing of Aboriginal Self-Government."

71 Prince, "Federal Expenditures and First Nations Experiences," 278–9; and Alberts, "Indian Affairs Fails to Monitor $3.6B in Native Funding."

72 Alberts, "AFN Signs Accountability Agreement."

73 Canada Mortgage and Housing Corporation, *Housing Conditions of Aboriginal People*, 3, 5, A-2.

74 Ponting, *First Nations in Canada*, 95.

75 Frideres, *Aboriginal Peoples in Canada*, 169.

76 Anderssen, "How the Sawridge Millions Tore Apart a Native Community." The people being kept out are non-status Indians whose status was restored by Bill C-31 in 1985.

77 *Canadian Aboriginal Economic Development Strategy*, 18.

78 Buckley, *From Wooden Ploughs to Welfare*, 16.

79 Notzke, *Indian Reserves in Canada*, 48–9, 53–4.

80 Cornell and Kalt, *What Can Tribes Do?* 29.

81 Ibid., 31–2.

82 Cienski, "High Stakes on the Reserve."

83 Egan, "New Prosperity Brings New Conflict to Indian Country."

84 Beaty, "Feds Predict $3.5M Deficit for Stoney Reserve Budget."

85 Mill, *On Liberty*, 6.

CHAPTER SEVEN

1 Quoted in Pipes, *Property and Freedom*, 19–20.

2 Cited in Donald, "Liberty, Equality, Fraternity," 145.

3 Ridley, *Origins of Virtue*, 213.

4 Wilson, "What Chief Seattle Said," 1452.

5 Ibid., 1458.

6 Pipes, *Property and Freedom*, 88.

7 Anderson, *Property Rights and Indian Economies*.

8 Demsetz, "Toward a Theory of Property Rights," 347–8.

9 Ibid., 350.

10 Pipes, *Property and Freedom*, 81.

11 DeLong, *Property Matters*, 25–6.

12 Dyson-Hudson and Smith, "Human Territoriality."

13 Bell and Asch, "Challenging Assumptions," 69, citing the textbooks of two noted anthropologists, Marvin Harris and Lucy Mair.

14 Benson, "Customary Indian Law," 34.

15 Demsetz, "Toward a Theory of Property Rights," 351–3; Dyson-Hudson and Smith, "Human Territoriality," 31; and Harold Hickerson, *Land Tenure of the Rainy Lake Chippewa*, 60.

16 Trigger, *Huron Farmers of the North*, 30–2.

17 Donald, *Aboriginal Slavery*, 26.

18 Newell, *Tangled Webs*, 41–2.

19 Donald, *Aboriginal Slavery*.

20 Many of these early documents are described in Slattery, *Land Rights of Indigenous Canadian Peoples*, 70–99.

21 Kinney, *A Continent Lost*, 6–15.

22 Royal Proclamation of 7 October 1763, in Slattery, *Land Rights*, 366–8.

23 Borrows, "Wampum at Niagara," 161–5. The author's argument that the Royal Proclamation is really a treaty seems far-fetched to me.

24 Henry Ellis, quoted in Slattery, *Land Rights*, 191.

25 Donald B. Smith, "Aboriginal Rights in 1885."
26 Quoted in ibid., 31.
27 *St Catherine's Milling and Lumber Company v. The Queen* [1888], 14 A.C., 54.
28 Ibid., 55
29 Ibid., 59.
30 Tennant, *Aboriginal Peoples and Politics*, 17–38.
31 Ibid., 43.
32 All the cases mentioned in this paragraph are described and excerpted in Isaac, *Aboriginal Law*.
33 Melvin H. Smith, *Our Home or Native Land?* 125–7.
34 Cited in Burns, "*Delgamuukw*: A Summary of the Judgment," 33.
35 Quoted in Foster, "It Goes without Saying," 138.
36 Melvin H. Smith, *Our Home or Native Land?* 136.
37 Herb George, oral presentation at Fraser Institute conference, "The Delgamuukw Case," 26 May 1999.
38 I was assisted in understanding this complex case by Strother, "The *Delgamuukw* Case"; McDonald, "Compensation after *Delgamuukw*"; McNeil, "Defining Aboriginal Title in the 90's"; and Slattery, "Aboriginal Title."
39 *Delgamuukw v. The Queen* [1997], 153 D.L.R. (4th), 251–2.
40 Ibid., 243.
41 Ibid., 253–5.
42 Ibid., 242.
43 Ibid., 246.
44 Ibid., 247.
45 Conversation with Brian Slattery, 26 May 1999.
46 Ibid., 264–5.
47 Ibid., 265
48 Ibid., 265–6.
49 Tanner, "Impact of Delgamuukw in Newfoundland and Labrador," 5.
50 Warby, *Past Wrongs, Future Rights*, 120.
51 McNeil, "Defining Aboriginal Title in the 90's," 19.
52 Mel Smith, oral presentation, Fraser Institute conference, "The Delgamuukw Case," 27 May 1999.

CHAPTER EIGHT

1 Kindred et al., *International Law*, 115. The new law on treaties came into force in 1980.

2 Vattel, *Law of Nations,* vol. 3, 160.

3 *R. v. Sioui,* in Isaac, *Aboriginal Law,* 132.

4 For example, *R. v. Sikyea,* in Isaac, *Aboriginal Law,* 106.

5 *The Constitution Act, 1982,* s. 35(1).

6 RCAP, *Report,* vol. 2, 18.

7 Francis Jennings et al., *History and Culture of Iroquois Diplomacy.*

8 Isaac, *Aboriginal Law,* 129–30.

9 RCAP, *Report,* vol. 1, 123.

10 Daugherty, *Maritime Indian Treaties,* 45–7.

11 In ibid., 67–8.

12 Ibid., 24, 45–6.

13 Quoted in *R. v. Paul,* decision of Justice Turnbull, New Brunswick Court of Queen's Bench, 28 October 1997, online version, paragraph 13.

14 Quoted in *R. v. Paul,* decision of Justice Turnbull, New Brunswick Court of Queen's Bench, 28 October 1997, online version, paragraph 71.

15 *R. v. Paul* [1998], 158 D.L.R. (4th), 241–2.

16 Whyte, "Supreme Court Refuses to Hear Native Case."

17 Daugherty, *Maritime Indian Treaties,* 78.

18 *R. v. Marshall,* 17 September 1999, paragraph 59, www.droit.umontreal.ca

19 Scofield, "Scope of Aboriginal Ruling"; and Szklarski, "Fishing Rights."

20 J. Hugh Faulkner to the President of the New Brunswick Association of Métis and Non-status Indians, 2 February 1979, quoted in Gould and Semple, *Our Land,* 111.

21 Allan J. MacEachen to Harry Daniels, 28 March 1979, quoted in ibid., 137.

22 Hamilton, "Mi'kmaq to Show They Never Gave Up Land."

23 Chris Morris, "Micmacs Take Down Barricades in Quebec"; and Cox, "N.B. Pact Allows Native Logging."

24 Séguin, "Micmac Protesters Refuse to Dismantle Highway Barricade"; and Anderssen, "Why the N.B. Micmacs Won't Give Up the Trees."

25 Cayo, "Rights and Wrongs," 12.

26 Surtees, "Land Cessions," 1763–1830, 97.

27 Department of Indian Affairs, *Indian Treaties and Surrenders,* vol. 1, 1.

28 Surtees, "Land Cessions, 1763–1830," 112.
29 Department of Indian Affairs, *Indian Treaties and Surrenders*, vol. 1, 251–2.
30 Surtees, "Land Cessions, 1763–1830," 112–13.
31 Hawthorn et al., *Survey of the Contemporary Indians of Canada*, vol. 1, 238.
32 Ibid., 238–9.
33 Robinson Superior and Huron Treaties, in Alexander Morris, *Treaties of Canada with the Indians*, 302–9.
34 Quoted in Cumming and Mickenberg, *Native Rights in Canada*, 148.
35 The text is in Alexander Morris, *Treaties of Canada with the Indians*, 299–300.
36 Flanagan, *Metis Lands in Manitoba*, 14.
37 Pevar, *Rights of Indians and Tribes*, 38–9.
38 Quoted in Chamberlin, "Culture and Anarchy in Indian Country," 36.
39 Flanagan, "Adhesion to Canadian Indian Treaties and the Lubicon Lake Dispute," 185–205.
40 Treaty 7, in Alexander Morris, *Treaties of Canada with the Indians*, 368–9.
41 Alexander Morris, *Treaties of Canada with the Indians*, 369.
42 Ibid., 296–7.
43 Melvin H. Smith, *Our Home or Native Land?* 121.
44 RCAP, *Report*, vol. 2, 623.
45 Isaac, *Aboriginal Law*, 42.
46 Laird, "Outlaw Judge," 66–8.
47 Arnot, "Honour of the Crown," 345.
48 Treaty 7, in Alexander Morris, *Treaties of Canada with the Indians*, 370; and Melvin H. Smith, *Our Home or Native Land?* 110.
49 Treaty 7, in Alexander Morris, *Treaties of Canada with the Indians*, 371; and Melvin H. Smith, *Our Home or Native Land?* 110.
50 ICC news release, 20 March 1998, at www.indianclaims.ca.
51 RCAP, *Report*, vol. 2, 613.
52 Anderssen, "Fearing Big Costs, Ottawa Stalls Native Land Promise."
53 Ross and Sharvit, "Forest Management in Alberta," 648–9. For a similar summary, see Macklem, "Impact of Treaty 9 on Natural Resource Development in Ontario," 98–100.

54 *R. v. Horse* [1988] 2 w.w.r., 300.
55 For example, Ross and Sharvit, "Forest Management in Alberta," 648; Pratt, "Numbered Treaties and Extinguishment," 41–3; and RCAP, *Report,* vol 2, 29.
56 Venne, "Understanding Treaty 6," 173.
57 *R. v. Marshall,* 17 September 1999, paragraph 11, www.droit.umontreal.ca
58 RCAP, *Report,* vol. 2, 18.
59 Ibid., 19.
60 Ibid., 20–1.
61 Ibid., 35.
62 Asch and Zlotkin, "Affirming Aboriginal Title," 209.
63 RCAP, *Report,* vol. 2, 45.
64 Chief Harold Turner, testimony before the RCAP, 20 May 1992, cited in Zlotkin, "*Delgamuukw* and the Interpretation of the Prairie Treaties," 7.
65 Zlotkin, "*Delgamuukw* and the Interpretation of the Prairie Treaties," 7.
66 RCAP, *Report,* vol. 2, 47.
67 Ibid., 50.
68 Fumoleau, *As Long as This Land Shall Last,* 13.
69 Trial transcript, p. 157. Glenbow Alberta Institute, William G. Morrow Papers, M 1865, box 1, file 1.
70 Declaration of Intent by the Treaty 8 First Nations of Alberta, as Represented by the Grand Chief, and Her Majesty the Queen in Right of Canada, as Represented by the Minister of Indian Affairs and Northern Development, 22 June 1998.
71 *R. v. Catarat and Sylvestre,* Provincial Court of Saskatchewan, 26 August 1998, typescript, 39.
72 Originating Notice, *Ahyasou et al. v. RioAlto et al.,* 13 February 1998, s. 5.
73 Madill, *Treaty Eight,* 128.
74 Ibid., 122–3.
75 Statement of claim, s. 12, cited in Tyler, "Will *Delgamuukw* Eclipse the Prairie Sun?" 5.
76 Statement of claim, ss. 39–40, cited in ibid., 6.
77 Macklem, "Impact of Treaty 9 on Natural Resource Development in Ontario," 97.
78 Ibid., 116.

79 Ibid., 133.
80 Price, *Spirit of the Alberta Indian Treaties;* Treaty 7 Elders, *True Spirit and Original Intent of Treaty 7.*
81 For example, the Saskatchewan oral history program described in Stonechild and Waiser, *Loyal till Death.*
82 Opekokew, "Review of Ethnocentric Bias Facing Indian Witnesses," 197.
83 *R. v. Horse* [1988] 2 W.W.R., 300.
84 *R. v. Badger* [1996] 133 D.L.R. (4th), 344.
85 *Delgamuukw v. British Columbia* [1997], 153 D.L.R. (4th), 235.
86 Ibid., 232. For a critique, see von Gernet, "What My Elders Taught Me," 16–23.
87 Von Gernet, "What My Elders Taught Me," 16.
88 Ibid., 22.
89 *Delgamuukw v. British Columbia* [1997], 153 D.L.R. (4th), 231.
90 Ibid., 232.
91 Ibid., 232–3.
92 RCAP, *Report,* vol. 1, 34–5.
93 Cruikshank, "Oral Tradition and Oral History," 410.
94 Price, *Spirit of the Alberta Indian Treaties,* 122.
95 Ibid., 126.
96 Flanagan, "Analysis of Plaintiffs' Experts' Reports in the Case of *Chief Victor Buffalo v. Her Majesty the Queen et al.*," 17–18.
97 Trial transcript, p. 157. Glenbow Alberta Institute, William G. Morrow Papers, M 1865, box 1, file 1.
98 Price, *Spirit of the Alberta Indian Treaties,* 146.
99 Ibid., 159.
100 Von Gernet, *Oral Narratives and Aboriginal Pasts,* 20.
101 Ibid., 16.
102 Quoted in Gover and Macaulay, "'Snow Houses Leave No Ruins,'" 67.
103 Price, *Spirit of the Alberta Indian Treaties,* xiv.
104 Treaty 7 Elders, *True Spirit and Original Intent of Treaty 7.*
105 See also von Gernet, "What My Elders Taught Me."

CHAPTER NINE

1 Madill, *Treaty Eight,* 3–5.
2 Fumoleau, *As Long as This Land Shall Last,* 264–8.

3 Quoted in Tough, 'As Their Natural Resources Fail,' 193.
4 Weaver, "The Iroquois: The Grand River Reserve in the Late Nineteenth and Early Twentieth Centuries," 223.
5 Rogers, "Algonquian Farmers of Southern Ontario," 138–9.
6 Alfred, Heeding the Voices, 55–6.
7 Dyck, Administration of Federal Indian Aid.
8 Hall, "Clifford Sifton and Canadian Indian Administration," 143 n. 73.
9 Carter, Lost Harvests.
10 See also Buckley, From Wooden Ploughs to Welfare.
11 For examples of agricultural prosperity at this time, see Dempsey, Gentle Persuader, 71, and Tom Three Persons, 86–7.
12 Flanagan, "Analysis of Plaintiffs' Experts' Reports in the Case of Chief Victor Buffalo v. Her Majesty the Queen et al."
13 John Snow, These Mountains Are Our Sacred Places, 108–9.
14 RCAP, Report, vol. 1, 14.
15 Hawthorn, Survey of the Contemporary Indians of Canada, vol. 1, 314.
16 Indian Act, R.S.C. 1985, c. I-5, s. 89(1), in Isaac, Aboriginal Law, 276.
17 Buckley, From Wooden Ploughs to Welfare, 71.
18 Moscovitch and Webster, "Aboriginal Social Assistance Expenditures," 212.
19 Quoted in Hawthorn, Survey of the Contemporary Indians of Canada, vol. 1, 318.
20 Moscovitch and Webster, "Aboriginal Social Assistance Expenditures," 212–13.
21 Ibid., 214.
22 Hawthorn, Survey of the Contemporary Indians of Canada, vol. 1, 319.
23 Moscovitch and Webster, "Aboriginal Social Assistance Expenditures," 218–19; and RCAP, Report, vol. 2, 800–1.
24 Simpson, "Aboriginal Conundrum."
25 For example, a 1980 Indian Affairs publication stated that "in 1974, 55 per cent of the total Indian population on reserves was receiving social assistance or welfare payment." Department of Indian and Northern Affairs, Indian Conditions, 28.
26 Moscovitch and Webster, "Aboriginal Social Assistance Expenditures," 220.
27 Ibid., 224.

28 Ibid.

29 Roberts, "Native Drama 'Hits Close to Home.'"

30 RCAP, *Report*, vol. 4, 212.

31 Hawthorn, *Survey of the Contemporary Indians of Canada*, vol. 1, 165.

32 Ibid., vol. 1, 6.

33 Ibid., 168.

34 Ibid., 176.

35 Ibid., 178.

36 Ibid., 164.

37 Ibid., 6.

38 Ibid., 163. In order to improve comparability with later years, I have subtracted interest payments on the federal debt.

39 Adams, *Understanding the Nisga'a Agreement*, 12.

40 RCAP, *Report*, vol. 5, 60.

41 Ibid., vol. 2, 826.

42 Ibid., 902.

43 Ibid., 828.

44 Ibid., 827.

45 Ibid., 828.

46 Ibid., 970–92.

47 Ibid., 971.

48 Hawthorn, *Survey of Contemporary Indians of Canada*, vol. 1, 324.

49 McMahon, *Looking the Gift Horse in the Mouth*, 10.

50 RCAP, *Report*, vol. 5, 30.

51 Warby, *Past Wrongs, Future Rights*, 115.

52 Partington, *Hasluck v. Coombs*, 125–6.

53 Galligan, "Review of John Reeves, *Building on Land Rights for the Next Generation*," 13.

54 Duff, *Maori*.

55 The figure for 1989 comes from *Canadian Aboriginal Economic Development Strategy*, 18. The figure for 1998 comes from Lowey, "Natives Operate 20,000 Firms." The same figure was stated by David Roy Newhouse at a C.D. Howe consultation on "Setting an Agenda for Research on Aboriginal Issues," Toronto, 6 March 1998.

56 St Eugene Mission Resort, "Project Information Brief"; and "Resort to Boost East Kootenays."

57 Gray, "Roller-Coaster Ride to Economic Autonomy."

58 Walton, "Tsuu T'ina Company Taps Munitions Disposal Market."

59 Sowell, *Preferential Policies*, 156–7.

CHAPTER TEN

1 Tully, *Strange Multiplicity.*
2 Sowell, *Race and Economics,* 128.
3 Loney, *Pursuit of Division,* 111.

CHAPTER ELEVEN

1 Steve Olsen, *Mapping Human History: Discovering the Past through Our Genesis* (Boston: Houghton Miflin, 2002), 203.
2 Thomas D. Dillehay, *The Settlement of the Americas: A New Prehistory* (New York: Basic Books, 2000); J. M. Adovasio (with Jake Page), *The First Americans: In Pursuit of Archaeology's Greatest Mystery* (New York: Random House, 2002).
3 Brian Fagan, *The Long Summer: How Climate Changed Civilization* (New York: Basic Books, 2004), 52.
4 Tom Koppel, *Lost World: Rewriting Prehistory – How New Science Is Tracing America's Ice Age Mariners* (New York: Atria Books, 2003).
5 Tom Flanagan, "Harper and the N-Word," *Maclean's,* 11 December 2006.
6 *R. v. Powley,* [2003] 2 S.C.R. 207, 2003 SCC 43, para. 12.
7 Alberta Aboriginal Affairs and Northern Development (2004). "Interim Métis Harvesting Agreement," http://www.aand.gov.ab.ca/AANDNonFlash/Files/IMHA_MNAA_Sep28_04.pdf.
8 Thomas Flanagan, *Metis Lands in Manitoba* (Calgary: University of Calgary Press, 1991).
9 *Manitoba Metis Federation Inc. et al. v. Attorney General of Canada et al.,* 2007 MBQB 293, para. 588–594.
10 See Métis Law Summary 2006, http://www.metisnation.ca/pdfs/MLS-2006.pdf.
11 Library of Parliament, Legislative Summary of Bill C-7, http://www.parl.gc.ca/common/bills_ls.asp?Parl=37&Ses=2&ls=c7#1governancetxt.
12 Indian Affairs media release, "Government of Canada Moves to Deliver Human Rights Protection for Aboriginal Canadians, Again," http://www.marketwire.com/mw/release.do?id=792237.
13 Congress of Aboriginal Peoples website, "CAP Policy: Section 67 of the Canadian Human Rights Act," http://www.abo-peoples.org/policy/Section_67.html.

14 See any press release on the AFN website, http://www.afn.ca.

15 Mary C. Hurley, "The Nisga'a Final Agreement," Library of Parliament, 24 September 2001.

16 *Gordon Campbell et al. v. Attorney General of British Columbia, Attorney General of Canada, and the Nisga'a Nation et al.*, 2000 BCSC 1123.

17 Canadian Constitution Foundation news release, "Nisga'a Chief wins in B.C. Court of Appeal," 9 October 2007.

18 John Graham and Jodi Bruhn, "In Praise of Taxes: The Link between Taxation and Good Governance in a First Nations Context," Institute on Governance, 31 March 2008 (draft), 7.

19 Ibid., 27.

20 Thomas Flanagan and Christopher Alcantara, "Individual Property Rights on Canadian Indian Reserves," *Queen's Law Journal* 29 (2004), 489-532.

21 Thomas Flanagan and Christopher Alcantara, "Customary Land Rights on Canadian Indian Reserves," in Terry L. Anderson, Bruce L. Benson, and Thomas E. Flanagan, eds., *Self-Determination: The Other Path for Native Americans* (Stanford: Stanford University Press, 2006), 134-58.

22 Indian Act, R.S.C., c. I-5, s. 89(1).

23 Indian and Northern Affairs Canada, media release, April 20, 2007, http://www.ainc-inac.gc.ca/nr/prs/j-a2007/2-2872-eng.asp.

24 *Musqueam Indian Band v. Glass* [2000], 2 S.C.R. 633.

25 "Prime Minister Harper announces major reforms to address the backlog of Aboriginal treaty claims."12 June 2007, http://pm.gc.ca/eng/media.asp?id=1695.

26 *Negotiation or Confrontation: It's Canada's Choice – Final Report of the Standing Senate Committee on Aboriginal Peoples Special Study on the Federal Specific Claims Process* in 2006.

27 Bill C-30, s. 6(2).

28 Bill C-30, s. 19.

29 Calvin Helin, *Dances with Dependency: Indigenous Success through Self-Reliance* (Vancouver: Orca Spirit, 2006), 264.

30 http://www.cbc.ca/news/background/caledonia-landclaim/historical-timeline.html.

31 http://www.cbc.ca/story/canada/national/2006/06/16/caledonia-bought.html.

32 http://www.cbc.ca/canada/toronto/story/2008/01/14/six-nations.html.

33 Flanagan, *First Nations? Second Thoughts*, 132.

34 *Mitchell v. M.N.R.*, [2001] 1 S.C.R. 911, 2001 SCC 33, para. 38.

35 *R. v. Marshall; R. v. Bernard*, [2005] 2 S.C.R. 220, 2005 SCC 43, para. 34.

36 Ibid., para. 58.

37 Haida Nation v. British Columbia (Minister of Forests), 2004 SCC 73, [2004] 3 S.C.R. 511, headnote.

38 "Native groups launch $1 billion lawsuit against Ontario," *Ottawa Citizen*, 19 September 2007.

39 Treaty 8, in Dennis F.K. Madill, *Treaty Research Report: Treaty Eight* (Ottawa: Treaties and Historical Research Centre, Indian and Northern Affairs Canada, 1986), 128.

40 *Mikisew Cree First Nation v. Canada* (Minister of Canadian Heritage), 2005 SCC 69, [2005] 3 S.C.R. 388, headnote.

41 Flanagan, *First Nations? Second Thoughts*, 189.

42 MacPherson Leslie & Tyerman LLP, MLP Insolvency Group 2004 in Review, http://www.mlt.com/media/newsletters/05Q1Insolvency.pdf.

43 Dan Rubinstein, "The Road to Prosperity," *Tracks & Treads* (summer 2002), 15–17.

44 *Oil Daily*, 20 April 2006.

45 Helin, *Dances with Dependency*, 236–7.

46 Jacquelyn Thayer Scott, "'Doing Business with the Devil': Land, Sovereignty, and Corporate Partnerships in Membertou, Inc.," in Anderson, Benson, and Flanagan, *Self-Determination*, 242–72. Allison Hanes, "In Cape Breton, a success story," *National Post*, February 20, 2008.

47 Yale D. Belanger, *Gambling with the Future: The Evolution of Aboriginal Gaming in Canada* (Saskatoon: Purich Publishing, 2006).

48 Brett D. Fromson, *Hitting the Jackpot: The Inside Story of the Richest Indian Tribe in History* (New York: Atlantic Monthly Press, 2003).

49 André LeDressay to Tom Flanagan, 6 November 2007. Private email.

50 Brian Hutchinson, "Living Off the Band Land," *National Post*, 19 January 2008.

51 David D. Haddock and Robert J. Miller, "Sovereignty Can Be a Liability: How Tribes Can Mitigate the Sovereign's Paradox," in Anderson, Benson, and Flanagan, *Self-Determination*, 194–5.

52 Statistics Canada, *The Daily*, 15 January 2008, www.statcan.ca.

53 Ibid.

54 Sue Bailey, "Native Population Growing," *Toronto Star,*
15 January 2008. In fact, Statistics Canada enumerated only
564,870 status Indians, plus 133,155 who called themselves North
American Indian but were not registered under the Act. Statistics
Canada, *The Daily,* 15 January 2008, www.statcan.ca.

55 Stewart Clatworth, "Impacts of the 1985 Amendments to the
Indian Act on First Nations Populations," in Jerry P. White, Paul S.
Maxim, and Dan Beavon, eds., *Aboriginal Conditions: Research as
a Foundation for Public Policy* (Vancouver: UBC Press, 2003), 68.

56 Martin Cooke and Dan Beavon, "The Registered Indian Human
Development Index, 1981–2001," in Jerry P. White, Dan Beavon,
and Nicholas Spence, eds., *Aboriginal Well-Being: Canada's Continuing Challenge* (Toronto: Thompson Educational Publishing,
2007), 53.

57 Ibid., 55.

58 Erin O'Sullivan and Mindy McHardy, "The Community Well-being
Index (CWB): Well-being in First Nations Communities, Present,
Past, and Future," in White, Beavon, and Spence, *Aboriginal
Well-Being,* 114.

59 Ibid., 118.

60 Ibid., 128–9.

61 Jerry White, Nicholas Spence, and Paul Maxim, "Assessing the Net
Effects of Specific Claims Settlements in First Nations Communities in the Context of Community Well-being," in White, Beavon,
and Spence, *Aboriginal Well-Being,* 193.

62 Indian Affairs and Northern Development, *Basic Departmental
Data* (2004), table 2.1, p. 24.

63 Ibid., table 2.4, p. 31.

64 John Richards, *Creating Choice* (Toronto: C.D. Howe Institute,
2006), 34–5, 41; *Basic Departmental Data* (2004), table 2.3,
p. 29.

65 Statistics Canada, *Aboriginal Peoples in Canada in 2006*, Tables 21
and 22, on-line at www.statcan.ca.

66 John Richards, *Reducing Poverty: What Has Worked, and What
Should Come Next* (Toronto: C.D. Howe Institute Commentary,
October 2007), 9.

67 Indian and Northern Affairs Canada, *Basic Departmental Data*
(2000), tables 1.4 and 4.3, pp. 7, 46.

68 Richards, *Reducing Poverty,* 17; Indian Affairs, *Basic Departmental
Data* (2004), tables 1.4 and 4.3, pp. 9, 65.

69 Assembly of First Nations Blogger, "Numbers – Turns out you can't always count on 'em," http://assemblyoffirstnations.blogspot.com/2008/02/numbers-turns-out-you-cant-always-count.html.

70 Stéphane Godin, Senior Statistical Officer (Social Development and Indian Government Support), INAC, to Tom Flanagan, email message, 8 May 2008.

71 J. Rick Ponting, *First Nations in Canada: Perspectives on Opportunity, Empowerment, and Self-Determination* (Toronto: McGraw-Hill Ryerson, 1997), 98.

72 *Report of the Auditor General* (2000), 4-5.

73 *Report of the Auditor General* (2004), 5-1.

74 Educational Portrait of Canada, 2006 Census, pp. 19–23, www12.statcan.ca/english/census06/analysis/education/pdf/97-560-XIE2006001.pdf.

75 Michael Mendelson, "Improving Primary and Secondary Education on Reserves in Canada," Caledon Commentary, October 2006, 4.

76 Ibid., 5–6.

77 Richards, *Creating Choices*, ch. 4.

78 Helin, *Dances with Dependency*, 214.

79 Dan Beavon and Jerry White, "Aboriginal Well-being: Canada's Continuing Challenge," in White, Beavon, and Spence, *Aboriginal Well-Being*, 5.

80 Thomas Sowell, *A Conflict of Visions* (New York: William Morrow, 1987), 8.

81 Akwesasne website, http://www.akwesasne.ca/tworowwampum.html.

82 Jean Allard, *Big Bear's Treaty*, http://www.bigbearstreaty.ca.

83 Frances Widdowson and Albert Howard, *Disrobing the Aboriginal Industry: The Deception Behind Indigenous Cultural Preservation* (Montreal: McGill-Queen's University Press, 2008).

84 Helin, *Dances with Dependency*, 265.

References

Adams, Stuart. *Understanding the Nisga'a Agreement and Looking at Alternatives.* Vancouver: Fraser Institute Occasional Paper, no. 17, 1999.

Alberts, Sheldon. "AFN Signs Accountability Agreement." *Calgary Herald,* 31 March 1998.

– "Indian Affairs Fails to Monitor $3.6B in Native Funding." *National Post,* 21 April 1999.

– "Reserve Corrupt, Cree Charge." *Calgary Herald,* 13 September 1997.

– "Stoney Cleanup Costs $1.8 Million." *Calgary Herald,* 8 July 1988.

Alfred, Gerald R. *Heeding the Voices of Our Ancestors: Kahnawake Mohawk Politics and the Rise of Native Nationalism.* Toronto: Oxford University Press, 1995.

Anderson, Terry L. *Sovereign Nations or Reservations? An Economic History of American Indians.* San Francisco: Pacific Research Institute, 1995.

–, ed. *Property Rights and Indian Economies.* Lanham, Md: Rowman and Littlefield, 1992.

Anderssen, Erin. "Fearing Big Costs, Ottawa Stalls Native Land Promise." *Globe and Mail,* 16 November 1998.

– "How the Sawridge Millions Tore Apart a Native Community." *Globe and Mail,* 31 October 1998.

– "Why the N.B. Micmacs Won't Give Up the Trees." *Globe and Mail,* 27 April 1998.

Anderssen, Erin, and Edward Greenspon. "Federal Apology Fails to Mollify Native Leaders." *Globe and Mail,* 8 January 1998.

Arcand, Stanley. "Clobbering the First Nations with a New 'Frontier Thesis.'" *Globe and Mail,* 10 May 1999.

Arneil, Barbara. *John Locke and America: The Defence of English Colonialism.* Oxford: Clarendon Press, 1996.

Arnot, David M. "The Honour of the Crown." *Saskatchewan Law Review* 60 (1996): 339–47.

Asch, Michael, ed. *Aboriginal and Treaty Rights in Canada: Essays on Law, Equality, and Respect for Difference.* Vancouver: University of British Columbia Press, 1997.

Asch, Michael, and Norman Zlotkin. "Affirming Aboriginal Title: A New Basis for Comprehensive Claims Negotiations." In Asch, *Aboriginal and Treaty Rights.*

Barsh, Russel Lawrence, and James Youngblood Henderson. *The Road: Indian Tribes and Political Liberty.* Berkeley: University of California Press, 1980.

Beaty, Bob. "Feds Predict $3.5M Deficit for Stoney Reserve Budget." *Calgary Herald,* 21 March 1998.

– "Once-Rich Stoneys Open First Food Bank." *Calgary Herald,* 24 January 1998.

– "Province Takes Over Stoney Child Welfare." *Calgary Herald,* 5 February 1998.

– "Stoney Chief in Cardiology Ward." *Calgary Herald,* 27 January 1998.

Beaty, Bob, and Kim Lunman. "Stoney Chiefs Received $450,000." *Calgary Herald,* 24 December 1997.

Belabwi, Hazem, and Giacomo Luciani, eds. *The Rentier State.* London: Croom Helm, 1987.

Bell, Catherine, and Michael Asch. "Challenging Assumptions: The Impact of Precedent in Aboriginal Rights Litigation." In Asch, *Aboriginal and Treaty Rights.*

Bell, Stewart. "Elders Outraged after Native Leaders Used Health Grant to Play Stock Market." *National Post,* 30 April 1999.

Benedict, Ruth. *Patterns of Culture.* Boston: Houghton Mifflin, 1934.

Benson, Bruce L. "Customary Indian Law: Two Case Studies." In Anderson, *Property Rights and Indian Economies.*

Berger, Thomas R. *Village Journey: The Report of the Alaska Native Review Commission.* New York: Hill and Wang, 1985.

Boldt, Menno. *Surviving as Indians: The Challenge of Self-Government.* Toronto: University of Toronto Press, 1993.

Boldt, Menno, and J. Anthony Long, eds. *The Quest for Justice: Aboriginal Peoples and Aboriginal Rights.* Toronto: University of Toronto Press, 1985.

– "Tribal Traditions and European-Western Political Ideologies: The Dilemma of Canada's Native Indians." *Canadian Journal of Political Science* 17 (1984): 537–53.

Borrows, John. "Wampum at Niagara: The Royal Proclamation, Canadian Legal History, and Self-Government." In Asch, *Aboriginal and Treaty Rights*.

Brynen, Rex. "Economic Crisis and Post-Rentier Democratization in the Arab World: The Case of Jordan." *Canadian Journal of Political Science* 25 (1992):69–97.

– "The Neopatrimonial Dimension of Palestinian Politics." *Journal of Palestine Studies* 25 (1995): 23–36.

Buckley, Helen. *From Wooden Ploughs to Welfare: Why Indian Policy Failed in the Prairie Provinces.* Montreal and Kingston: McGill-Queen's University Press, 1992.

Burns, Peter T. "*Delgamuukw*: A Summary of the Judgment," in Cassidy, *Aboriginal Title in British Columbia*.

Campbell, Lyle. *American Indian Languages: The Historical Linguistics of Native America.* New York: Oxford University Press, 1997.

Canada Mortgage and Housing Corporation. *The Housing Conditions of Aboriginal People in Canada.* September 1996.

Canadian Aboriginal Economic Development Strategy. Ottawa: Minister of Supply and Services, 1989.

Cardinal, Harold. *The Rebirth of Canada's Indians.* Edmonton: Hurtig, 1977.

Carstens, Peter. *The Queen's People: A Study of Hegemony, Coercion, and Accommodation among the Okanagan of Canada.* Toronto: University of Toronto Press, 1991.

Carter, Sarah. *Lost Harvests: Prairie Indian Reserve Farmers and Government Policy.* Montreal and Kingston: McGill-Queen's University Press, 1990.

Cassidy, Frank. "Aboriginal Governments in Canada: An Emerging Field of Study." *Canadian Journal of Political Science* 23 (1990): 73–99.

–, ed. *Aboriginal Title in British Columbia: Delgamuukw v. The Queen.* Montreal: Institute for Research on Public Policy, 1992.

Cassidy, Frank, and Robert Bish. *Indian Government: Its Meaning in Practice.* Lantzville, B.C.: Oolichan Books, 1989.

Cavalli-Sforza, Luigi Luca, and Francesco Cavalli-Sforza. *The Great Human Diasporas: The History of Diversity and Evolution.* Reading, Mass.: Addison-Wesley, 1995.

Cayo, Don. "Rights and Wrongs: Finding a Just Middle Ground in Land Claims Disputes." Paper presented at Fraser Institute conference, "The Delgamuukw Case."

Ceci, Lynn. "Squanto and the Pilgrims: On Planting Corn 'in the Manner of the Indians.'" In Clifton, *Invented Indian*.

Chamberlin, J. Edward. "Culture and Anarchy in Indian Country." In Asch, *Aboriginal and Treaty Rights*.

– *The Harrowing of Eden: White Attitudes toward North American Natives*. Toronto: Fitzhenry and Whiteside, 1975.

Cheney, Peter. "How Money Has Cursed Alberta's Samson Cree." *Globe and Mail*, 24 April 1999.

– "The Money Pit: An Indian Band's Story." *Globe and Mail*, 24 October 1998.

Cienski, Jan. "High Stakes on the Reserve." *National Post*, 6 July 1999.

Clifton, James A., ed. *The Invented Indian: Cultural Fictions and Government Policies*. New Brunswick, N.J.: Transaction Publishers, 1990.

Comeau, Pauline, and Aldo Santin. *The First Canadians: A Profile of Canada's Native People Today*. 2nd ed. Toronto: James Lorimer, 1995.

Cornell, Stephen, and Joseph P. Kalt, eds. *What Can Tribes Do? Strategies and Institutions in American Indian Economic Development*. Los Angeles: American Indian Studies Center, 1992.

Cox, Kevin. "N.B. Pact Allows Native Logging." *Globe and Mail*, 11 June 1998.

Crosby, Alfred W. *Ecological Imperialism: The Biological Expansion of Europe, 900–1900*. Cambridge: Cambridge University Press, 1986.

Crowfoot, Strater. "Leadership in First Nation Communities: A Chief's Perspective on the Colonial Millstone." In Ponting, *First Nations in Canada*.

Crowley, Brian Lee. "Property, Culture, and Aboriginal Self-Government." In Drost, Crowley, and Schwindt, *Market Solutions for Native Poverty*.

Cruikshank, Julie. "Oral Tradition and Oral History: Reviewing Some Issues." *Canadian Historical Review* 75 (1994): 403–18.

Cumming, Peter A., and Neil H. Mickenberg. *Native Rights in Canada*. 2nd ed. Toronto: General Publishing, 1972.

Daniels, Harry W. *Native People and the Constitution of Canada: The Report of the Metis and Non-status Indian Constitutional Review Commission*. Ottawa: Mutual Press, April 1981.

Daugherty, W.E. *Maritime Indian Treaties in Historical Perspective*. Ottawa: Research Branch, Corporate Policy, Indian and Northern Affairs Canada, 1981.

Dawson, Alastair G. *Ice Age Earth: Late Quaternary Geology and Climate*. London: Routledge, 1992.

Degler, Carl N. *In Search of Human Nature: The Decline and Revival of Darwinism in American Social Thought*. New York: Oxford University Press, 1991.

DeLong, James V. *Property Matters: How Property Rights Are under Assault – and Why You Should Care.* New York: Free Press, 1997.

Dempsey, Hugh. *The Gentle Persuader: A Biography of James Gladstone, Indian Senator.* Saskatoon: Western Producer, 1986.

– *Tom Three Persons: Legend of an Indian Cowboy.* Saskatoon: Purich, 1997.

Dempster, Lisa. "Reserve in Battle over Timber Profits." *Calgary Herald*, 28 December 1997.

Demsetz, Harold. "Toward a Theory of Property Rights." *American Economic Review* 57 (1968): 347–59.

"Dene Declaration," in Watkins, *Dene Nation.*

Department of Indian Affairs. *Gathering Strength – Canada's Aboriginal Action Plan.* 1998. www.inac.gc.ca

– *Indian Treaties and Surrenders from 1680 to 1890.* Ottawa: King's Printer, 1905.

Department of Indian and Northern Affairs. *Indian Conditions: A Survey.* Ottawa, 1980.

Desbarats, Peter. "The 150-Year Gap." *Globe and Mail*, 14 January 1998.

DeWiel, Boris. "A Conceptual History of Civil Society: From Greek Beginnings to the End of Marx." *Past Imperfect* 6 (1997): 3–42.

Diamond, Jared. *Guns, Germs, and Steel: The Fates of Human Societies.* New York: W.W. North, 1997.

Dickason, Olive Patricia, ed. *The Native Imprint: The Contribution of First Peoples to Canada's Character.* Athabasca, Alta: Athabasca University Educational Enterprises, 1995.

Dickerson, Mark O., and Thomas Flanagan. *An Introduction to Government and Politics: A Conceptual Approach.* 5th ed. Toronto: ITP Nelson, 1998.

Donald, Leland. *Aboriginal Slavery on the Northwest Coast of North America.* Berkeley: University of California Press, 1997.

– "Liberty, Equality, Fraternity: Was the Indian Really Egalitarian?" In Clifton, *Invented Indian.*

Driben, Paul, and Robert S. Trudeau. *When Freedom Is Lost: The Dark Side of the Relationship between Government and the Fort Hope Band.* Toronto: University of Toronto Press, 1983.

Drost, Helmar; Brian Lee Crowley; and Richard Schwindt. *Market Solutions for Native Poverty: Social Policy for the Third Solitude.* Toronto: C.D. Howe Institute, 1995.

D'Souza, Dinesh. *The End of Racism: Principles for a Multiracial Society.* New York: Free Press, 1995.

Duff, Alan. *Maori: The Crisis and the Challenge.* Auckland: Harper-Collins, 1993.

Dust, Theresa M. "The Impact of Aboriginal Land Claims and Self-Government on Canadian Municipalities." *Canadian Public Administration* 40 (1997): 481–94.

Dyck, Noel Evan. *The Administration of Federal Indian Aid in the North-West Territories, 1879–1885.* M.A. thesis, University of Saskatchewan, 1970.

Dyson-Hudson, Rada, and Eric Alden Smith. "Human Territoriality: An Ecological Reassessment." *American Anthropologist* 80 (1978): 21–41.

Egan, Timothy. "New Prosperity Brings New Conflict to Indian Country." *New York Times*, 8 March 1998.

Engelstad, Diane, and John Bird, eds. *Nation to Nation: Aboriginal Sovereignty and the Future of Canada.* Concord, Ont.: Anansi, 1992.

Erasmus, Georges, and Joe Sanders. "Canadian History: An Aboriginal Perspective." In Engelstad and Bird, *Nation to Nation.*

Fagan, Brian M. *People of the Earth: An Introduction to World Prehistory.* 8th ed. New York: HarperCollins, 1995.

Flanagan, Tom. "Adhesion to Canadian Indian Treaties and the Lubicon Lake Dispute." *Canadian Journal of Law and Society* 7 (1992): 185–205.

– "The Agricultural Argument and Original Appropriation: Indian Lands and Political Philosophy." *Canadian Journal of Political Science* 22 (1989): 589–602.

– "Analysis of Plaintiffs' Experts' Reports in the Case of *Chief Victor Buffalo v. Her Majesty the Queen et al.*" Consulting report, July 1998.

– "Francisco de Vitoria and the Meaning of Aboriginal Rights." *Queen's Quarterly* 95 (1988): 421–30.

– "Indian Bands Unwise to Give Public Money to Political Parties." *Calgary Herald*, 7 April 1998.

– "The Inherent Problems of Aboriginal Self-Government." In Gérald-A. Beaudoin et al., eds., *Le fédéralisme de demain: réformes essentielles / Federalism for the Future: Essential Reforms.* Montreal: Wilson and Lafleur, 1998.

– "The Last Immigrants." *The Next City*, Summer 1998: 26–33, 47.

– *Louis 'David' Riel: 'Prophet of the New World.'* Rev. ed. Toronto: University of Toronto Press, 1996.

– "The Lubicon Lake Dispute." In Allan Tupper and Roger Gibbins, eds., *Government and Politics of Alberta*, 269–303. Edmonton: University of Alberta Press, 1992.

– *Metis Lands in Manitoba*. Calgary: University of Calgary Press, 1991.
– *Riel and the Rebellion: 1885 Reconsidered*. Saskatoon: Western Producer Prairie Books, 1983.
– "The Sovereignty and Nationhood of Canadian Indians: A Comment on Boldt and Long." *Canadian Journal of Political Science* 18 (1985): 367–74.
– "An Unworkable Vision of Self-Government," *Policy Options*, March 1997: 19–21.
Fontaine, Phil. "No Lessons Needed in Democracy." *Globe and Mail*, 11 December 1997.
Foot, Richard. "Ottawa Aims to Limit Supply of Free Drugs on Native Reserves." *National Post*, 13 November 1998.
Foster, Hamar. "It Goes without Saying: The Doctrine of Extinguishment by Implication in *Delgamuukw*." In Cassidy, *Aboriginal Title in British Columbia*.
Franks, C.E.S. *Public Administration Questions Relating to Aboriginal Self-Government*. Kingston: Institute of Intergovernmental Relations, 1987.
Fraser Institute colloquium. "The *Delgamuukw* Case: Questions of Compensation." Vancouver, 20 July 1998.
Fraser Institute conference. "The Delgamuukw Case: Aboriginal Land Claims and Canada's Regions." Ottawa, 26–27 May 1999.
Freeman, Derek. *Margaret Mead and Samoa: The Making and Unmaking of an Anthropological Myth*. Cambridge: Harvard University Press, 1983.
Frideres, James S. *Aboriginal Peoples in Canada*. 5th ed. Scarborough: Prentice Hall Allyn and Bacon Canada, 1998.
Fumoleau, René. *As Long as This Land Shall Last*. Toronto: McClelland and Stewart, n.d.
Galligan, Brian. "A Review of John Reeves, *Building on Land Rights for the Next Generation*." Unpublished manuscript.
Gamble, Clive. *Timewalkers: The Prehistory of Global Colonization*. Harmondsworth: Penguin, 1995; first published in 1993.
Gamboa, Melquiades J. *A Dictionary of International Law and Diplomacy*. New York: Oceana, 1973.
Gauthier, David. Review of William R. Shea and John King-Farlow, eds., *Contemporary Issues in Political Philosophy*. *Dialogue* 18 (1979).
Getty, Ian A.L., and Antoine S. Lussier, eds. *As Long as the Sun Shines and Water Flows: A Reader in Canadian Native Studies*. Vancouver: University of British Columbia Press, 1983.

Gibbins, Roger. "Citizenship, Political and Intergovernmental Problems with Indian Self-Government." In Ponting, *Arduous Journey*.

Gibbons, Ann. "Geneticists Trace the DNA Trail of the First Americans." In Dickason, *Native Imprint*.

Giraud, Marcel. *The Métis in the Canadian West*. Translated by George Woodcock. Edmonton: University of Alberta Press, 1986.

Gosse, Richard; James Youngblood Henderson; and Roger Carter, eds. *Continuing Poundmaker and Riel's Quest: Presentations Made at a Conference on Aboriginal Peoples and Justice*. Saskatoon: Purich, 1994.

Gould, Gary P., and Alan J. Semple, eds. *Our Land: The Maritimes*. Fredericton: Saint Annes Point Press, 1980.

Gover, Brian J., and Mary Locke Macaulay. "'Snow Houses Leave No Ruins.'" *Saskatchewan Law Review* 60 (1996): 47–89.

Gowlett, John A.J. *Ascent to Civilization: The Archaeology of Early Man*. New York: Alfred A. Knopf, 1984.

Gray, John. "The Roller-Coaster Ride to Economic Autonomy." *Globe and Mail*, 7 November 1998.

Green, L.C. *Claims to Territory in Colonial America*. In L.C. Green and Olive P. Dickason, *The Law of Nations and the New World*. Edmonton: University of Alberta Press, 1989.

Greenberg, Joseph H. *Language in the Americas*. Stanford, Calif.: Stanford University Press, 1987.

Ground, Derek T. "The Legal Basis for Aboriginal Self-Government." In Smart and Coyle, *Aboriginal Issues Today*.

Gruhn, Ruth. "Language Classification and Models of the Peopling of the Americas." In McConvell and Evans, *Archaeology and Linguistics*.

– "Linguistic Evidence in Support of the Coastal Route of Earliest Entry into the New World." In Dickason, *Native Imprint*.

Hall, D.J. "Clifford Sifton and Canadian Indian Administration." In Getty and Lussier, *As Long as the Sun Shines*.

Hamilton, Alexander; John Jay; and James Madison. *The Federalist*. New York: Modern Library, n.d.

Hamilton, Graeme. "Mi'kmaq to Show They Never Gave Up Land." *National Post*, 20 July 1999.

Harrington, Carol. "Cree Comic Pokes Funs at Own People." Review of CD recording. *Calgary Herald*, 9 June 1999.

Hawkes, David C. *Aboriginal Peoples and Government Responsibility: Exploring Federal and Provincial Roles*. Ottawa: Carleton University Press, 1989.

Hawthorn, H.B., ed. *A Survey of the Contemporary Indians of Canada.* Ottawa, Indian Affairs Branch, 1967.

Henderson, James Youngblood. "Impact of *Delgamuukw* Guidelines in Atlantic Canada." Paper presented at Fraser Institute conference, "The Delgamuukw Case."

Henry, William A., III. *In Defense of Elitism.* New York: Doubleday, 1994.

Hickerson, Harold. *Land Tenure of the Rainy Lake Chippewa at the Beginning of the 19th Century.* Washington, D.C.: Smithsonian Press, 1967; Smithsonian Contributions to Anthropology.

Hobbes, Thomas. *Leviathan.* New York: E.P. Dutton, 1950.

Howard, James H. *The Plains-Ojibwa or Bungi: Hunters and Warriors of the Northern Prairies with Special Reference to the Turtle Mountain Band.* Vermillion, S.D.: South Dakota Museum, Anthropological Papers, no. 1.

Huck, Barbara, and Doug Whiteway. *In Search of Ancient Alberta.* Winnipeg: Heartland, 1998.

Hume, Mark. "9,300 Years after His Death, This Man Sparks a Lively Fight." *National Post,* 31 October 1998.

Hylton, John H., ed. *Aboriginal Self-Government in Canada: Current Trends and Issues.* Saskatoon, Purich, 1994.

"Iroquois Wars." *The Canadian Encyclopedia.* Edmonton: Hurtig, 1985. Vol. 2, 904.

Isaac, Thomas, ed. *Aboriginal Law: Cases, Materials and Commentary.* Saskatoon: Purich, 1995.

Jackson, Lionel E., Jr, et al. "Cosmogenic 36_{Cl} Dating of the Foothills Erratics Train, Alberta, Canada." *Geology* 25 (March 1997): 195–9.

Jenness, Diamond. *The Indians of Canada.* 6th ed. Ottawa: National Museum of Canada, 1963; first published in 1932.

Jennings, Francis, et al. *The History and Culture of Iroquois Diplomacy: An Interdisciplinary Guide to the Treaties of the Six Nations and Their League.* Syracuse: Syracuse University Press, 1985.

Jennings, R.Y. *The Acquisition of Territory in International Law.* Manchester: Manchester University Press, 1963.

Joint Council of the National Indian Brotherhood. "Treaty and Aboriginal Rights Principles." In Getty and Lussier, *As Long as the Sun Shines.*

Jones, Peter. *History of the Ojebway Indians, with Especial Reference to Their Conversion to Christianity.* London: A.W. Bennett, 1861.

Jules, Chief Manny. "First Nations and Taxation." In Smart and Coyle, *Aboriginal Issues Today.*

Keller, Arthur S.; Oliver J. Lissitzyn; and Frederick J. Mann. *Creation of Rights of Sovereignty through Symbolic Acts, 1400–1800*. New York: Columbia University Press, 1937; reprinted by AMS Press, 1967.

Kesselman, Jonathan. "Living as Leaseholders, Living without Rights." *Vancouver Sun*, 14 August 1998.

Kickingbird, Kirke. "Indian Sovereignty: The American Experience." In Little Bear, Boldt, and Long, *Pathways to Self-Determination*.

Kindred, Hugh M., et al. *International Law, Chiefly as Interpreted and Applied in Canada*. 4th ed. Toronto: Emond Montgomery, 1987.

Kinney, J.P. *A Continent Lost – A Civilization Won: Indian Land Tenure in America*. New York: Octagon, 1975; first published in 1937.

Laird, Gordon. "The Outlaw Judge." *Saturday Night*, June 1998, 62–70.

Lauterpacht, E., ed. *International Law Reports*, vol. 59. Cambridge: Grotius Publications, 1980.

LaViolette, Forrest E. *The Struggle for Survival: Indian Cultures and the Protestant Ethic in British Columbia*. 2nd ed. Toronto: University of Toronto Press, 1973.

Lithman, Yngve Georg. *The Community Apart: A Case Study of a Canadian Indian Reserve Community*. Winnipeg: University of Manitoba Press, 1984.

Little Bear, Leroy; Menno Boldt; and J. Anthony Long, eds. *Pathways to Self-Determination: Canadian Indians and the Canadian State*. Toronto: University of Toronto Press, 1984.

Locke, John. *The Second Treatise of Government*. Indianapolis: Bobbs-Merrill, 1952.

Loney, Martin. *The Pursuit of Division: Race, Gender, and Preferential Hiring in Canada*. Montreal and Kingston: McGill-Queen's University Press, 1998.

Long, J. Anthony. "Political Revitalization in Canadian Native Indian Societies." *Canadian Journal of Political Science* 23 (1990).

Lowey, Mark. "Alexis Band Mired in Deepening Deficit." *Calgary Herald*, 28 June 1998.

– "Natives Operate 20,000 Firms." *Calgary Herald*, 2 June 1998.

– "New Stoney Politicians Say Voters Want Change." *Calgary Herald*, 12 December 1998.

– "Province May Revoke Child Care Authority." *Calgary Herald*, 22 November 1998.

– "Stoney Audit Will Last until Spring." *Calgary Herald*, 4 November 1997.

– "Stoneys Turn Around Child Care Crisis." *Calgary Herald*, 9 June 1998.

Lunman, Kim. "Stoney Probe Reveals Serious Problems." *Calgary Herald,* 13 August 1998.

Lunman, Kim, and Bob Beaty. "Arson Suspected in Stoney Reserve Fires." *Calgary Herald,* 10 February 1998.

– "Chief Used Public Funds for Nanny." *Calgary Herald,* 15 November 1997.

Lunman, Kim; Mark Lowey; and Bob Beaty. "The Stoney Saga." *Calgary Herald,* 27 December 1997.

McConvell, Patrick, and Nicholas Evans, eds. *Archaeology and Linguistics: Aboriginal Australia in Global Perspective.* Melbourne: Oxford University Press, 1997.

McDonald, Michael. "Compensation after *Delgamuukw:* Aboriginal Title's 'Inescapable Economic Component.'" Paper presented at Fraser Institute colloquium, "The *Delgamuukw* Case."

McFarlane, Peter. *Brotherhood to Nationhood: George Manuel and the Making of the Modern Indian Movement.* Toronto: Between the Lines, 1993.

Macklem, Patrick. "Distributing Sovereignty: Indian Nations and Equality of Peoples." *Stanford Law Review* 45 (1993): 1312–67.

McMahon, Fred. *Looking the Gift Horse in the Mouth: The Impact of Federal Transfers on Atlantic Canada.* Halifax: Atlantic Institute for Market Studies, 1996.

McNeil, Kent. "Defining Aboriginal Title in the 90's: Has the Supreme Court Finally Got It Right?" Robarts Lecture, Robarts Centre for Canadian Studies, 25 March 1998.

McNeill, William H. *Plagues and Peoples.* Garden City, N.Y.: Anchor Books, 1976.

– "The Impact of Treaty 9 on Natural Resource Development in Ontario." In Asch, *Aboriginal and Treaty Rights.*

Madill, Dennis F.K. *Treaty Research Report: Treaty Eight.* Ottawa: Treaties and Historical Research Centre, Indian and Northern Affairs Canada, 1986.

Manuel, George, and Michael Posluns. *The Fourth World: An Indian Reality.* Don Mills: Collier Macmillan Canada, 1974.

Maritain, Jacques. "The Concept of Sovereignty." In W.J. ed., Stankiewicz, ed., *In Defence of Sovereignty.* New York: Oxford University Press, 1969.

Martin, Lawrence. *The Antagonist: Lucien Bouchard and the Politics of Delusion.* Toronto: Penguin, 1997.

Maslove, Allan M., and Carolyn Dittburner. "The Financing of Aboriginal Self-Government." In Hylton, *Aboriginal Self-Government.*

Matthews, Hans, and Donald Wakefield. "Resource Development on Traditional Aboriginal Lands." In Smart and Coyle, *Aboriginal Issues Today.*

Mill, John Stuart. "Civilization." *London and Westminster Review,* April 1836. In Mill, *Dissertations and Discussions.* London: John W. Parker and Son, 1859.

– *On Liberty.* Indianapolis: Bobbs-Merrill, 1956.

– *Principles of Political Economy.* London: Routledge and Sons, 1891.

Miller, J.R. *Skyscrapers Hide the Heavens: A History of Indian-White Relations in Canada.* Toronto: University of Toronto Press, 1989.

Milloy, John S. *The Plains Cree: Trade, Diplomacy and War, 1790 to 1870.* Winnipeg: University of Manitoba Press, 1988.

Mitchell, Alanna. "Population Bomb Ticking on Reserves." *Globe and Mail,* 14 January 1998.

More, Thomas. *Utopia.* Translated by Paul Turner. Harmondsworth: Penguin, 1965.

Morris, Alexander. *The Treaties of Canada with the Indians of Manitoba and the North-West Territories.* Toronto: Belfords, Clarke, 1880.

Morris, Chris. "Micmacs Take Down Barricades in Quebec." *Globe and Mail,* 18 August 1998.

Morrison, R. Bruce, and C. Roderick Wilson, eds. *Native Peoples: The Canadian Experience.* 2nd ed. Toronto: McClelland and Stewart, 1995.

Morton, A.S. "The New Nation, the Métis." *Transactions of the Royal Society of Canada,* series 3, section II, vol. 33 (1930).

Moscovitch, Allan, and Andrew Webster. "Aboriginal Social Assistance Expenditures." In Susan D. Phillips, ed., *How Ottawa Spends, 1995–96: Mid-Life Crises.* Ottawa: Carleton University Press, 1995.

Murphy, Robert F. *Cultural and Social Anthropology: An Overture.* 3rd ed. Englewood Cliffs, N.J.: Prentice-Hall, 1989.

Newell, Dianne. *Tangled Webs of History: Indians and the Law in Canada's Pacific Coast Fisheries.* Toronto: University of Toronto Press, 1993.

Nichols, Johanna. "Linguistic Diversity and the First Settlement of the New World." *Language* 66 (1990): 475–521.

Notzke, Claudia. *Indian Reserves in Canada: Development Problems of the Stoney and Peigan Reserves in Alberta.* Marburg/Lahn: Geographisches Institut der Universität Marburg, 1985.

Opekokew, Delia. *The First Nations: Indian Government and the Canadian Federation.* Saskatoon: Federation of Saskatchewan Indians, 1980.

– "A Review of Ethnocentric Bias Facing Indian Witnesses." In Gosse, Henderson, and Carter, *Continuing Poundmaker and Riel's Quest.*

Paenson, Isaac. *Manual of the Terminology of Public International Law (Law of Peace) and International Organizations*. Brussels: Emile Bruylant, 1983.

Partington, Geoffrey. *Hasluck v. Coombs: White Politics and Australia's Aborigines*. Sydney: Quakers Hill Press, 1996.

Pearce, Roy Harvey. *Savagism and Civilization: A Study of the Indian and American Mind*. Berkeley and Los Angeles: University of California Press, 1988; first published in 1953.

Peoples, James, and Garrick Bailey. *Humanity: An Introduction to Cultural Anthropology*. 3rd ed. Minneapolis/St Paul: West Publishing, 1994.

Pevar, Stephen L. *The Rights of Indians and Tribes: The Basic ACLU Guide to Indian and Tribal Rights*. 2nd ed. Carbondale: Southern Illinois University Press, 1992.

Pipes, Richard. *Property and Freedom: The Story of How through the Centuries Private Ownership Has Promoted Liberty and the Rule of Law*. New York: Alfred A. Knopf, 1999.

Plain, Fred. "Rights of the Aboriginal Peoples of North America." In Boldt and Long, *Quest for Justice*.

Pocklington, T.C. *The Government and Politics of the Alberta Metis Settlements*. Regina: Canadian Plains Research Center, 1991.

Ponting, J. Rick. *First Nations in Canada: Perspectives on Opportunity, Empowerment, and Self-Determination*. Toronto: McGraw-Hill Ryerson, 1997.

–, ed. *Arduous Journey: Canadian Indians and Decolonization*. Toronto: McClelland and Stewart, 1986.

Ponting, J. Rick, and Roger Gibbins. *Out of Irrelevance: A Socio-Political Introduction to Indian Affairs in Canada*. Toronto: Butterworths, 1980.

Pratt, Alan. "Federalism in the Era of Aboriginal Self-Government." In Hawkes, *Aboriginal Peoples*.

– "The Numbered Treaties and Extinguishment: A Legal Analysis." Discussion Paper for the Royal Commission on Aboriginal Peoples, May 1995.

Price, Richard, ed. *The Spirit of the Alberta Indian Treaties*. Montreal: Institute for Research on Public Policy, 1979.

Prince, Michael J. "Federal Expenditures and First Nations Experiences." In Susan D. Phillips, ed., *How Ottawa Spends, 1994–95: Making Change*. Ottawa: Carleton University Press, 1994.

Purich, Donald. *The Metis*. Toronto: James Lorimer, 1988.

Ray, A.J. *I Have Lived Here Since the World Began*. Toronto: Key Porter & Lester, 1996.

Renfrew, Colin. *Archaeology and Language: The Puzzle of Indo-European Origins*. New York: Cambridge University Press, 1987.

"Resort to Boost East Kootenays." *Calgary Herald*, 11 December 1998.

Reynolds, Henry. *Aboriginal Sovereignty: Reflections on Race, State and Nation*. St Leonards, N.S.W.: Allen and Unwin, 1996.

– *The Law of the Land*. Harmondsworth: Penguin, 1992; first published in 1987.

Ridley, Matt. *The Origins of Virtue: Human Instincts and the Evolution of Cooperation*. Harmondsworth: Penguin, 1996.

Roberts, David. "Native Drama 'Hits Close to Home.'" *Globe and Mail*, 21 October 1998.

Rogers, Edward S. "The Algonquian Farmers of Southern Ontario." In Rogers and Smith, *Aboriginal Ontario*.

Rogers, Edward S., and Donald B. Smith, eds. *Aboriginal Ontario: Historical Perspectives on the First Nations*. Toronto: Dundurn, 1994.

Ross, Monique M., and Cheryl Y. Sharvit. "Forest Management in Alberta and Rights to Hunt, Trap and Fish under Treaty 8." *Alberta Law Review* 36 (1998): 645–91.

Royal Commission on Aboriginal Peoples. *Report*. Ottawa: Minister of Supply and Services, 1996, 5 vols.

Ruhlen, Merritt. *The Origin of Language: Tracing the Evolution of the Mother Tongue*. New York: John Wiley and Sons, 1994.

Russell, Peter H. "The Dene Nation and Confederation." In Watkins, *Dene Nation*.

St Eugene Mission Resort. "Project Information Brief." Ktunaxa/Kinbasket Tribal Council, February 1998, 17-page photocopy.

Sanders, Douglas. "The Indian Lobby." In Keith Banting and Richard Simeon, eds., *And No One Cheered: Federalism, Democracy and the Constitution Act*. Toronto: Methuen, 1983.

Sanderson, Stephen K. *Social Evolutionism: A Critical History*. Oxford: Basil Blackwell, 1990.

Schapiro, J. Salwyn. *Liberalism: Its Meaning and History*. New York: Van Nostrand Reinhold, 1958.

Schouls, Tim; John Olthuis; and Diane Engelstad. "The Basic Dilemma: Sovereignty or Assimilation." In Engelstad and Bird, *Nation to Nation*.

Scofield, Heather. "Scope of Aboriginal Ruling in Dispute." *Globe and Mail*, 23 October 1999.

Scott, Shirley V. "*Terra Nullius* and the *Mabo* Judgement of the Australian High Court: A Case Study of the Operation of Legalist Reasoning as a Mechanism of Political-Legal Change." *Australian Journal of Politics and History* 42 (1996): 385–401.

Séguin, Rhéal. "Micmac Protesters Refuse to Dismantle Highway Barricade." *Globe and Mail,* 10 August 1998.

Shafer, Boyd C. *Faces of Nationalism: New Realities and Old Myths.* New York: Harcourt Brace Jovanovich, 1972.

Sheremata, Davis. "Flag of Inconvenience." *Alberta Report,* 10 August 1998.

Simpson, Jeffrey. "Aboriginal Conundrum." *Globe and Mail,* 15 October 1998.

Simsarian, James. "The Acquisition of Legal Title to Terra Nullius," *Political Science Quarterly* 53 (1938): 111–28.

Skari, Andrea. "The Tribal Judiciary: A Primer for Policy Development." In Cornell and Kalt, *What Can Tribes Do?*

Slattery, Brian. "Aboriginal Title." Paper presented at Fraser Institute conference, "The Delgamuukw Case."

– *The Land Rights of Indigenous Canadian Peoples, as Affected by the Crown's Acquisition of Their Territories.* Oxford: ph.D. thesis, 1979.

Slomanson, William R. *Fundamental Perspectives on International Law.* Minneapolis/St Paul: West Publishing, 1990.

Smart, Stephen B., and Michael Coyle, eds. *Aboriginal Issues Today: A Legal and Business Guide.* North Vancouver: Self-Counsel Press, 1997.

Smith, Derek G. *Canadian Indians and the Law: Selected Documents, 1663–1972.* Toronto: McClelland and Stewart, 1975.

Smith, Donald B. "Aboriginal Rights in 1885: A Study of the *St. Catharine's [sic] Milling* or Indian Title Case." In R.C. Macleod, ed., *Swords and Ploughshares: War and Agriculture in Western Canada.* Edmonton: University of Alberta Press, 1993.

Smith, Melvin H. *Our Home or Native Land? What Governments' Aboriginal Policy Is Doing to Canada.* Victoria: Crown Western, 1995.

Snow, Alpheus Henry. *The Question of Aborigines in the Law and Practice of Nations.* Northbrook, Ill.: Metro Books, 1972; first published in 1919.

Snow, John. *These Mountains Are Our Sacred Places: The Story of the Stoney Indians.* Toronto: Samuel Stevens, 1977.

Sowell, Thomas. *Preferential Policies: An International Perspective.* New York: William Morrow, 1990.

– *Race and Economics.* New York: David McKay, 1957.

Stanley, George F.G., et al. *The Collected Writings of Louis Riel.* 5 vols. Edmonton: University of Alberta Press, 1985.

Stonechild, Blair, and Bill Waiser. *Loyal till Death: Indians and the North-West Rebellion.* Calgary: Fifth House, 1997.

Stringer, Christopher, and Robin McKie. *African Exodus: The Origins of Modern Humanity.* New York: Henry Holt, 1996.

Strother, Robert C. "The *Delgamuukw* Case: Potential Impact on Forestry." Paper presented at Fraser Institute colloquium, "The *Delgamuukw* Case," 1998.

Surtees, Robert J. "Land Cessions, 1763–1830." In Rogers and Smith, *Aboriginal Ontario*.

Szklarski, Cassandra. "Fishing Rights are Just the Start: Micmac Rep." *Montreal Gazette*, 25 October 1999.

Tanner, Adrian. "The Impact of Delgamuukw in Newfoundland and Labrador." Paper presented at Fraser Institute conference, "The Delgamuukw Case."

Tennant, Paul. *Aboriginal Peoples and Politics: The Indian Land Question in British Columbia, 1849–1989*. Vancouver: University of British Columbia Press, 1990.

– "Delgamuukw and Diplomacy: First Nations and Municipalities in British Columbia." Paper presented at Fraser Institute conference, "The Delgamuukw Case."

Tibbets, Janice. "Feds Say 150 Bands Need Financial Aid." *Calgary Herald*, 20 November 1998.

Tough, Frank. '*As Their Natural Resources Fail': Native Peoples and the Economic History of Northern Manitoba, 1870–1930*. Vancouver: University of British Columbia Press, 1996.

Treaty 7 Elders. *The True Spirit and Original Intent of Treaty 7*. Montreal and Kingston: McGill-Queen's University Press, 1996.

Trigger, Bruce G. *The Huron Farmers of the North*. 2nd ed. Fort Worth: Holt, Rinehart and Winston, 1990.

– *Natives and Newcomers: Canada's "Heroic Age" Reconsidered*. Kingston and Montreal: McGill-Queen's University Press, 1985.

Truscott, Richard. "Native Bands: Where Has All the Money Gone?" *The Taxpayer*, April 1999, 37.

Tully, James. *Strange Multiplicity: Constitutionalism in an Age of Diversity*. Cambridge: Cambridge University Press, 1995.

Tyler, Ken. "Will *Delgamuukw* Eclipse the Prairie Sun? The Implications of the Supreme Court's Decision for the Prairie Treaties." Paper presented at Fraser Institute conference, "The Delgamuukw Case."

Varcoe, Chris. "Stoney Nation, Velvet Exploration Sign Gas Deal." *Calgary Herald*, 18 July 1988.

Vattel, E. de. *The Law of Nations or the Principles of Natural Law Applied to the Conduct and to the Affairs of Nations and of Sovereigns*. New York: Oceana, 1964.

Venne, Sharon. "Understanding Treaty 6: An Indigenous Perspective." In Asch, *Aboriginal and Treaty Rights*.

von Gernet, Alexander. *Oral Narratives and Aboriginal Pasts: An Inter-disciplinary Review of the Literature on Oral Traditions and Oral Histories.* Ottawa: Research and Analysis Directorate, Indian and Northern Affairs Canada, 1996.

– "What My Elders Taught Me: Oral Traditions as Evidence in Aboriginal Litigation." Paper presented at Fraser Institute conference, "The Delgamuukw Case."

Waite, P.B. *The Confederation Debates in the Province of Canada/1865.* Toronto: McClelland and Stewart, 1963.

Walton, Dawn. "Tsuu T'ina Company Taps Munitions Disposal Market." *Calgary Herald,* 10 May 1998.

Warby, Michael. *Past Wrongs, Future Rights: Anti-discrimination, Native Title and Aboriginal and Torres Strait Islander Policy, 1975–1997.* Melbourne: Tasman Institute, 1997.

Watkins, Mel, ed. *Dene Nation: The Colony Within.* Toronto: University of Toronto Press, 1977.

Weaver, Sally M. "The Iroquois: The Grand River Reserve in the Late Nineteenth and Early Twentieth Centuries." In Rogers and Smith, *Aboriginal Ontario.*

White, Philip L. "What Is a Nationality?" *Canadian Review of Studies in Nationalism* 12 (1985):1–23.

Whyte, Murray. "Supreme Court Refuses to Hear Native Case." *National Post,* 6 November 1998.

Wilkins, Kerry. "Take Your Time and Do It Right: *Delgamuukw* and the Dynamics of Self-Government Advocacy." Paper presented at Fraser Institute conference, "The Delgamuukw Case."

Williams, Raymond. *Keywords: A Vocabulary of Culture and Society.* London: Fontana, 1976.

Wilson, C. Roderick, and Carl Urion. "First Nations Prehistory and Canadian History." In Morrison and Wilson, *Native Peoples.*

Wilson, Paul S. "What Chief Seattle Said." *Environmental Law* 22 (1992): 1451–68.

"Word Study Bolsters Theory of Several Native Migrations from Asia." *Globe and Mail,* 10 November 1998.

Zdeb, Chris. "Alberta Car Insurer Refusing to Renew Reserve's Coverage." *National Post,* 11 October 1999.

Zlotkin, Norman. "*Delgamuukw* and the Interpretation of the Prairie Treaties." Paper presented at Fraser Institute conference, "The Delgamuukw Case."

Index